PAUL KRETZMANN

Popular Commentary on Exodus and Leviticus

First published by Just and Sinner 2020

www.jspublishing.org

First edition

ISBN: 978-1-952295-07-2

This book was professionally typeset on Reedsy. Find out more at reedsy.com

Contents

II The Book of Leviticus

I

The Book of Exodus

The Second of the Five Books of Moses

1

Introduction

The second book of Moses, called Exodus (going out, departure), has been recognized as a distinct book since the time of the Jewish Church. It is not a continuation, but a sequel of the Book of Genesis, a long interval of time being passed over without record. The family of Jacob had now grown into a .large nation, and the inspired author proceeds to show how the Lord carried out His promise of leading the children of Israel back to the land where Abraham, Isaac, and Jacob had been strangers. Gen. 15, 13-16; 35, 11. 12; 48, 21. 22; 50, 25. The main purpose of the book is to relate how the theocracy, the direct government of God, was established among the people of Israel by the solemn giving of the Law on Mount Sinai, the act by which God made and confirmed the covenant which He had hinted at to the patriarchs. The book tells the history of Israel from the time that God arranged for their departure out of Egypt until the time that the Tabernacle had been dedicated near Mount Horeb. A large part of the book is devoted to the legislation on Mount Sinai, which included not only the giving of the Moral, or Natural, Law in the form of the Ten Commandments, but also the Ceremonial, or Levitical, Law, which prescribed all forms of divine worship which were to be observed by the people of God in the centuries before the coming of Christ, and the Civil Law, which was given to the children of Israel as a separate people among the nations of the earth and which regulated their political affairs and provided for sanitary rules throughout the country.

"Exodus is the Book of Redemption. The chosen people are in hopeless bondage in the land of Egypt, having no power to deliver themselves. But God says: 'I have seen the affliction of My people, I have heard their cry, I know their sorrows; I am come down to deliver them out of the hand of the Egyptians, and to bring them up into a good land,' Ex. 3, 7. 8. It is a beautiful picture of the soul redeemed from the bondage of Egypt into the glorious liberty of the children of God. God is revealed to us as the Deliverer and Leader of His people, a God near at hand, dwelling among them, concerned with the affairs of their daily life." (Hodgkin.)

The Book of Exodus is especially rich in Messianic types and symbols. The burning bush, chap.3, is a picture of the incarnation of Jesus Christ. The Passover Lamb, chap. 12, is a type of Christ and His redemption, 1 Cor. 5, 7. 8; 1 Pet. 1, 18. 19. The manna, chap. 16, is a type which Jesus applies to Himself, John 6, 48-51, when He says: "I am the Bread of Life." The smitten rock, chap. 17, is referred to 1 Cor. 10, 4: "They drank of that spiritual Rock that followed them; and that Rock was. Christ." Moses himself, the central personage of Exodus, is a type of the great Prophet of the New Testament, Deut. 18, 15. 18. The high priest Aaron was a type of our great High Priest, Jesus Christ, whose atoning sacrifice reconciled the whole world to God. The Tabernacle in the wilderness, built according to the design furnished by God Himself, was a picture and shadow of heavenly things, Heb. 8, 5. It was the outward sign of God's presence, God's tent in the midst of the tents of the children of Israel, the meeting-place between God and man.

The contents of the book may be briefly summarized: The departure out of Egypt, including the narrative of the oppression, of the birth and education of Moses, of his flight, call, and equipment, of the ten plagues, of the institution of the Passover, of the passage through the Red Sea and the destruction of Pharaoh; the wilderness journey to Mount Sinai, including the stop at Marah, the quails, manna, water from the rock, the battle with Amalek; the solemn legislation on Mount Sinai, including the preparations, the Ten Commandments, the rights of Israel, and the making of the covenant; the building and the dedication of the Tabernacle, including the sin of Aaron and the people, the making of the Tabernacle coverings and appointments, the erection and the dedication of the Tabernacle.[1]

---

[1] Cp. *Concordia Bible Class.* Feb. 1919; Fuerbringer, *Einleitung in das Alte Testament,* 24. 25.

2

Exodus 1

The Oppression of Israel in Egypt.

T HE RAPID GROWTH OF THE PEOPLE. - **V. 1. Now these are the names of the children of Israel which came into Egypt; every man and his household came with Jacob: V.2. Reuben, Simeon, Levi, and Judah, v. 3. Issachar, Zebulun, and Benjamin, v. 4. Dan, and Naphtali, Gad, and Asher. V. 5. And all the souls that came out of the loins of Jacob were seventy souls; for Joseph was in Egypt already.** The order is: the sons of Leah, the son of Rachel, the sons of Rachel's handmaid, the sons of Leah's handmaid. As in Gen. 46, 27, seventy souls are mentioned as the forefathers of the children of Israel, it being expressly stated that the sons came, each with his family, with his wife and children. The small number serves as a fine contrast over against the immense multitude that is spoken of at the time of the

Exodus. V. 6. **And Joseph died, and all his brethren and all that generation.** Joseph died at the age of one hundred and ten years, Gen. 50, 26, apparently the first one of the brothers to be taken away; but he was soon followed by the other members of his own generation, Levy dying about twenty years after him, Ex. 6, 16. **V. 7. And the children of Israel were fruitful, and increased abundantly, and multiplied, and waxed exceeding mighty; and the land was filled with them.** The heaping of the expressions, five different terms being used to emphasize this point, indicates the extraordinary growth of the people, a factor brought about not only by natural fertility and the eagerness for children, but above all by the fulfillment of God's promise to all the patriarchs. They filled the entire land, particularly Goshen, so that the country swarmed with their numbers. God's promises never fail, and it is a matter of wisdom to trust in them with firm confidence.

PHARAOH PLANS TO CURB THE GROWTH. - **V. 8. Now there arose up a new king over Egypt which knew not Joseph.** The expression "arose up" indicates either that the new Pharaoh adopted entirely new policies with reference to the strange people within the boundaries of his land, or that a new dynasty was founded by conquest or by the overthrow of that which had been friendly to the people of Joseph, the savior of Egypt. This new Pharaoh knew not Joseph, either because he was entirely unfamiliar with the history of the strange people in Goshen, or because he determined to set aside the high regard in which the strangers had been held. A careful comparison of Biblical and secular history seems to show that Thothmes I must have been the Pharaoh of the oppression, while the Pharaoh of the Exodus was Amenhotep II. **V. 9. And he said unto his people, to the high officials and representatives of the people, who were his counselors, Behold, the people of the children of Israel are more and mightier than we.** This was an exaggeration to emphasize the unwelcome growth of the Israelites which showed the abject fear of the despot. **V. 10. Come on, let us deal wisely with them,** make use of political sagacity combined with despotic craftiness and malice, **lest they multiply, and it come to pass that, when there falleth out any war, they join also unto our enemies, and fight against us, and so get them up out of the land.** The children of Israel were no citizens of Egypt, they had never become Egyptianized, neither in language nor in religion nor in customs, and so the new despot scented a danger which his policy bade him remove in time. He did not fear the conquest of his own country, but merely the departure of the Jews in case of a war. He considered the Israelites subject to his jurisdiction to the extent of treating them as serfs and bondmen. **V. 11. Therefore they did set over them taskmasters to afflict them with their burdens.** The counselors advised impressing the Israelites into peonage, practically into slavery, by setting officers over them, the purpose being to enfeeble the people, both in body and mind, by enforced labor, to take the heart out of them by the grievousness of their burdens. **And they built for Pharaoh treasure cities, Pithom and Raamses.** Certain cities had been set aside as places to store the annual tax of the harvest which Joseph had introduced, Pithom, which was situated on the canal connecting the Nile with the Arabian Gulf, and Raamses, later known as Heroopolis, in Goshen, about twenty-two miles east of Pithom, as nearly as may be determined at the present time. **V. 12. But the more they afflicted them, the more they multiplied and grew.** God spoiled the success of the Egyptians' plans by continuing to bless the Israelites in spite of all the measures intended to destroy their fruitfulness. **And they were grieved because of the children of Israel.** They were not merely disgusted at them, but they felt an increasing horror of the mysterious power that was aiding the children of Israel. **V. 13. And the Egyptians made the children of Israel to serve with rigor; v. 14. and they made their lives bitter with hard bondage, in mortar and in brick and in all manner of service in the field; all their service wherein they made them serve was with rigor.** Chagrined at the failure of their first plan, the Egyptians added ill treatment and cruelty to oppression. Two new forms of service were laid upon them, brick-making, which included both the preparing of the clay and the drying of the brick, and the hard field labor on the soil which had to be irrigated. Thus all the work which the Egyptians performed through the Israelites was done under hard pressure upon the latter. To this day tribulation and persecution is the lot of the people of God, but such crosses bring them only blessing and gain.

THE COMMAND TO KILL ALL THE :MALE CHIL-DREN. - **V. 15. And the king of Egypt spake to the Hebrew midwives, of which the name of the one was Shiphrah, and the name of the other Puah,** their names being recorded to their lasting honor; **v. 16. and he said, When ye do the office of a midwife to the Hebrew women, and see them upon the stools,** in determining the sex; **if it be a son, then ye shall kill him,** the male children should be killed right after birth; **but if it be a daughter,**

then she shall live. Whether these two women were the only midwives in Israel, or whether they were the heads of the order of midwives, is immaterial, the devilish command to use inhuman violence referred to all male children among the Hebrews. **V. 17. But the midwives feared God, and did not as the king of Egypt commanded them, but saved the men children alive.** They placed the reverential fear of God before the slavish fear of the tyrant. **V. 18. And the king of Egypt called for the midwives,** he stormed at them with an angry cry, **and said unto them, Why have ye done this thing, and have saved the men children alive? V. 19. And the midwives said unto Pharaoh, Because the Hebrew women are not as the Egyptian women; for they are lively,** full of life and energy, **and are delivered ere the midwives come in unto them.** This was not a mere evasion or deception, but agreed with the general experience, although in this case art untruth would have been defensible. **V. 20. Therefore God dealt well with the midwives,** gave them evidence of His goodness; **and the people multiplied, and waxed very mighty** under their ministrations, the remarkable growth of the children of Israel continued. **V. 21. And it came to pass, because the midwives feared God, that He made them houses.** He blessed them with abundant prosperity. **V. 22. And Pharaoh charged all his people, saying, Every son that is born** (to the Hebrews) **ye shall cast into the river** (Nile), **and every daughter ye shall save alive.** Since his first plan had failed, he made use of open, violent brutality in not only giving permission, but even a command that his people might at any time drown the male babies of the Israelites. No Christian will permit himself to be made the instrument of a tyrant who seeks to destroy the Church of God. And it will be found that it is to the advantage of believers to obey God rather than men, even here in time.

3

Exodus 2

The Birth, Upbringing, Flight, and Marriage of Moses.

The birth of Moses. — V.1. **And there went a man of the house of Levi, and took to wife a daughter of Levi.** Amram, a grandson of Levi, married his aunt Jochebed, the daughter of Levi; in spite of the troublous times he had dared to enter into the state of marriage, and the marriage, as the later history shows, had been blessed with a daughter and a son. The special reference is here to the time when the cruel mandate of Pharaoh went into effect. V.2. **And the woman conceived, and bare a son; and when she saw him that he was a goodly child,** a handsome, well-proportioned baby, that also gave promise of fine development, **she hid him three months,** in the hope of saving his life somehow, Acts 7, 20; Heb.11, 23. V.3. **And when she could not longer hide him, she took for him an ark of bulrushes, and daubed it with slime and with pitch, and put the child therein; and she laid it in the**

12

flags by the river's brink. When it became increasingly difficult to hide the boy from the eyes and ears of prying Egyptians, the mother constructed for him a small chest, or ark, out of the papyrus reeds that grew on the banks of the Nile, making it water-tight by means of asphalt and pitch, and placed this in the rushes on the brink of the river. V.4. **And his sister stood afar off to wit what would be done with him.** Miriam had thus reached an age at which she could volunteer to watch over the baby, to find out what would happen to him. The place chosen by the anxious mother was one frequented by the daughter of Pharaoh for bathing, and this fact entered into her plans. She trusted in the Lord that He would take care of her son, for faith will dare many things for the sake of a thing which has the approval of God.

Moses adopted by Pharaoh's daughter. — V.5. **And the daughter of Pharaoh came down to wash herself at the river,** for such bathing in the open stream accords well with the customs of ancient Egypt; **and her maidens,** the attending slaves, **walked along by the river's side; and when she saw the ark among the flags, she sent her maid to fetch it.** The other maids being engaged in patrolling the neighborhood against any disturbance, the attendant of the princess was sent to get the chest which had aroused the curiosity of Pharaoh's daughter. V.6. **And when she had opened it, she saw the child; and, behold, the babe wept. And she had compassion on him and said, This is one of the Hebrews' children.** She guessed the reason for the exposure of the child at once, but the natural motherly feeling asserted itself; she was filled with loving pity for the lonely, hungry child. V.7. **Then said his**

sister, who had quietly drawn near during the excitement, **to Pharaoh's daughter, Shall I go and call to thee a nurse of the Hebrew women that she may nurse the child for thee?** She managed to make her question so casual that no one suspected her of being in the neighborhood by design, and her inquiry contained just enough of the suggestion necessary to direct the thoughts of Pharaoh's daughter as she wished matters to proceed. V.8. **And Pharaoh's daughter said to her, Go.** In her deep pity for the crying child she readily acted upon the suggestion offered her. **And the maid went and called the child's mother,** the best arrangement that could have been devised. V.9. **And Pharaoh's daughter said unto her, Take this child away,** carry it away with you, **and nurse it for me, and I will give thee thy wages. So the boy's own mother was engaged to be his nurse, obviously by the dispensation of God. And the woman took the child, and nursed it.** V.10. **And the child grew,** he reached the age at which he was weaned, **and she brought him unto Pharaoh's daughter, and he became her son,** was formally adopted by the princess, but not before he had been informed of his descent and of his deliverance, for with his mother's milk he drank in the Hebrew spirit. **And she called his name Moses; and she said, Because I drew him out of the water.** This Egyptian name, Mousheh, which means saved, that is, delivered from the water, became in the Hebrew Mosheh, which means deliverer, a name with prophetic significance. As the adopted son of Pharaoh's daughter Moses was educated according to the highest Egyptian standards, and became mighty in words and deeds, Acts 7, 22. Thus God holds His sheltering hand over them that are His and saves them in the midst of great perils.

Moses attempts to deliver his people. — V.11. **And it came to pass in those days, when Moses was grown, that he went out unto his brethren, and looked on their burdens; and he spied an Egyptian smiting an Hebrew, one of his brethren.** Moses grew to manhood fully conscious of his derivation, and therefore an Israelite at heart, although a prince of the nation to all appearances. The Israelites were his brethren, as the text emphasizes by the repetition of the word, and the enforced labor under which they were groaning hurt him deeply. He restrained himself, however, until he saw an Egyptian overseer strike down a Hebrew workman. V.12. **And he looked this way and that way,** to be sure that there were no unwelcome witnesses present, **and when he saw that there was no man, he slew the Egyptian,** thus avenging the murder which the latter had just committed, **and hid him in the sand.** Although the act of Moses cannot be labeled murder, Acts 7, 24. 25, yet he anticipated divine providence by his rash act. V.13. **And when he went out the second day, behold, two men of the Hebrews strove together,** they were engaged in a fight; **and he said to him that did the wrong,** the one that was in the wrong in the quarrel, **Wherefore smitest thou thy fellow?** V.14. **And he said, Who made thee a prince and a judge over us?** He plainly told Moses that he had no business to interfere, not having any authority over the Israelites. **Intendest thou to kill me as thou killedst the Egyptian?** So there must have been a witness on the previous day who had escaped the watchful eye of Moses. **And Moses feared and said, Surely this thing is known.** How did this matter become known? V.15. **Now when**

Pharaoh heard this thing, he sought to slay Moses. But Moses fled from the face of Pharaoh, and dwelt in the land of Midian. And he sat down by a well. The land of the Midianites had no definite boundaries, but may be said to have extended eastward from the Aelanitic Gulf; some tribes, however, were found on the Peninsula of Sinai. He chose this country for his sojourn, pitching his tent near a well, apparently the only source of water for a long distance. This experience of Moses was to serve him in good stead in later years, for it is God's way of preparing great men for their life's work.

Moses in the land of Midian. — **V. 16. Now the priest of Midian had seven daughters; and they came and drew water, and filled the troughs to water their father's flock.** This man is called a priest, but the Midianites apparently had not retained the pure religion of Abraham, chap. 4, 25. 26, although the tradition of the true God persisted, as the name Reuel shows. The seven daughters of this priest, as dwellers in the wilderness, performed the work which the unmarried daughters of the Arab tribes do to this day. V.17. **And the shepherds came and drove them away,** for the saying that might makes right held good in the wilderness; **but Moses stood up and helped them, and watered their flock.** V.18. **And when they came to Reuel, their father, he said, How is it that ye are come so soon today?** It seems that the shepherds made ungallant behavior their daily practise. V.19. **And they said, An Egyptian,** for as such they regarded Moses from his dress and probably from his speech, **delivered us out of the hand of the shepherds, and also drew water enough for us, and watered the flock.** In comparing this passage with

Num. 10, 29 and Ex. 18, it should be noted that Reuel (friend of God) was the given name of this priest and Jethro, or Jether, his official title, while Hobab was the name of his son, the brother-in-law of Moses. V.20. **And he said unto his daughters, And where is he? Why is it that ye have left the man? Call him that he may eat bread.** They had offended against desert hospitality in not inviting Moses to the home of their father, especially after he had shown them such kindness. V.21. **And Moses was content to dwell with the man,** he consented to accept the urgent invitation; **and he gave Moses Zipporah, his daughter.** V.22. **And she bare him a son, and he called his name Gershom** (always a sojourner, ever a stranger); **for he said, I have been a stranger in a strange land.** The birth of this son is of particular interest, inasmuch as at various times the Lord threatened to destroy the children of Israel and to make the descendants of Moses a great nation. Through the long period of trial and humiliation Moses clung to his faith in the true God and learned to submit unconditionally to the will of God.

The Lord resolves to deliver Israel. — V.23. **And it came to pass: in process of time that the king of Egypt died,** the Pharaoh on whose account Moses had found it necessary to flee; **and the children of Israel sighed by reason of the bondage, and they cried, and their cry came up unto God by reason of the bondage.** This was many days, about forty years, after the flight of Moses. The oppression of the children of Israel continued also under the new Pharaoh, and since they had hoped for some relief, their crying arose to heaven with all the greater fervency. V.24. **And God heard their groaning, and God remembered**

His covenant with Abraham, with Isaac, and with Jacob.
He had, of course, never forgotten it, but He took occasion
to reflect and to act upon it. V.25. **And God looked upon
the children of Israel, and God had respect unto them.**
He looked into the case and was constrained to interfere in
behalf of His people. When God's hour of deliverance has
come, He always sees to it that the temptation is speedily
brought to a close.

4

Exodus 3

The Call of Moses.

The burning bush. — V.1. **Now Moses kept,** was pasturing, **the flock of Jethro, his father-in-law, the priest of Midian,** whose given name was Reuel, chap. 2, 18; **and he led the flock to the backside of the desert,** beyond the wilderness which separated the country of the Midianites from the Sinaitic mountain range, **and came to the mountain of God, even to Horeb,** named so here on account of its later importance in the history of Israel. Even after the lower valleys are dried up, the upper regions of these mountains are still green with rich pastures. V.2. **And the Angel of the Lord, the Son of God Himself, appeared unto him in a flame of fire out of the midst of a bush,** the fire being a symbol of the purifying affliction and of the chastening justice of God. **And he looked, and, behold, the bush burned with fire, and the bush was not consumed.** The obvious miracle of a desert thorn-bush which was burning, while at the same time the flames left it intact, drew and held his attention. V.3. **And Moses said, I will now turn aside, and see this great sight, why the bush is not burned.** It was an appearance or vision decidedly worth investigating. V.4. **And when the Lord saw that he turned aside to see, God called unto him out of the midst of the bush and said, Moses, Moses. And he said, Here am I.** So the Angel of the Lord of v. 2 is here identified with Jehovah, with God Himself, who addresses Moses with words of solemn warning. V.5. **And He said, Draw not nigh hither; put off thy shoes from off thy feet, for the place whereon thou standest is holy ground.** The places where the Lord deigns to appear to sinful men are ever afterward set apart in their eyes and may not be desecrated by irreverent behavior, for man owes to God the highest degree of veneration. Throughout the Orient, the custom of removing the shoes before entering into a place dedicated to divine service, whether true or false, is still observed. V.6. **Moreover, He said, I am the God of thy father, the God of Abraham, the God of Isaac, and the God of Jacob.** This was the formal declaration of majesty and power. Where deliverance, salvation, is required, there the Angel of the Lord, Jehovah, the mighty God Himself, must come to the rescue of weak and sinful men. But where God is present and visits His children in mercy, there the safety of all those that put their trust in Him is assured. **And Moses hid his face; for he was afraid to look upon God.** Sinful man cannot endure the sight of the holy God, and the eye is naturally overcome by the splendor which reflects the glory of the Lord.

The command to go to Egypt. — **V. 7. And the Lord said,**

I have surely seen, "seeing I have seen," a very emphatic expression, **the affliction of My people which are in Egypt,** the burdens which they were forced to bear, **and have heard their cry by reason of their taskmasters,** in the presence of the cruel drivers; **for I know their sorrows,** the pains and the suffering which they were enduring; v.8. **and I am come down to deliver them out of the hand of the Egyptians, and to bring them up out of that land unto a good land and a large, unto a land flowing with milk and honey; unto the place of the Canaanites, and the Hittites, and the Amorites, and the Perizzites, and the Hivites, and the Jebusites.** Cp. Gen. 10, 19; 15, 18. The land of Canaan, which was now inhabited by the Canaanitish tribes enumerated here, was to the children of Israel the Land of Promise, a good land on account of its great fertility, and a large or wide land in contrast to the present condition of oppression in the land of Egypt, a land overflowing with milk and honey, supremely rich in flowery and nourishing pastures. V.9. **Now, therefore, behold, the cry of the children of Israel is come unto Me; and I have also seen the oppression wherewith the Egyptians oppress them.** V.10. **Come now, therefore, and I will send thee unto Pharaoh, that thou mayest bring forth My people, the children of Israel, out of Egypt.** This was the object of the Lord's explanation, to make Moses the leader of the people in effecting their deliverance from the bondage of Egypt. With. out the command and call of God no man should venture to undertake work in His kingdom. Even Christ glorified not Himself to be made a High Priest, Heb. 5, 5. 6. Moses received an immediate call from God; His method at the present time is that of the mediate call, through

21

the congregations or their representatives.

The emphatic commission. — V.11. **And Moses said unto God, Who am I that I should go unto Pharaoh, and that I should bring forth the children of Israel out of Egypt?** Moses certainly had learned humility in. the school of Midian, not unmixed with dejection; all his youthful rashness was forgotten. "He who once would, when as yet he ought not, now will no longer when he ought." V.12. **And He said, Certainly I will be with thee,** the presence, the power, and the wisdom of God was to accompany Moses; **and this shall be a token unto thee that I have sent thee: When thou halt brought forth the people out of Egypt, ye shall serve God upon this mountain.** This was literally fulfilled, for it was on almost the identical spot then occupied by Moses that the children of Israel were encamped when they entered into the formal relation of worshipers of Jehovah. But Moses had another objection. V.13. **And Moses said unto God, Behold, when I come unto the children of Israel and shall say unto them, The God of your fathers hath sent me unto you, and they shall say unto me, What is His name? what shall I say unto them?** The name God Almighty was too general to distinguish the true God from the idols of Egypt, and therefore the inquiry for the name has the purpose of obtaining some expression on the part of God which would indicate His essence and the actual manifestation of the divine essence toward His people, by which they might understand and apprehend Him. V.14. **And God said unto Moses, I AM THAT I AM; and He said, Thus shalt thou say unto the children of Israel, I AM hath sent me unto you.** It is a majestic declaration in which God reveals His essence to Moses as the unchangeable, eternally faithful covenant God. From past to future, from everlasting to everlasting, He is the same merciful Lord over all, without change or shadow of turning. V.15. **And God said, moreover, unto Moses, Thus shalt thou say unto the children of Israel, The Lord God of your fathers, the God of Abraham, the God of Isaac, and the God of Jacob, hath sent me unto you; this is My name forever and ever, and this is My memorial unto all generations.** Forward into the endless future, and backward into the past without beginning: there is only that one true God as He should be accepted by all men. V.16. **Go, and gather the elders of Israel together, and say unto them, The Lord God of your fathers, the God of Abraham, of Isaac, and of Jacob, appeared unto me, saying, I have surely visited you,** visiting I have visited you, **and seen that which is done to you in Egypt;** v.17. **and I have said, I will bring you up out of the affliction,** the burden, **of Egypt unto the land of the Canaanites, and the Hittites, and the Amorites, and the Perizzites, and the Hivites, and the Jebusites, unto a land flowing with milk and honey.** The apparently cumbersome repetition of the name of God and the long enumeration of the Canaanitish tribes all serve for emphasis to bring out the certainty of the fulfilment. V.18. **And they shall hearken to thy voice; and thou shalt come, thou and the elders of Israel, unto the king of Egypt, and ye shall say unto him, The Lord God of the Hebrews hath met with us,** for the present revelation of God to Moses concerned, and had significance for, all the people; **and now let us go, we beseech thee, three days' journey into the wilderness, that we may sacrifice to the Lord, our God.** This request was not a deception, but

23

agreed with the plan of God, for because the Lord knew the hard heart of Pharaoh, Moses and the elders were, at the beginning, not to ask more than a leave of absence, for Pharaoh's denial of this petition would then reveal the hardness of his heart. God intended to make Pharaoh an example for all time.

THE PROMISE OF DELIVERANCE. V.19. **And I am sure that the king of Egypt will not let you go, no, not by a mighty hand.** The omniscient God knew that Pharaoh would not permanently submit to Him, not even after the ten plagues, but would deliberately harden himself against his better knowledge and thus invite destruction upon himself. V.20. **And I will stretch out My hand and smite Egypt with all My wonders which I will do in the midst thereof.** The Lord announces that He will glorify Himself by means of great miracles which He would perform in the midst of Egypt, thus letting all men know that He was supreme. **And after that he will let you go.** V.21. **And I will give this people favor in the sight of the Egyptians; and it sha11 come to pass that, when ye go, ye shall not go empty;** v.22. **but every woman shall borrow,** that is, ask, request, **of her neighbor, and of her that sojourneth in her house, jewels of silver, and jewels of gold, and raiment; and ye shall put them upon your sons and upon your daughters; and ye shall spoil the Egyptians.** By God's dispensation, the Egyptian women would show their Israelite neighbors all kindness in readily bringing forth all the jewelry and the vessels of precious metals which they desired, this spoiling of the Egyptians being intended by God to compensate the Israelites for the many years of serfdom and slavery. It may often seem that there is neither right nor

24

justice in the world, but the righteousness of God will always bring deliverance to His children, very often with a greater blessing than they expected.

5

Exodus 4

The Mission of Moses to the Children of Israel.

God gives Moses miraculous powers. — **V. 1 And Moses answered and said, But, behold, they will not believe me, nor hearken unto my voice; for they will say, The Lord hath not appeared unto thee.** The fear and anxiety of Moses here discovered another objection, that based upon the fact that the people were no longer accustomed to prophetic voices and would therefore not acknowledge his call. V.2. **And the Lord said unto him, What is that in thine hand? And he said, A rod.** Moses held his shepherd's staff in his hand. V.3. **And He said, Cast it on the ground. And he cast it on the ground, and it became a serpent; and Moses fled from before it.** The serpent was no delusion, but a fact, and looked dangerous enough to fill the heart of Moses with fear. V.4. **And the Lord said unto Moses, Put forth thine hand, and take it by the tail. And he**

put forth his hand and caught it, and it became a rod in his land; v.5. **that they may believe that the Lord God of their fathers, the God of Abraham, the God of Isaac, and the God of Jacob, hath appeared unto thee.** The simple shepherd's staff, according to the will of God, became the instrument by which Pharaoh and his land were punished, for the miracle showed that God would deliver His people from the hostile power which was holding it captive. Moses received the commission, the power. to overcome the might, the wickedness of Satan, and this fact could not be hidden from the eyes of the children of Israel: they were bound to acknowledge his call. V.6. **And the Lord said furthermore unto him, Put now thy hand into thy bosom. And he put his hand into his bosom; and when he took it out, behold, his hand was leprous as snow,** infected with the white leprosy, Lev. 13, 3. V.7. **And he said, Put thine hand into thy bosom again. And he put his hand into his bosom again; and plucked it out of his bosom, and, behold, it was turned again as his other flesh.** Thereby the Lord signified that He intended to cleanse His people, the children of Israel, of the spiritual leprosy of sin by the sacrifices and purifications which typified the cleansing through the redemption of Christ. V.8. **And it shall come to pass, if they will not believe thee, neither hearken to the voice of the first sign,** to its unmistakable evidence, **that they will believe the voice of the latter sign.** V.9. **And it shall come to pass, if they will not believe also these two signs, neither hearken unto thy voice, that thou shalt take of the water of the river** (Nile), **and pour it upon the dry land; and the water which thou takest out of the river shall become blood upon the dry land.**

The Nile was given the veneration of a god in Egypt on account of the fact that the fertility of the entire country depended upon its annual overflow. If Moses, therefore. had the power to turn this water of blessing into blood, he commanded a power which exceeded that of Pharaoh: death and destruction upon the tyrants was in his hand. The same almighty power of God is able to deliver us from every evil work and to give us the possession of the saints in light.

The fears of Moses reproved. — **V. 10. And Moses said unto the Lord, O my Lord, I am not eloquent, neither heretofore nor since Thou hast spoken unto Thy servant; but I am slow of speech and of a slow tongue.** The great fear of Moses now made him protest his oratorical inability. which made it impossible for him to do justice to the message of the Lord and therefore threatened failure to the whole plan. He lacked both the natural gift of facile speech and the practice before an audience, and this ability had not been imparted to him in the course of this conversation. **V. 11 And the Lord said unto him, Who hath made man's mouth? Or who maketh the dumb, or deaf, or the seeing, or the blind? Have not I, the Lord?** The excuse of Moses might have weight with men, but not with the Lord, who has absolute power over all the senses, being able to give the full use of them or to withdraw this in whole or in part. V.12. **Now, therefore, go, and I will be with thy mouth, and teach thee what thou shalt say.** It was an easy matter for the Lord to impart divine eloquence to Moses, both as to facility of speech and as to choice of the most fitting words. All reasonable objections of Moses were now removed. V.13. **And he said, O my Lord, send, I pray Thee, by the hand of him whom Thou wilt send.**

The misgivings of Moses were still so great that he wanted the mission to be taken care of by anyone else than himself. The weakness of his flesh was so overpowering that his words sound like a flat refusal. V.14. **And the anger of the Lord was kindled against Moses, and He said, Is not Aaron, the Levite, thy brother?** The Lord implied that Aaron surely was more worthy of being called a descendant of Levi than Moses with his hesitation**. I know that he can speak well. And also, behold, he cometh forth to meet thee,** for the Lord had arranged for this; **and when he seeth thee, he will be glad in his heart.** Aaron could indeed make fine speeches, and he would be delighted to be connected with this mission as the spokesman. V.15. **And thou shalt speak unto him, and put words in his mouth; and I will be with thy mouth and with his mouth and will teach you what ye shall do.** V.16. **And he shall be thy spokesman unto the people; and he shall be, even he shall be to thee instead of a mouth, and thou shalt be to him instead of God,** to make known to him both the form and the contents of his speeches to the people. As Moses, the prophet, speaks only what God commands him to say, thus Aaron was to defer to Moses in stating only what Moses told him. "He that has the Word of God and is a believer has the Spirit and the power of God, also divine wisdom, truth, heart, mind, and disposition, and everything that pertains to God." (Luther.) V.17. **And thou shalt take this rod in thine hand, wherewith thou shalt do signs.** The shepherd's staff was to be a symbol of the divine signs which were to be performed by the hand of Moses. The Lord has patience with our weakness and does not expect too much of us, but strengthens us to remain steadfast in His service and obedience.

Moses dismissed by Jethro. — **V. 18. And Moses went and returned to Jethro, his father-in-law, and said unto him, Let me go, I pray thee, and return unto my brethren which are in Egypt, and see whether they be yet alive.** The faithfulness, the sense of duty in Moses would not have permitted him to leave the flocks in the wilderness and to go to Egypt without leave-taking, even for a short while. He told Jethro as much of the truth as the latter needed to know at that time, for he would hardly have found a complete understanding of his object and of the divine revelation in the home of his relatives by marriage. **And Jethro said to Moses, Go in peace.** V.19. **And the Lord said unto Moses in Midian,** for Moses apparently delayed his journey even now, **Go, return into Egypt; for all the men are dead which sought thy life.** This disclosure was intended to reassure Moses, to take away the last shred of his hesitation, although his mind had been made up even before. V.20. **And Moses took his wife and his sons,** Gershom and Eliezer, chap. 18, 4, **and set them upon an ass, and he returned to the land of Egypt,** he started out on his trip to the country of his birth, **and Moses took the rod of God in his hand,** for so he regarded the staff with which he was to perform miracles. V.21. **And the Lord said unto Moses, When thou goest to return into Egypt, see that thou do all those wonders before Pharaoh which I have put in thine hand.** The first commission was here repeated and explained, in order to impress every detail upon Moses' mind. After his return to Egypt he was to perform all the wonders, all the terrible signs, which the Lord had placed in his hand to do. There would be need of great firmness and courage in dealing with Pharaoh. **But I will harden his heart that he shall not let the people go.** In His omniscience the Lord here anticipates. He knew that Pharaoh would harden his heart willfully and maliciously, would refuse to heed the successive appeals that would be made, and therefore God announces the final judgment upon the Egyptian king, the condemnation which would make it impossible for him to be converted in the end. V.22. **And thou shalt say unto Pharaoh, Thus saith the Lord, Israel is My son, even my first-born;** v.23. **and I say unto thee, Let My son go that he may serve me; and if thou refuse to let him go, behold, I will slay thy son, even thy first-born.** This threat looks forward to the last of the Egyptian plagues. The fact that Israel is called God's first-born son suggests, even here, that the Lord would later choose others, that He would gain spiritual children out of the heathen nations. V.24. **And it came to pass by the way in the inn that the Lord met him, and sought to kill him.** In the place where Moses and his family encamped for the night while on the journey, the Lord threatened to take his life by a sudden disease, because he had neglected to circumcise his second son, Eliezer. Circumcision was the sign of the covenant between God and His people, and could not be omitted without grave consequences. **V. 25. Then Zipporah took a sharp stone,** a stone knife, **and cut off the foreskin of her son, and cast it at his feet,** laid it down so that it touched the feet of Moses, **and said, Surely a bloody husband art thou to me.** The entire incident seems to have been a source of great displeasure to Zipporah, and her words indicate that she considered her husband regained by the blood of her child. V.26. **So He let him go. Then she said,**

31

A bloody husband, or bridegroom, **thou art, because of the circumcision.** She vented her displeasure after the recovery of Moses was assured. It seems that this incident caused Moses to reconsider his intention of taking his family along to Egypt. At any rate, it was not until his return to the peninsula of Sinai that his father-in-law brought his family to him, chap. 18, 2. As circumcision was a sacrament in the Old Testament, so Baptism is a sacrament of the New Testament, and the Lord's zeal for the use of the means of grace is as great as ever.

Moses and Aaron before the people. — V.27. **And the Lord said to Aaron, Go into the wilderness to meet Moses.** This showed that the favor of the Lord had once more turned to Moses. His wife was not in full accord with him and his belief at that time, but Aaron's coming would be a great comfort to him. And he went, and met him in the mount of God, on Mount Horeb, **and kissed him,** this cordial greeting being all the more natural since the brothers had not seen each other for about forty years. V.28. **And Moses told Aaron all the words of the Lord, who had sent him, and all the signs which He had commanded him.** Aaron thus became familiar with the situation just as the Lord had presented it to Moses. V.29. **And Moses and Aaron went and gathered together all the elders of the children of Israel,** as the Lord had commanded, chap. 3, 16; v.30. **and Aaron spake all the words which the Lord had spoken unto Moses, and did the signs in the sight of the people.** V.31. **And the people believed,** they were convinced by the words of Aaron, as they were substantiated by the miraculous signs given to Moses. **And when they heard that the Lord had visited the children of Israel,** that He had investigated their condition in the land of their bondage, **and that He had looked upon their affliction,** their distressing burdens, **then they bowed their heads and worshiped.** The promise of the patriarchs was still alive in their hearts, they took new hope for the future, and they thanked God for the prospect of a speedy deliverance. This new hope at the same time welded the people together into one organization by making them conscious once more of their position. Thus the believers will ever accept all the promises of God in His Word with a thankful heart and place their confidence in Him without wavering.

6

Exodus 5

The Increase of the Oppression.

The taskmasters instructed to burden the people. — V.1. **And afterward Moses and Aaron went in and told Pharaoh, Thus saith the Lord God of Israel, Let My people go that they may hold a feast unto Me in the wilderness.** Moses and Aaron here acted not only as representatives of the children of Israel, who had acknowledged their commission from God, but as the ambassadors of the Lord Himself. Their question distinctly stated by whose authority they were acting, namely, by that of Jehovah, the God of Israel. V.2. **And Pharaoh said, Who is the Lord that I should obey His voice to let Israel go? I know not the Lord, neither will I let Israel go.** Although Pharaoh's answer was given with the understanding that the gods governed the countries, and that therefore the Israelites belonged under the jurisdiction of the Egyptian gods and had no business to have a God of their own, Pharaoh here showed an impious, selfish, blasphemous mind, and proved himself a religious tyrant. V.3. **And they said, The God of the Hebrews hath met with us,** He had disclosed, revealed Himself to them in glory, He, the ancient God of the free Hebrews. **Let us go, we pray thee, three days' journey into the desert, and sacrifice unto the Lord, our God, lest He fall upon us with pestilence or with the sword.** The plea was that Jehovah would look upon their neglect to bring Him sacrifices as a deliberate act of disobedience, and would therefore come upon them, as their enemy, with severe punishments. Thus both ideas are brought out, that Jehovah was a jealous, and that He was a powerful God. V.4. **And the king of Egypt said unto them, Wherefore do ye, Moses and Aaron, let the people from their works,** attempt to secure for them a vacation from their labors, release them from their duties? **Get you unto your burdens,** your servile labor. He addressed them as though they themselves were slaves, and at the same time intimated that their request was a vain pretext. **you want to secure for them a vacation, a period of rest, and their great numbers caused such a period to result in losses to the crown. The words reveal a boundless contempt for the common people. V.6. And Pharaoh commanded the same day the taskmasters, the overseers who drove them to their work and while they were at work, and their officers, saying, v.7. Ye shall no more give the people straw to make brick, as heretofore, chopped straw being used for binding the clay in the bricks before they were dried in the sun; let them go and gather straw for themselves. In the past this straw had been furnished by the Egyptian overseers, and the**

Hebrew officers had kept a record of the work done by their countrymen. V.8. And the tale of the bricks which they did make heretofore ye shall lay upon them; ye shall not diminish aught thereof, the Israelites were to make and to deliver to the Egyptian overseers the same number of bricks as had always been required of them; for they be idle; therefore they cry, saying, Let us go and sacrifice to our God. Thus Pharaoh ascribed their request to be allowed to worship their God to a lack of sufficient occupation, to the fact that time was hanging heavy on their hands. V.9. Let there more work be laid upon the men that they may labor therein, literally: Let the service rest heavily upon the men and keep them busy therewith; and let them not regard vain words, let them not listen to the lying representations of that man Moses. Similar charges are preferred against the Christians to this day, namely, that they are restless, dissatisfied people, having only worship and prayer in mind and neglecting their duties as citizens — false accusations all of them.

The people complain to Pharaoh. — V.10. And the taskmasters of the people went out and their officers, the Egyptian overseers and their Hebrew subordinates, and they spake to the people, saying, Thus saith Pharaoh, I will not give you straw. The royal decree was to be carried out to the letter not a single straw was to be furnished. The Jewish scribes, or officers, had by this time become willing tools in the hands of the despots. V.11. Go ye, get you straw where ye can find it; yet not aught of your work shall be diminished. There is an emphasis on the pronoun:

Ye yourselves go, not others, as heretofore. V.12. So the people were scattered abroad throughout all the land of Egypt to gather stubble instead of straw. They did not even have access to straw-stacks, but were obliged to go out into the harvested fields and collect the stubble. V.13. And the taskmasters hasted them, urged them forward vehemently, saying, Fulfil your works, your daily tasks, the amount of labor which had been allotted them day by day, for each day, as when there was straw, when the necessary material for binding the clay was furnished. V.14. And the officers of the children of Israel which Pharaoh's taskmasters had set over them, as their own subordinates, were beaten, and demanded, Wherefore have ye not fulfilled your task in making brick both yesterday and today, as heretofore? When the number of bricks allotted to any company of the Israelites was not forthcoming, because it was a physical impossibility both to provide the straw and to make the bricks, the Jewish officers were held responsible and were punished. V.15. Then the officers of the children of Israel came and cried unto Pharaoh, saying, Wherefore dealest thou thus with thy servants? It was an attempt to protest against the tyrannical injustice of the measure. V.16. There is no straw given unto thy servants, and they say to us, Make brick; and, behold, thy servants are beaten; but the fault is in thine own people, the sin is that of thy people. Their cry was an indirect complaint against the king himself, whom they did not dare to reproach outright. V.17. But he said, Ye are idle, ye are idle; therefore ye say, Let us go and do sacrifice to the

Lord. He emphatically repeated his baseless charge, v.8. V.18. Go, therefore, now, and work; for there shall no straw be given you, yet shall ye deliver the tale of bricks. The unjust order was not only not remanded, but repeated by Pharaoh's own mouth, So that there could be no mistake about it. V.19. And the officers of the children of Israel did see that they were in evil case, literally, they were in bad, their position was now worse than it was before, after it was said, Ye shall not minish aught from your bricks of your daily task. The fact that the oppression of the children of Israel was increased in this manner was a last severe trial for them. God wanted to test their faith in the certainty of His promise regarding the deliverance which was near.

The officers reproach Moses and Aaron. — V.20. And they met Moses and Aaron, who stood in the way as they came forth from Pharaoh, anxious to hear the result of the meeting with the king. V.21. And they said unto them, The Lord look upon you and judge, because ye have made our savor to be abhorred in the eyes of Pharaoh and in the eyes of his servants to put a sword in their hand to slay us. It was a reproach of bitterness and despair: Ye have made us to stink, ye have brought us into ill repute. The king and his servants now had nothing but ill will and abhorrence for them, and this feeling was bound to find its outlet in acts of cruelty, in punishment and bloodshed. V.22. And Moses returned unto the Lord, turned to Jehovah with a cry of distress, and said, Lord, wherefore hast Thou so evil entreated this people? Why is it that Thou hast sent me? It is an appeal coming from the depths of humility and despair, but also a prayer of faith which clings to the Lord in spite of all adversities. V.23. For since I came to Pharaoh to speak in Thy name, he hath done evil to this people; neither hast Thou delivered Thy people at all; the Lord had apparently taken no steps to bring about the deliverance of His people from the house of bondage. Thus the Christians will often be inclined to be vexed and impatient in the midst of the trials and tribulations of this world. But God is merciful and patient and does not withdraw His almighty hand.

7

Exodus 6

The Renewal of God's Promise to His People.

The Lord sends a comforting message. — V.1. **Then the Lord said unto Moses,** in answer to his cry of anxiety, **Now shalt thou see what I will do to Pharaoh; for with a strong hand shall he let them go, and with a strong hand shall he drive them out of his land.** That was God's answer as to the eventual method which would be adopted by Pharaoh in dealing with the children of Israel. He would not only dismiss Israel out of his country, but he would do so with impatience, he would expel them. V.2. **And God spake unto Moses** in a solemn declaration, **and said unto him, I am the Lord;** v.3. **and I appeared unto Abraham, unto Isaac, and unto Jacob by the name of God Almighty, but by My name Jehovah was I not known to them.** To the patriarchs the Lord had not revealed Himself in His specific capacity as Jehovah, although the name was not unknown to them. Now He wanted to give actual evidence, definite proof, of Himself in fulfilling His promises, in carrying out the conditions of the Messianic covenant, at least in its typical form. V.4. **And I have also established my covenant with them to give them the land of Canaan, the land of their pilgrimage, wherein they were strangers.** This covenant had been made with Abraham, with Isaac, and with Jacob, as their history abundantly shows, while they were still strangers in the Land of Promise. But the time of four generations, of which the Lord had spoken to Abraham, Gen. 15, 16, was now drawing to a close, and so His words must now be fulfilled. V.5. **And I have also heard the groaning of the children of Israel, whom the Egyptians keep in bondage; and I have remembered my covenant.** That was the second factor which decided the Lord, the lamenting, the wailing, of the children of Israel under the burden of their bondage in Egypt. V.6. **Wherefore say unto the children of Israel, I am the Lord;** He wanted to prove Himself as Jehovah. **And I will bring you out from under the burdens of the Egyptians, and I will rid you out of their bondage, and I will redeem you with a stretched-out arm and with great judgments.** The expression "arm stretched out" is even stronger than "arm of strength" of verse 1, since it is the aim of the Lord to reassure the people beyond the shadow of a doubt. V.7. **And I will take you to Me for a people, and I will be to you a God; and ye shall know that I am the Lord, your God, which bringeth you out from under the burdens of the Egyptians.** This formal acceptance of the children of Israel as the people of the covenant took place at Mount Sinai, chap. 19, 5. 6. The Lord here repeats the definite statement that He would lead

Israel out from under, entirely away from, the oppressive burdens of the Egyptians. V.8. **And I will bring you in unto the land concerning the which I did swear to give it to Abraham, to Isaac, and to Jacob; and I will give it you for an heritage,** for a permanent possession; **I am the Lord.** This, then, was the Lord's threefold promise: to deliver His people from the bondage of Egypt; formally to adopt them as His people; to bring them into Canaan, their future possession. Thus the Lord comforts His children in the midst of their afflictions with the promise of the everlasting deliverance, whereby His covenant, His Word, remains alive in their hearts.

God's charge to Moses and Aaron. — V.9. **And Moses spake so unto the children of Israel; but they hearkened not unto Moses for anguish of spirit and for cruel bondage,** literally, for shortness of breath and for hard slavery. It was not merely physical affliction with which they were suffering, but their spirit was almost broken with the unendurable harshness of the treatment which they received. V.10. **And the Lord spake unto Moses, saying,** v.11. **Go in, speak unto Pharaoh, king of Egypt, that he let the children of Israel go out of his land.** It was a direct command to lay aside all faint-heartedness and to undertake the task of delivering the people with all energy. V.12. **And Moses spake before the Lord, saying, Behold, the children of Israel have not hearkened unto me; how, then, shall Pharaoh hear me, who am of uncircumcised lips?** He argues that if the less difficult was impossible for him, the harder task would certainly be far above his ability. He assigns the reason for his failure to his uncircumcised, his unregenerate lips, which made it impossible for him to transmit the words of the Lord to Aaron with the proper ease and fluency and in all their stainless purity. V.13. **And the Lord spake unto Moses and unto Aaron, and gave them a charge unto the children of Israel, and unto Pharaoh, king of Egypt, to bring the children of Israel out of the land of Egypt.** It was a comprehensive command intended to beat down the last feeling of hesitation which Moses still felt. It is no small matter to proclaim the will of the Lord to defiant, obstinate men, but when the Lord commands, His will must be done.

The genealogy of Moses and Aaron. — V.14. **These be the heads of their father's houses.** The tribes were considered as branching off first into families, or clans, or heads of the father-houses; these again branch off into the father-houses themselves. **The sons of Reuben, the first-born of Israel: Hanoch, and Pallu, Hezron, and Carmi; these be the families of Reuben.** Cp. Gen. 46, 9; 1 Chron. 5, 3. V.15. **And the sons of Simeon: Jemuel, and Jamin, and Ohad, and Jachin, and Zohar, and Shaul, the son of a Canaanitish woman; these are the families of Simeon.** Cp. Gen. 46, 10; 1 Chron. 4. 24. V.16. **And these are the names of the sons of Levi according to their; generations: Gershon, and Kohath, and Merari,** Gen. 46, 11; **and the years of the life of Levi were an hundred and thirty and seven years. V.17. The sons of Gershon: Libni and Shimi, according to their families.** V.18. **And the sons of Kohath: Amram, and Izhar, and Hebron, and Uzziel; and the years of the life of Kohath were an hundred thirty and three years. V.19. And the sons of Merari: Mahali and Mushi; these are the families of Levi according to their generations.** V.20.

43

And Amram took him Jochebed, his father's sister, to wife; and she bare him Aaron and Moses; and the years of the life of Amram were an hundred and thirty and seven years. Cp. 1 Chron. 6, 1–3. Note that the sum of the ages of these three generations, plus the age of Moses at the time of the Exodus, is four hundred eighty-seven years; so there is no difficulty in making Bible chronology fit. Of the three children of Amram and Jochebed, Aaron was three years older than Moses, and Miriam was older than either. V.21. **And the sons of Izhar: Korah, and Nepheg, and Zichri.** V.22. **And the sons of Uzziel: Mishael, and Elzaphan, and Zithri.** These were the cousins of Moses and Aaron. V.23. **And Aaron took him Elisheba, daughter of Amminadab, sister of Naashon, to wife,** a woman of the tribe of Judah, 1 Chron. 2, 10; **and she bare him Nadab, and Abihu, Eleazar, and Ithamar.** V.24. **And the sons of Korah: Assir, and Elkanah, and Abiasaph; these are the families of the Korhites. V. 25. And Eleazar, Aaron's son, took him one of the daughters of Putiel to wife; and she bare him Phinehas. These are the heads of the fathers of the Levites according to their families,** the heads of the father-houses. V.26. **These are that Aaron and Moses to whom the Lord said, Bring out the children of Israel from the land of Egypt according to their armies.** Although the heads of the father-houses of Reuben and Simeon were also mentioned, the genealogy was here inserted chiefly for the sake of showing the family relations of Moses and Aaron. V.27. **These are they which spake to Pharaoh, king of Egypt, to bring out the children of Israel from Egypt; these are that Moses and Aaron,** Moses being mentioned in first place again on account of his leadership at the time of the Exodus. The men through whom the Lord performed such great works occupy a place of honor in the history of the Lord's kingdom.

The Lord again commissions Moses. — V.28. **And it came to pass on the day when the Lord spake unto Moses in the land of Egypt,** v.29. **that the Lord spake unto Moses, saying, I am the Lord; speak thou unto Pharaoh, king of Egypt, all that I say unto thee.** The narrative is here resumed with another emphatic commission of the Lord, in which He bids Moses transmit His exact words to Pharaoh. V.30. **And Moses said before the Lord, Behold, I am of uncircumcised lips, and how shall Pharaoh hearken unto me?** It is the same objection as in verse 12, declaring his complete unfitness for the task which the Lord had laid upon him. When the Lord calls, His servants should at all times heed His call with all eagerness and not consult with flesh and blood.

8

Exodus 7

God's Judgment upon Pharaoh Begins.

Moses as God's ambassador to Pharaoh. — V.1. **And the Lord said unto Moses, See, I have made thee a god to Pharaoh,** He had given him authority as His ambassador, with power to carry out His judgments; **and Aaron, thy brother, shall be thy prophet,** by acting as spokesman of the revelations given to Moses. V.2. **Thou shalt speak all that I command thee,** communicate the commands and the revelations of God to Aaron; **and Aaron, thy brother, shall speak unto Pharaoh, that he send the children of Israel out of his land.** That aim Aaron was always to keep in mind, to induce the king of Egypt to permit the emigration of Israel. V.3. **And I will harden Pharaoh's heart, and multiply My signs and wonders in the land of Egypt.** Because Pharaoh would harden his heart in the first place, the Lord intended to punish him by leaving him in this sin of obduracy. In this way the glory of the Lord would be increased by the many miracles which were to be performed before Pharaoh. V.4. **But Pharaoh shall not hearken unto you,** on account of his condition of hard-heartedness, **that I may lay My hand upon Egypt, and bring forth Mine armies,** the hosts that were to wage the Lord's battles, **and My people, the children of Israel, out of the land of Egypt by great judgments.** The Lord would judge, condemn, and punish the entire land of Egypt because the people consented to the sins of their king. V.5. **And the Egyptians shall know that I am the Lord when I stretch forth Mine hand upon Egypt,** in avenging justice and in almighty power, **and bring out the children of Israel from among them. V. 6. And Moses and Aaron did as the Lord commanded them, so did they.** They accepted the commission given them. V.7. **And Moses was fourscore years old and Aaron fourscore and three years old when they spake unto Pharaoh.** This concludes the narrative of the call of Moses and Aaron. Both of them now willingly placed themselves under the direction of the Lord, just as all true servants of God perform His will whenever He commands.

The miracles in the presence of Pharaoh. — V.8. **And the Lord spake unto Moses and unto Aaron, saying,** v.9. **When Pharaoh shall speak unto you, saying, Show a miracle for you, then thou shalt say unto Aaron, Take thy rod and cast it before Pharaoh, and it shall become a serpent.** This miracle, chap. 4, 3–5, was to substantiate the words of the ambassadors, to give definite proof of their divine commission. V.10. **And Moses and Aaron went in unto Pharaoh, and they did so as the Lord had commanded; and Aaron cast down his rod before**

Pharaoh, the shepherd's staff which Moses had brought along and had entrusted to Aaron for that purpose, **and before his servants, and it became a serpent,** a large,. poisonous snake. V.11. **Then Pharaoh also called the wise men and the sorcerers,** the men versed in occult arts and witchcraft. **Now the magicians of Egypt, they also did in like manner with their enchantments,** for the devil is also able to perform what seems like miracles, with the sufferance of God. v.12. **For they cast down every man his rod, and they became serpents,** there being, to all appearances, no difference between the miracles. **But Aaron's rod swallowed up their rods,** God thus indicating that He was the mightier. Cp. 2 Tim. 3, 8, where the names of the chief sorcerers of Pharaoh are supplied as having been Jannes and Jambres. V.13. **And He hardened Pharaoh's heart, that he hearkened not unto them; as the Lord had said.** The fact that his wise men with their witchcraft succeeded in imitating the miracle of Aaron was enough to decide Pharaoh against the Lord, the result being a hardening of his heart. Even so many an unbeliever in our days is confirmed in his opposition to the Gospel by the claims advanced by a false science.

The plague of blood. — V.14. **And the Lord said unto Moses, Pharaoh's heart is hardened, he refuseth to let the people go.** V.15. **Get thee unto Pharaoh in the morning; lo, he goeth out unto the water, to the river Nile; and thou shalt stand by the river's brink against he come,** he should stand ready to meet him as Pharaoh approached**; and the rod which was turned to a serpent thou shalt take in thine hand.** V.16. **And thou shalt say unto him, The Lord God of the Hebrews hath sent**

me unto thee, saying, **Let My people go that they may
serve Me in the wilderness,** chap. 3, 12. 18; **and, behold,
hitherto thou wouldest not hear.** V.17. **Thus saith
the Lord, In this thou shalt know that I am the Lord:
behold, I will smite with the rod that is in mine hand
upon the waters which are in the river, and they shall
be turned to blood,** not merely be given a blood-red color
through the presence of microscopic animals or particles of
red clay, but actually be changed into blood, that the river
throughout the length of Egypt would flow with the liquid
which commonly pulses through the arteries and veins of
men and beasts. V.18. **And the fish that is in the river
shall die, and the river shall stink; and the Egyptians
shall loathe to drink of the water of the river.** With their
life element taken from them, the fishes could no longer
live, and their decaying carcasses would infect the river and
cause an insufferable stench. V.19. **And the Lord spake
unto Moses, Say unto Aaron, Take thy rod,** the same staff
which had served before, **and stretch out thine hand upon
the waters of Egypt, upon their streams, upon their
rivers, and upon their ponds, and upon all their pools
of water, that they may become blood.** Thus not only
the Nile with its various arms was involved, but also the
canals of the Nile, all lakes or ponds that had been formed
by the overflow of the Nile, And that there may be blood
throughout all the land of Egypt, both in vessels of wood
and in vessels of stone, in all pails, jugs, and tubs, in which
water was kept for use in the homes. V.20. **And Moses and
Aaron did so, as the Lord commanded; and he lifted up
the rod, and smote the waters that were in the river, in
the sight of Pharaoh,** who was thus to witness the cause and

to note the effect, **and in the sight of his servants; and all the waters that were in the river were turned to blood. V.21. And the fish that was in the river died; and the river stank, and the Egyptians could not drink of the water of the river; and there was blood throughout all the land of Egypt.** The Nile was the one source of fertility and life in Egypt, and therefore the Lord indicated by this miracle that it was an easy matter for Him to change all the blessings of the country into curses. The very Nile to which the Egyptians gave divine honor was subject to the command of the God of the Hebrews, and this fact was to be impressed upon them forcibly. V.22. **And the magicians of Egypt did so with their enchantments,** probably over the water of the wells dug by the Egyptians, v.24. **and Pharaoh's heart was hardened, neither did he hearken unto them, as the Lord had said.** V.23. **And Pharaoh turned and went into his house, neither did he set his heart to this also. His heart was in no manner moved to grant the request of Moses and Aaron.** V.24. **And all the Egyptians digged round about the river for water to drink;** they quickly dug wells in the hope that the underground springs were still pure or that the seepage water had not turned into blood; for they could not drink of the water of the river. V.25. **And seven days were fulfilled, after that the Lord had smitten the river,** for it was He whose curse rested upon the land, and the miracle had been performed in His power. The plague lasted seven days and may to this day be regarded as an example of warning to all unbelievers.

9

Exodus 8

The Second, Third, and Fourth Plagues.

The plague of the frogs. — V.1. **And the Lord spake unto Moses, Go unto Pharaoh, and say unto him, Thus saith the Lord, Let My people go that they may serve Me.** This command became a formula in the course of the plagues and was intended to impress Pharaoh by its very repetition. V.2. **And if thou refuse to let them go, behold, I will smite all thy borders, the entire country to the extremest boundaries, with frogs;** v.3. **and the river,** otherwise the source of fertility and blessing, **shall bring forth frogs abundantly,** it would swarm with frogs, **which shall go up and come into thine house, and into thy bedchamber, and upon thy bed, and into the house of thy servants, and upon thy people, and into thine ovens, and into thy kneading-troughs;** v.4. **and the frogs shall come up both on thee, and upon thy people, and upon all thy servants.** As the frogs came up out of the water and the mire of the Nile, there was not a spot in Egypt safe from their clammy presence, not even the inner bedrooms of the houses, not even the large wooden vessels in which the Egyptian women kneaded the bread-dough, not even the very persons of the Egyptians: the frogs would persist in creeping everywhere. V.5. **And the Lord spake unto Moses, Say unto Aaron, Stretch forth thine hand with thy rod over the streams, over the rivers, and over the ponds, almost as in the first plague, and cause frogs to come up upon the land of Egypt.** V.6. **And Aaron stretched out his hand over the waters of Egypt; and the frogs came up, and covered the land of Egypt.** There was one immense expanse of frogs as far as one could see. V.7. **And the magicians did so with their enchantments,** with their verses of incantation, **and brought up frogs upon the land of Egypt.** They could imitate the miracle on a small scale, but they were unable to remove the plague. V.8. **Then Pharaoh called for Moses and Aaron and said, Intreat the Lord that He may take away the frogs from me and from my people.** He was forced to admit, not only that Jehovah actually existed, but that this plague was His punishment, and that He was the only one able to remove its horror. **And I will let the people go that they may do sacrifice unto the Lord.** The promise was pressed from him by the great emergency which was upon him. V.9. **And Moses said unto Pharaoh, Glory over me,** be magnified above me, an expression used by Moses to refer all honor to Jehovah; **when shall I intreat for thee, and for thy servants, and for thy people, to destroy,** literally to cut off, to put away definitely, **the frogs from thee and thy houses, that they may remain in the river only?** The fact that Pharaoh was even permitted to set the time for the deliverance from the plague was to direct his thoughts to the superior power of the God of the Hebrews. V.10. **And he said, To-morrow,** thinking, perhaps, that it would be impossible to remove the frogs in such a short time. **And he said, Be it according to thy word; that thou mayest know that there is none like unto the Lord, our God.** Moses hoped that the fulfillment of his definite promise would have some influence upon the king. V.11. **And the frogs shall depart from thee, and from thy houses, and from thy servants, and from thy people; they shall remain in the river only.** As persistently as the clammy creatures had sought the company of men, so rapidly they would turn back to their natural haunts. V.12. **And Moses and Aaron went out from Pharaoh; and Moses cried unto the Lord,** with a loud and insistent appeal, **because of the frogs which He had brought against Pharaoh.** V.13. **And the Lord did according to the word of Moses,** He stood by His servant in granting his request; **and the frogs died out of the houses,** literally away from the houses, **out of the villages,** or courts, **and out of the fields.** V.14. **And they gathered them together upon heaps,** by the bushel; **and the land stank** from the odor of decay. V.15. **But when Pharaoh saw that there was respite,** there was relief from the pressure of the plague and he could once more get his breath, **he hardened his heart and hearkened not unto them; as the Lord had said.** Thus it happens even in our days that obstinate sinners will cry for help when the hand of God rests heavily upon them. But there is no real change of heart in their case, and as soon as they feel relief, they forget all their solemn promises.

The plague of the lice. — V.16. **And the Lord said unto Moses, Say unto Aaron, Stretch out thy rod, and smite the dust of the land, that it may become lice throughout all the land of Egypt.** The insects referred to are very small gnats, which crawl on the skin, and even into the noses and ears, and inflict painful stings. These tiny animals were, by a special creative act of God, to come up out of the dust in countless millions, like the dust. V.17. **And they did so; for Aaron stretched out his hand with his rod, and smote the dust of the earth, and it became lice in man and in beast; all the dust of the land became lice throughout all the land of Egypt.** The Nile had twice become the source of a plague, and here the very land which yielded such rich harvests brought forth an insect pest which was unbearable. V.18. **And the magicians did so with their enchantments,** they also smote the dust while they murmured verses of incantation, **to bring forth lice, but they could not; so there were lice upon man and upon beast.** In this case the Lord did not consent to their imitating His miracle, and so they were unable to perform the apparently simple feat. V.19. **Then the magicians said unto Pharaoh, This is the finger of God.** They were forced to declare their impotence in the face of God's almighty power, to acknowledge that the God of the Hebrews was mightier than they. **And Pharaoh's heart was hardened, and he hearkened not unto them; as the Lord had said.** In spite of all the evidence, in spite of the confession of his wisest sorcerers, he persisted in his obstinacy. Even the blind children of this world are obliged to acknowledge occasionally that God's punishments strike the world, and yet they refuse to repent.

The plague of the flies. — V.20. **And the Lord said unto Moses, Rise up early in the morning, and stand before Pharaoh; lo, he cometh forth to the water,** the river Nile, probably for purposes of worship; **and say unto him, Thus saith the Lord, Let My people go that they may serve Me.** It is a monotonous repetition intended to wear down the hard heart of the king. V.21. **Else, if thou wilt not let My people go, behold, I will send swarms of flies upon thee, and upon thy servants, and upon thy people, and into thy houses; and the houses of the Egyptians shall be full of swarms of flies, and also the ground whereon they are.** As nearly as can be determined, the flies here referred to are the dog-flies or blood sucking gad-flies, whose sting is particularly painful. The grievousness of the plague, moreover, would be increased by the fact that the flies would come in such great numbers as to fill the land and cover the ground. V.22. **And I will sever in that day the land of Goshen, in which My people dwell, that no swarms of flies shall be there;** the Lord intended to make a miraculous distinction in favor of the children of Israel; **to the end thou mayest know that I am the Lord in the midst of the earth,** therefore possessing absolute power also over the land of Egypt as the omnipotent Sovereign over all. V.23. **And I will put a division between My people and thy people,** set a redemption in favor of the children of Israel, to deliver them from the plague; **to-morrow shall this sign be.** V.24. **And the Lord did so; and there came a grievous swarm of flies into the house of Pharaoh, and into his servants' houses, and into all the land of Egypt; the land was corrupted by reason of the swarm of flies.** Not only were the people tortured with the severe stings, as well as the animals, but the vegetation was attacked by the maggots that developed from the eggs deposited on it. V.25. **And Pharaoh called for Moses and for Aaron, and said, Go ye, sacrifice to your God in the land.** The fierceness of the plague drove Pharaoh to this first concession, at least to grant the children of Israel a few days of rest for a sacrificial festival. V.26. **And Moses said, It is not meet so to do,** to do so would have been against the rule which the Lord wanted to have observed; **for we shall sacrifice the abomination of the Egyptians to the Lord, our God,** for the Egyptians were highly scandalized if animals sacred to them were offered; **lo, shall we sacrifice the abomination of the Egyptians before their eyes, and will they not stone us?** The idea of offering sacrifices to Jehovah in Egypt, where the true God was not accepted, was in itself an abomination to the Egyptians, and they would not have hesitated about making known their objections. V.27. **We will go three days' journey Into the wilderness, and sacrifice to the Lord, our God, as He shall command us.** Moses refused to recede from his original demand in any manner. V.28. **And Pharaoh said, I will let you go, that ye may sacrifice to the Lord, your God, in the wilderness; only ye shall not go very far away,** a restriction which he was cautious to add; **intreat for me.** He feigned a compliance which was far from that which the situation demanded. V.29. **And Moses said, Behold, I go out from thee, and I will lntreat the Lord that the swarms of files may depart from Pharaoh, from his servants, and from his people, to-morrow; but let not Pharaoh deal deceitfully any more in not letting the people go to sacrifice to the Lord.** This was a warning against the trickery which Pharaoh had exhibited before, v.15. and indicated that Moses was master of the situation. V.30. **And Moses went out from Pharaoh, and intreated the Lord.** V.31. **And the Lord did according to the word of Moses; and He removed the swarms of flies,** the obnoxious vermin, **from Pharaoh, from his servants, and from his people; there remained not one.** It was another miraculous removal of a plague. V.32. **And Pharaoh hardened his heart at this time also, neither would he let the people go.** It may happen now and then that obstinate sinners will declare themselves willing to reform in the one or the other thing which is offensive to the Lord; but such outward changes do not affect the heart, which remains hardened in sins as before. There is only one thing for Christians to do, namely, to serve the Lord in the manner which He prescribes in His Word. All self-chosen worship is an abomination to the Lord.

10

Exodus 9

The Fifth, Sixth, and Seventh Plagues.

The plague of the pestilence of beasts. — V.1. **Then the Lord said unto Moses, Go in unto Pharaoh and tell him, Thus saith the Lord God of the Hebrews, Let My people go that they may serve Me.** This was now the standing formula of demand. V.2. **For if thou refuse to let them go and wilt hold them still,** hold them back, using force upon them, in spite of the fact that Jehovah had made known His will so emphatically, v.3. **behold, the hand of the Lord is upon thy cattle which is in the field,** the domestic animals of every variety, **upon the horses, upon the asses, upon the camels, upon the oxen, and upon the sheep,** upon the flocks; **there shall be a very grievous murrain,** a destructive pestilence, against which human skill would avail nothing. V.4. **And the Lord shall sever between the cattle of Israel and the cattle of Egypt,** set a sharp line of distinction; **and there shall nothing die**

of all that is the children's of Israel. The fact that this exception of Israel's cattle was predicted and came to pass in just that way was to impress upon Pharaoh and upon all the Egyptians the unlimited power of the true God. V.5. **And the Lord appointed a set time, saying, Tomorrow the Lord shall do this thing in the land.** This was further evidence of His omnipotence. V.6. **And the Lord did that thing on the morrow, and all the cattle of Egypt died,** the various kinds were destroyed in such great numbers that there was only a negligible quantity remaining, v. 19; **but of the cattle of the children of Israel died not one.** V.7. **And Pharaoh sent, and, behold, there was not one of the cattle of the Israelites dead.** The words of the Lord had again been fulfilled literally. **And the heart of Pharaoh was hardened, and he did not let the people go.** He was further confirmed in his obduracy and incidentally showed his tyrannical disposition, since the plague, which struck chiefly his poor subjects, affected him very little, although he had convinced himself of the miraculous sparing of the Israelites. A person who is hardened against God will also lose his feeling of affection toward his fellow-men.

The plague of boils and blains. — V.8. **And the Lord said unto Moses and unto Aaron, Take to you handfuls of ashes of the furnace,** soot from the ovens, **and let Moses sprinkle it toward the heaven in the sight of Pharaoh,** who should again know the cause and note the effect. V.9. **And it shall become small dust in all the land of Egypt, and shall be a boil breaking forth with blains upon man and upon beast throughout all the land of Egypt.** The soot, reduced to fine black dust and increased a thousandfold, was to infect both man and beast throughout Egypt with inflammatory pustules or ulcers, painful boils and sores, probably on the order of smallpox. V.10. **And they took ashes of the furnace, and stood before Pharaoh; and Moses sprinkled it up toward heaven, and it became a boil breaking forth with blains upon man and upon beast,** an inflammation coming to a head in pustules, filled with a watery fluid. V.11. **And the magicians could not stand before Moses because of the boils; for the boil was upon the magicians and upon all the Egyptians.** Far from being able to imitate the miracle in this case, the Egyptian sorcerers were not even able to protect themselves against the ulcerous inflammation. V.12. **And the Lord hardened the heart of Pharaoh,** He placed the curse upon him which his obduracy deserved, **and he hearkened not unto them, as the Lord had spoken unto Moses.** If a sinner consistently rejects repentance and a change of heart, the Lord finally inflicts this obduracy upon him as a curse.

The hail threatened. — V.13. **And the Lord said unto Moses, Rise up early in the morning, and stand before Pharaoh, and say unto him, Thus saith the Lord God of the Hebrews, Let My people go that they may serve Me.** The same demand repeated, with maddening emphasis. V.14. **For I will at this time send all My plagues upon thine heart and upon thy servants and upon thy people, that thou mayest know that there is none like Me in all the earth.** The threat in this case is more fearful, and seems to include all the remaining plagues, which were to be directed against the obdurate heart of the king, but were also to affect his servants and all his people, since they all consented to the sins of Pharaoh. The final purpose was to establish the fact that the Lord God of the Hebrews was the one true God in all the earth. V.15. **For now I will stretch out My hand that I may smite thee and thy people with pestilence, and thou shalt be cut off from the earth.** Pharaoh was even now doomed to death, and if the Lord had so chosen, it would have been an easy matter for Him to destroy him before this. V.16. **And, in very deed, for this cause have I raised thee up,** God intended to set Pharaoh forth, as it were, as an example before the whole world and for all times, **for to show in thee My power, and that My name be declared throughout all the earth.** The manner in which the Lord would carry out the punishment upon Pharaoh would reveal His almighty power and cause His name to be extolled throughout the earth. After this general, impressive threat the Lord turns to the specific case in hand. V.17. **As yet exaltest thou thyself against My people that thou wilt not let them go?** There is a bit of terrible sarcasm here, that a puny man should so proudly glorify and exalt himself as to venture to set himself up as a dam against the will of God. V.18. **Behold, to-morrow about this time I will cause it to rain a very grievous hail, such as hath not been in Egypt since the foundation thereof even until now.** Since the day that the Egyptians had been organized as a nation such an extremely heavy and devastating hail had not been experienced in the land. Pharaoh was given only twenty-four hours' time for reflection, to save himself and his people from the plague. V.19. **Send, therefore, now, and gather thy cattle, and all that thou hast in the field,** he should put the cattle which had remained after the great pestilence in a safe place, and secure whatever part of the crop could be saved upon such short notice; **for upon every man and beast which shall** be found in the field, and shall not be brought home, the hail shall come down upon them, and they shall die. By adopting such measures of precaution as the Lord here advised, the Egyptians would be able to save at least a part of their property in the terrible destruction. V.20. He that feared the word of the Lord among the servants of Pharaoh made his servants and his cattle flee into the houses; v.21. and he that regarded not the word of the Lord, whose heart was not set upon the dire prediction and warning, left his servants and his cattle in the field. So the words of Moses and the plagues that had preceded the present one had at least produced a wholesome fear of the Lord, if they had not worked repentance.

The plague of the hail. — V.22. And the Lord said unto Moses, Stretch forth thine hand toward heaven, as a sign before all men that the plague was now to begin, that there may be hail in all the land of Egypt, upon man, and upon beast, and upon every herb of the field, plants of every kind, throughout the land of Egypt. V.23. And Moses stretched forth his rod, his hand which held his shepherd's staff, toward heaven: and the Lord sent thunder and hail, He gave forth voices accompanied with hail, as a most powerful revelation of His divine omnipotence. And the fire ran along upon the ground in the form of ball lightning which is particularly destructive; and the Lord rained hail upon the land of Egypt. It is a sublime description of a thunderstorm accompanied with a terrific fall of hail, causing a devastation such as no ordinary storm will bring about. V.24. So there was hail, and fire mingled with the hail, in addition to the hail, very grievous, such as there was none like it in all the land of Egypt since it

became a nation. V.25. And the hail smote, throughout all the land of Egypt, all that was in the field, both man and beast; they were not only struck down, but killed; **and the hail smote every herb of the field,** all the smaller plants, **and brake every tree of the field,** not only by stripping the trees of their foliage, but by cutting off twigs and branches. V.26. **Only in the land of Goshen, where the children of Israel were, was there no hail.** The Lord did not include His people in the plague. V.27. **And Pharaoh sent, and called for Moses and Aaron, and said unto them, I have sinned this time; the Lord is righteous, and I and my people are wicked.** That was not the voice of true repentance, but merely of slavish fear, of abject terror, a confession intended only to secure deliverance from the destruction of the plague. V.28. **Entreat the Lord (for it is enough) that there be no more mighty thundering and hail; and I will let you go, and ye shall stay no longer.** He immediately attaches the condition that they should not ask for, nor extend, the time of their festival beyond the three days originally named. A truly repentant heart will humbly bow under the punishment of the Lord, and will not presume to say when the limit has been reached. V.29. **And Moses said unto him, As soon as I am gone out of the city, I will spread abroad my hands unto the Lord,** in a gesture of earnest pleading; **and the thunder shall cease, neither shall there be any more hail; that thou mayest know how that the earth is the Lord's,** that all the land and all the powers of nature are in His hand, that He controls them as He pleases. V.30. **But as for thee and thy servants, I know that ye will not fear the Lord God;** it was obvious that their repentance was not of the right kind. V.31. **And the flax and the barley was smitten,** that was the extent of the damage done by the hail; **for the barley was in the ear,** the stalks had made heads, **and the flax was boiled,** it was in bloom. In their case, therefore, there was a total loss. V.32. **But the wheat and the rye,** or spelt, **were not smitten; for they were not grown up,** they belong to the late grains. V.33. **And Moses went out of the city from Pharaoh, and spread abroad his hands unto the Lord; and the thunders and hail ceased, and the rain was not poured upon the earth.** V.34. **And when Pharaoh saw that the rain and the hail and the thunders were ceased, he sinned yet more, and hardened his heart, he and his servants.** They added to their former sin and deliberately made their obduracy greater. V.35. **And the heart of Pharaoh was hardened, neither would he let the children of Israel go, as the Lord had spoken by Moses.** The man who hardens his heart against the influence of God's Word thereby invites the judgment of the Lord upon him. making it impossible for him to repent in truth. The condition of Pharaoh's heart may also be seen from the fact that he broke his promise to Moses. Where there is no fear of the Lord, all obligations of morality and decency are discarded.

11

Exodus 10

The Eighth and Ninth Plagues.

The locusts threatened. — V.1. **And the Lord said unto Moses, Go in unto Pharaoh; for I have hardened his heart, and the heart of his servants, that I might show these My signs before him,** v.2. **and that thou mayest tell in the ears of thy son and of thy son's son what things I have wrought in Egypt, and My signs which I have done among them; that ye may know how that I am the Lord.** Since Pharaoh had hardened his heart in the first place, the Lord now gave him up to the doom which he had chosen for himself, and the last plagues had the purpose of completing his obduracy. Of this fact Moses was informed, lest he become discouraged. At the same time the Lord had His own glorification in view; for the children of Israel, throughout their generations, should preserve the memory of the Egyptian plagues, in order to keep the fear of the Lord before them all the time. V.3. **And**

Moses and Aaron came in unto Pharaoh and said unto him, Thus saith the Lord God of the Hebrews; How long wilt thou refuse to humble thyself before Me? Let My people go that they may serve Me. It is the same formula, but preceded by a threatening question, spoken in a much severer tone than heretofore. Would Pharaoh never learn to humble himself before the almighty power of the true God? V.4. **Else, if thou refuse to let My people go, behold, to-morrow will I bring the locusts into thy coast.** It is again a definite prediction, which marks the plague as a miracle. V.5. **And they shall cover the face of the earth,** literally, the eye of the earth, which is pictured as looking upon man in the ornament of its rich vegetation, **that one cannot be able to see the earth; and they shall eat the residue of that which is escaped, which remaineth unto you from the hail,** all the plants whose foliage had been stripped, but which had recovered from the plague of the hail, **and shall eat every tree which groweth for you out of the field,** the foliage and the fruit of the trees, down to the very bark. V.6. **And they shall fill thy houses, and the houses of all thy servants, and the houses of all the Egyptians; which neither thy fathers, nor thy fathers' fathers have seen since the day that they were upon the earth unto this day.** Besides working utter devastation in the land, the locusts would, in addition, fill all the dwellings with their nauseating presence, thus proving themselves a pest upon men as well as upon vegetation. **And he** (Moses) **turned himself and went out from Pharaoh.** He added no appeal to his announcement, the simple statement of the fact coming with crushing force. V.7. **And Pharaoh's servants said unto him, How long shall this man be a**

snare unto us? They compared Moses to a trap, or snare, for catching animals and birds, and themselves to his victims. **Let the men go that they may serve the Lord, their God. Knowest thou not yet that Egypt is destroyed?** The blind obstinacy of Pharaoh was plunging the entire nation into destruction. Their advice was evidently that the king should grant the request and dismiss the Israelites. V.8. **And Moses and Aaron were brought again unto Pharaoh; and he said unto them, Go, serve the Lord, your God.** He acted as though he were ready to accede to their desire. **But who are they that shall go?** literally, "Who and who else are those going?" He wanted exact information on that point. V.9. **And Moses said, We will go with our young and with our old, with our sons and with our daughters, with our flocks and with our herds will we go; for we must hold a feast unto the Lord,** literally, "A feast of Jehovah is to us." It was again a simple statement of fact, for Moses was no longer the humble supplicant. V.10. **And he said unto them, Let the Lord be so with you, as I will let you go and your little ones.** That was bitter blasphemy, that Jehovah should be their assistance in the same degree as Pharaoh was dismissing them; for he had no such intention, and he defied the Lord. **Look to it; for evil is before you.** He meant to say that he saw through their design of withdrawing the people from their labors. V.11. **Not so; go now, ye that are men, and serve the Lord; for that ye did desire.** He intimated that he had understood them as asking only for leave of absence for the men. **And they were driven out from Pharaoh's presence.** The tyrant acted in a purely arbitrary manner and against better knowledge; for such is the way of unbelievers in waging war against the

Lord's people.

The plague of locusts. — V.12. **And the Lord said unto Moses, Stretch out thine hand over the land of Egypt for the locusts that they may come up upon the land of Egypt,** like a hostile military force, or like clouds carried by the wind, **and eat every herb of the land, even all that the hail hath left.** V.13. **And Moses stretched forth his rod,** his hand with the shepherd's staff, **over the land of Egypt; and the Lord brought an east wind upon the land all that day and all that night.** So it was really the Lord, the Performer of all miracles, who drove the wind from the eastern desert over Egypt. **And when it was morning, the east wind brought the locusts.** V.14. **And the locusts went up over all the land of Egypt, and rested,** settled down to devour and devastate, **in all the coasts of Egypt. Very grievous were they; before them there were no such locusts as they, neither after them shall be such,** for it was a miraculous plague from the Lord. This is shown not only by the fact that the locusts came from very far, the wind blowing for twenty-four hours, but also that they covered the entire land, whereas ordinarily they will attack only certain regions and then move on. V.15. **For they covered the face of the whole earth, so that the land was darkened;** daylight was shut out by the density of the swarms as they came on; **and they did eat every herb of the land, and all the fruit of the trees which the hail had left; and there remained not any green thing in the trees or in the herbs of the field through all the land of Egypt.** It was a complete devastation of the land, a punishment whose severity had been increased over the preceding plagues. V.16. **Then Pharaoh called for Moses**

and Aaron in haste; and he said, I have sinned against the Lord, your God, and against you. This is a distinct confession of sin, for Pharaoh was not lacking in knowledge of his transgression, but in willingness to repent. V.17. **Now, therefore, forgive, I pray thee, my sin only this once, and intreat the Lord, your God, that He may take away from me this death only.** Here was more hypocrisy; for Pharaoh did not desire forgiveness of his sins in order to turn to the Lord for mercy, but only to be delivered from this terrible plague, which gave him a feeling of utter helplessness. Only this time he wanted to be delivered from the deadly ruin staring him in the face, an expression which afterward condemned him. V.18. **And he** (Moses) **went out from Pharaoh and intreated the Lord.** V.19. **And the Lord turned a mighty strong west wind, which took away the locusts and cast them into the Red Sea,** on the eastern boundary of Egypt, where they were destroyed in the water; there remained not one locust in all the coasts of Egypt. This sudden deliverance was again indisputable evidence of the almighty power of Jehovah, the God of the Hebrews. V.20. **But the Lord hardened Pharaoh's heart,** as He had said, v.1. **so that he would not let the children of Israel go.** Jehovah was not yet done with His mighty miracles upon Pharaoh and upon Egypt. The condemnation of obduracy was upon the king, and he was being reserved for the final punishment.

The plague of darkness. — V.21. **And the Lord said unto Moses, Stretch out thine hand toward heaven that there may be darkness over the land of Egypt, even darkness which may be felt.** Without previous announcement or warning this plague came upon Egypt as another sign of

God's almighty power. It was a supernatural, miraculous darkness, so heavy that all light from whatever source was cut off completely and all men were reduced to the necessity of feeling their way. V.22. **And Moses stretched forth his hand toward heaven; and there was a thick darkness in all the land of Egypt three days; v.23. they saw not one another, neither rose any from his place for three days.** This was another sign of God's great anger and one of those that point forward to the last Judgment, a heavy, continuous darkness, which was not illumined by a single ray of light for three days. **But all the children of Israel had light in their dwellings;** the land of Goshen, where they dwelt, was not included in the plague. V.24. **And Pharaoh called unto Moses,** he summoned him in great fear, **and said, Go ye, serve the Lord; only let your flocks and your herds be stayed; let your little ones also go with you.** The cattle and sheep of the Israelites were to be a pledge of their return, for they were to be kept in certain designated places in charge of Egyptians. V.25. **And Moses said, Thou must give us also sacrifices and burnt offerings that we may sacrifice unto the Lord, our God;** for that was the reason substantiating their request to depart from Egypt. V.26. **Our cattle also shall go with us; there shall not an hoof be left behind.** It was a bold utterance, such as behooved the ambassador of the most high God. And the explanation should have satisfied the king; **for thereof must we take to serve the Lord, our God; and we know not with what we must serve the Lord until we come thither.** They would know what offerings the Lord desired only when they had arrived at the place where the Lord would reveal Himself to them. V.27. **But the Lord hardened Pharaoh's**

heart, and he would not let them go. God's punishment upon Pharaoh was going forward without abatement, to the bitter end. V.28. **And Pharaoh said unto him, Get thee from me, take heed to thyself, see my face no more; for in that day thou seest my face thou shalt die.** Thus the tyrant flew into a rage; having lost, he gave way to his temper. That is the final state of obduracy, if sinners repudiate the messengers of God entirely and will not hear another word of God's truth. V.29. **And Moses said, Thou hast spoken well, I will see thy face again no more.** He accepted the dismissal by answering: Just as thou hast said, let it be even so. It was the calmness of spiritual and moral superiority, the consciousness of having the Lord on his side, which gave Moses the courage to speak so at this time. If the believers have God's assurance of help, they will fear no evil.

12

Exodus 11

The Last Definite. Message of Deliverance.

V.1. **And the Lord said unto Moses, Yet will I bring one plague more upon pharaoh and upon Egypt; afterwards he will let you go hence. When he shall let you go, he shall surely thrust you out hence altogether.** The plague which the Lord had in mind was to be a final blow of such severity as to cause Pharaoh not only to dismiss the children of Israel, but even to drive them out. V.2. **Speak now in the ears of the people, and let every man borrow of his neighbor, and every woman of her neighbor, jewels of silver and jewels of gold.** This was one of the points which the Lord had mentioned as early as the time of Moses' call. The people were to demand of their Egyptian neighbors silverware and vessels of gold, jewelry of every kind. V.3. **And the Lord gave the people favor in the sight of the Egyptians.** He influenced the Egyptians in such a manner as to make them willing to give up their most costly treasures. Thus it happened that, in a way at least, the children of Israel received compensation for their years of severe toil. **Moreover, the man Moses was very great in the land of Egypt, in the sight of Pharaoh's servants and in the sight of the people.** This fact also had much weight in causing the Egyptians to part with their treasures so willingly: they stood in awe of Moses, because they saw the power of God in him. V.4. **And Moses said,** he made this solemn announcement to Pharaoh before he left his presence with the confident answer of chap. 10, 29: **Thus saith the Lord, About mid-night will I go out into the midst of Egypt,** He intended now to interfere personally in the affairs of Egypt, to execute judgment with His almighty arm. V.5. **And all the first-born in the land of Egypt shall die,** all the natural heads and representatives of families, all that was first-born, **from the first-born of Pharaoh that sitteth upon his throne, even unto the first-born of the maid-servant that is behind the mill,** the slave that was engaged in grinding meal on a hand-mill; **and all the first-born of beasts.** There Would be no exception, from the highest to the lowest the Egyptians must suffer. V.6. **And there shall be a great cry throughout all the land of Egypt, such as there was none like it, nor shall be like it any more.** The blow would be so sharp and would be so universally felt that the lamentation would arise on all sides, as it had never done in the same degree before. V.7. **But against any of the children of Israel shall not a dog move his tongue, against man or beast,** the proverbial expression of a dog's sharpening his tongue indicating that not the slightest trouble would be experienced, not the least disturbance would be suffered by the Jews; **that ye may know how that**

the Lord doth put a difference between the Egyptians and Israel. The just revenge of God will finally strike all the unrepentant children of unbelief, delivering them to death and destruction, while He holds His sheltering hand over those that are His. V.8. **And all these thy servants shall come down unto me, and bow down themselves unto me, saying, Get thee out, and all the people that follow thee,** literally, under thy feet, under thy jurisdiction; **and after that I will go out. And he went out from Pharaoh in a great anger.** That was a just and holy indignation, for it is no small matter for unbelievers to reject the Word of the Lord. Pharaoh's time of grace was now coming to an end, and the wrath of the Lord would soon descend upon him. V.9. **And the Lord said unto Moses, Pharaoh shall not hearken unto you,** heed not even his last terrible threat; **that My wonders may be multiplied in the land of Egypt.** When the Lord is finally obliged to resort to the destruction of the wicked, such righteous punishment redounds to the glory of His holiness and justice. V.10. **And Moses and Aaron did all these wonders before Pharaoh,** all those that have been related till now; **and the Lord hardened Pharaoh's heart, so that he would not let the children of Israel go out of his land.** That was a part of the final punishment upon the obstinate king, a foretaste of the last terrible wrath and endless destruction.

13

Exodus 12

The Preparation and the Departure from Egypt.

The ordinances concerning the Passover. — V.1. **And the Lord spake unto Moses and Aaron in the land of Egypt, saying,** v.2. **This month shall be unto you the beginning of months; it shall be the first month of the year to you.** This was the first and fundamental law for the congregation of Jehovah. Up to that time the children of Israel had reckoned their year in a different manner, even as they begin their civil year in the fall to this day. By God's order their church-year was to begin with the month of which He was then speaking, and all their church festivals were reckoned according to this new division of time. V.3. **Speak ye unto all the congregation of Israel, saying, In the tenth day of this month they shall take to them every man a lamb** (or kid), **according to the house of their fathers, a lamb for an house.** From this time the children of Israel were considered the congregation of Jehovah. Every housefather was to take, to separate from the flock, a lamb or a kid. The practise was afterward narrowed to include lambs only. V.4. **And if the household be too little for the lamb, let him and his neighbor next unto his house take it according to the number of the souls; every man according to his eating shall make your count for the lamb.** If the number of members in anyone household, including the children and the servants, was so small as to make their disposing of an entire lamb improbable, then two small families having about the same number of souls might unite. Custom afterwards fixed the number of participants at the meal at about ten to twelve, but the fundamental unit was the family. V.5. **Your lamb shall be without blemish,** sound in body and limb, **a male of the first year,** literally, a son of a year, one born the previous year; **ye shall take it from the sheep or from the goats;** the choice at that time was immaterial. V.6. **And ye shall keep it until the fourteenth day of the same month,** separated from the rest of the flock, in order to keep it from contamination and infection; **and the whole assembly of the congregation of Israel,** all the housefathers as household priests and representatives of the children of Israel, **shall kill it in the evening,** literally, "between the two evenings," at twilight. Custom later fixed the time at between three in the afternoon and sundown. V.7. **And they shall take of the blood, and strike it on the two side-posts and on the upper doorpost of the houses, wherein they shall eat it.** The blood of the animal was drawn, kept from coagulating by constant stirring, and then applied to the door-posts by sprinkling or painting. V.8. **And they shall eat the flesh in that night, roast with fire, and**

76

**unleavened bread; and with bitter herbs they shall eat
it.** Those were the three dishes expressly commanded by
God, the bitter herbs being a salad of wild lettuce, endive,
and other vegetables with which the roast meat apparently
was garnished. V.9. **Eat not of it raw, nor sodden at
all with water, but roast with fire; his head with his
legs and with the purtenance thereof,** whole, not cut in
pieces, no bone broken, and the entrails in place, although,
of course, cleaned. The animal, as a whole, represented
the unity of Israel. V.10. **And ye shall let nothing of it
remain until the morning; and that which remaineth
of it until the morning ye shall burn with fire.** Down to
the very last morsel the meat should, if possible, be eaten, that
which remained in spite of all the efforts of the assembled
household being consigned to the fire. The instructions were
purposely exact and detailed, in order that there might be
no misunderstanding.

The precept pertaining to unleavened bread. — V.11. **And
thus shall ye eat it: with your loins girded, your shoes
on your feet,** literally, "shod on your feet," **and your staff
in your hand; and ye shall eat it in haste,** in hasty flight,
as such that were about to flee, in readiness for speedy flight.
It is the Lord's Passover. These instructions concerned
the celebration in Egypt and were afterward dropped as
unessential. Only the name for the festival, the Passover
of the Lord, was not changed, a perpetual reminder of the
miracle which the Lord performed in delivering His people.
V.12. **For I will pass through the land of Egypt this night,
and will smite all the first-born in the land of Egypt,
both man and beast; and against all the gods of Egypt I
will execute judgment. I am the Lord.** As the avenging,

almighty Judge the Lord intended to traverse the entire land of Egypt, to strike down all the first-born, to punish the princes with the common people, and thus to expose all the Egyptian idols as helpless delusions. V.13. **And the blood shall be to you for a token upon the houses where ye are; and when I see the blood, I will pass over you, and the plague shall not be upon you to destroy you, when I smite the land of Egypt.** Thus the Lord Himself explained the meaning of the Passover. Wherever there was a sign of blood, as He had commanded, there He would pass by, or over, and the blow would not strike the inmates of a house thus designated to work destruction in their midst. The slaughter would come upon the land of the Egyptians only. V.14. **And this day shall be unto you for a memorial,** the evening of the fourteenth day of Abib; **and ye shall keep it a feast to the Lord throughout your generations,** a festival of commemoration from one generation to the next; **ye shall keep it a feast by an ordinance forever.** It was to be celebrated as the festival of Israel's redemption and of its being set aside as the people of God's covenant. V.15. **Seven days shall ye eat unleavened bread; even the first day ye shall put away leaven out of your houses; for whosoever eateth leavened bread from the first day until the seventh day, that soul shall be cut off from Israel.** This is the solemn ordinance relating to the Feast of Unleavened Bread, which was thus from the beginning connected with the Festival of Passover. The exact period of the seven days is later fixed by many further ordinances. V.16. **And in the first day there shall be an holy convocation, a solemn festival assembly, and in the seventh day there shall be an holy convocation to you,** another service of worship; **no manner of work shall be done in them, save that which every man must eat, that only may be done of you.** That was the only labor which was permitted, that connected with the preparation of foods, according to the necessities of the day, the ordinance thus being less strict than that concerning the Sabbath. Cp. Lev. 23, 7. v. **17. And ye shall observe the Feast of Unleavened Bread; for in this selfsame day have I brought your armies out of the land of Egypt; therefore shall ye observe this day in your generations by an ordinance forever.** While the Passover commemorated the dreadful night of judgment and deliverance, the Feast of Unleavened Bread, so closely connected with it, reminded the children of Israel of the Exodus itself, of the chief circumstances connected with the departure of their armies out of Egypt. V.18. **In the first month, on the fourteenth day of the month at even, ye shall eat unleavened bread, until the one and twentieth day of the month at even.** V.19. **Seven days shall there be no leaven found in your houses;** that was the order which was to apply for the future, when they would have reached the Land of Promise; **for whosoever eateth that which is leavened,** in any solid food, **even that soul shall be cut off from the congregation of Israel, whether he be a stranger or born in the land.** The naturalized, that is, the circumcised foreigner was obliged to submit to the ordinance in just the same manner as the native Israelite. V.20. **Ye shall eat nothing leavened; in all your habitations shall ye eat unleavened bread.** The ordinance was certainly not lacking in clearness and emphasis, for it was the intention of the Lord to symbolize the entire consecration of His people, as based upon their redemption. **2)**

The people accept the ordinances. — V.21. **Then Moses called for all the elders of Israel and said unto them,** as the representatives of the children of Israel who transmitted the will of God to them, **Draw out,** select, take out from the flock, **and take you a lamb according to your families, and kill the Passover;** for the name of the festival was applied to the lamb or kid as the chief sacrifice. V.22. **And ye shall take a bunch of hyssop,** a plant to which cleansing properties were ascribed, **and dip it in the blood that is in the basin,** which was caught when the animal was slaughtered, **and strike the lintel and the two side-posts with the blood that is in the basin,** thus applying the blood as a paint. **And none of you shall go out at the door of his house until the morning,** as a measure of safety, for they were protected only inside the house, behind the blood of sacrifice. V.23. **For the Lord will pass through to smite the Egyptians; and when He seeth the blood upon the lintel and on the two side-posts, the Lord will pass over the door, and will not suffer the destroyer to come in unto your houses to smite you.** With the blood on their door, destruction would not strike them, not because the blood in itself had such extraordinary powers, but because it was the type of the perfect, holy blood of propitiation, that of Christ. V.24. **And ye shall observe this thing for an ordinance to thee and to thy sons forever.** This precept concerning the Passover in its essential features was to be a fixed rule in their midst in their new home, an observance to be transmitted from generation to generation. V.25. **And it shall come to pass, when ye be come to the land which the Lord will give you, according as He hath promised,** that ye shall keep this service. V.26. **And it shall come to pass, when your children shall say unto you, What mean ye by this service?** v.27. **that ye shall say, It is the sacrifice of the Lord's Passover, who passed over the houses of the children of Israel in Egypt when He smote the Egyptians and delivered our houses.** Note that religious observances should not be performed in a mechanical manner, but with a proper understanding of their origin and their meaning. **And the people bowed the head and worshiped.** They accepted the words of the Lord in grateful adoration. V.28. **And the children of Israel went away, and did as the Lord had commanded Moses and Aaron, so did they.** This section is of more than usual interest to us Christians, because the Passover lamb is a type of Jesus Christ, the Lamb of God. Christ was a true man, born of the Virgin Mary. But He was, at the same time, holy, harmless, undefiled, separate from sinners, and made higher than the heavens. He is the Lamb which was sacrificed for the deliverance of all mankind. The blood of Jesus Christ protects us against wrath, against death and destruction; it reconciles us with God, it makes us members of His Church. This Lamb we should eat, we should receive Christ into our hearts as our Redeemer, therefore also purge out the old leaven, and be His own in sincerity and truth. Thus we obtain strength for our pathway through the wilderness of this world to the true Canaan above.

The slaughter of the first-born and the exodus. — V.29. **And it came to pass that at midnight the Lord smote all the firstborn in the land of Egypt, from the firstborn of Pharaoh that sat on his throne unto the first-born of the captive that was in the dungeon, and all the first-**

born of cattle. It was a supernatural visitation, a divine punishment which was here meted out, in spite of all the attempts to explain the facts in a natural way. The very fact that the firstborn only was stricken in every case, from the highest to the lowest, shows that it could not have been a mere accident of the Egyptian pest, nor would it have struck both man and beast all in the same night. V.30. **And Pharaoh rose up in the night, he and all his servants and all the Egyptians; and there was a great cry in Egypt,** there was lamenting from one end of the country to the other; **for there was not a house where there was not one dead.** God's punishment spared none. V.31. **And he called for Moses and Aaron by night,** the matter would not even wait for the coming of the morning, and said, **Rise up and get you forth from among my people, both ye and the children of Israel; and go, serve the Lord, as ye have said.** It was now not a mere permission, but a royal mandate, which showed signs of extreme excitement. The children of Israel were to have free hand to act as they thought best, to worship the Lord as they had indicated. V.32. **Also take your flocks and your herds, as ye have said, and be gone; and bless me also.** All the former conditions were forgotten, and his terror reduced Pharaoh to the state where he begged to be left the blessing of Jehovah as a guarantee against further plagues. V.33. **And the Egyptians were urgent upon the people, that they might send them out of the land in haste,** they almost resorted to violence in hurrying the departure of the children of Israel; **for they said, We be all dead men.** That is often the effect when God visits His enemies with such a terrible destruction, that even the survivors are filled with a dread and panic which sees nothing but death on all sides. V.34. **And the people** (the children of Israel) **took their dough before it was leavened, their kneading-troughs being bound up in their clothes upon their shoulders.** "They had already put enough unleavened dough for seven days into the baking pans, and carried these on their shoulders, wrapped up in their outer garments, or rather in wrapping-cloths, such as might be used for mantles or wallets." (Lange.) V.35. **And the children of Israel did according to the word of Moses; and they borrowed of the Egyptians jewels of silver and jewels of gold, costly vessels and jewelry, and raiment;** v.36. **and the Lord gave the people favor in the sight of the Egyptians, so that they lent unto them such things as they required.** The children of Israel simply demanded, and the Egyptians readily gave what was asked, glad, apparently, that they could give, if only it would mean the removal of the strangers out of their midst. **And they spoiled the Egyptians,** they took along all these treasures as rich plunder and as a well earned compensation, as a blessing of God.

The journey to Succoth. — V.37. **And the children of Israel journeyed from Rameses,** the neighborhood of the city or the district where they had been living in Egypt, to Succoth, on the edge of the wilderness toward the east, where the Suez Canal now passes through, **about six hundred thousand on foot that were men, beside children,** the Hebrew word including all of those that did not travel on foot, but on beasts of burden or in wagons. The entire number of the people may well have exceeded two million souls. V.38. **And a mixed multitude went up also with them,** a company of people that were not Israelites, a mixture of various peoples, chiefly adventurers of a low type, Num. 11, 4, a medley, a great rabble; **and flocks and herds, even very much cattle.** V.39. **And they baked unleavened cakes of the dough which they brought forth out of Egypt, for it was not leavened;** these unleavened cakes were the only provision they had, for their deliverance came upon them much more quickly than they had looked for; **because they were thrust out of Egypt, and could not tarry, neither had they prepared for themselves any victual.** Thus they celebrated, for the first time, the Feast of Unleavened Bread. And so the name of the Lord was magnified by this great deliverance, which remained a source of inspiration to the Hebrew poets for many hundreds of years, even as we Christians sing the praises of the eternal redemption which was gained for us by Christ.

Further precepts concerning the Passover. — V.40. **Now the sojourning of the children of Israel who dwelt in Egypt was four hundred and thirty years,** four long or ten short generations as they were then reckoned. V.41. **And it came to pass at the end of the four hundred and thirty years, even the selfsame day it came to pass, that all the hosts of the Lord,** the great armies that were to wage His wars, **went out from the land of Egypt.** The departure of them all took place on the same day, on the fifteenth of Abib, the day after the Passover Festival. V.42. **It is a night to be much observed unto the Lord for bringing them out from the land of Egypt; this is that night of the Lord to be observed,** year after year, **of all the children of Israel in their generations.** V.43. **And the Lord said unto Moses and Aaron, This is the ordinance of the Passover: There shall no stranger eat thereof.** The statute of the Lord confined participation strictly to the members of the children of Israel. V.44. **But every man's servant that is bought for money, when thou hast circumcised him,** whereby he became a member of the Jewish nation and church, **then shall he eat thereof.** V.45. **A foreigner,** a non-Israelite merely living in the country, and an hired servant, one merely engaged for a while, **shall not eat thereof.** V.46. **In one house shall it be eaten. Thou shalt not carry forth aught of the flesh abroad out of the house, neither shall ye break a bone thereof.** The idea of the communion and of the union was to be maintained, and the fact that no bone was broken pointed forward to Christ, John 19, 36. V.47. **All the congregation of Israel shall keep it,** shall do and observe what God had here instituted. V.48. **And when a stranger shall sojourn with thee, and will keep the Passover to the Lord, let all his males be circumcised** and thus be received into the Jewish Church, **and then let him come near and keep it; and he shall be as one that is born in the land; for no uncircumcised person shall eat thereof;** the privilege was limited to such as had accepted the Jewish doctrines, that believed in the God of the Jews. V.49. **One law shall be to him that is home-born, and unto the stranger that sojourneth among you.** V.50. **Thus did all the children of Israel; as the Lord commanded Moses and Aaron, so did they;** that became the custom among them in after-years, Num. 9, 5; Josh. 5, 10. V.51. **And it came to pass the selfsame day, this fifteenth day of Abib, that the Lord did bring the children of Israel out of the land of Egypt by their armies.** Herewith ends the story of the Exodus proper, and the story of the events following is next taken up. The people were now separated unto the

Lord, to be unto Him a kingdom of priests and a holy nation. This is true also of the New Testament Church until the end of time, as Peter shows, 1 Pet. 2, 9.

14

Exodus 13

Various Ordinances Given at the Time of the Exodus.

Concerning the feast of unleavened bread. — **V.1. And the Lord spake unto Moses, saying, v.2. Sanctify unto Me all the first-born, whatsoever openeth the womb among the children of Israel, both of man and of beast; it is Mine.** This is not said of the general sanctification of the people as God's own nation, but of the consecrating, of the setting apart, of the first-born, both of men and of animals, for the specific service of Jehovah. They were the Lord's not only by virtue of creation, but because He spared them in the great slaughter in Egypt. The first-born sons were to serve the Lord as priests, until this right was vested in the descendants of Levi, when they were obliged to redeem themselves by payment of a sacrifice of exemption; the first-born beasts were to be sacrificed to the Lord. **V.3. And Moses said unto the people, Remember this day, in which ye came**

out from Egypt, out of the house of bondage. The Lord here repeats His ordinance respecting the Feast of Unleavened Bread with impressive solemnity, His name for Egypt being "house of slaves"; for that was the relation in which they had stood to Pharaoh and to all the Egyptians, that of practical slavery. **For by strength of hand the Lord brought you out from this place.** The expression is more emphatic than the usual "by a strong hand." **There shall no leavened bread be eaten,** not only during the present days, but also at every anniversary of the occasion. V.4. **This day came ye out, in the month Abib,** the fifteenth day of the first month of the church-year. V.5. **And it shall be when the Lord shall bring thee into the land of the Canaanites, and the Hittites, and the Amorites, and the Hivites, and the Jebusites, which He sware unto thy fathers to give thee, a land flowing with milk and honey, that thou shalt keep this service in this month.** Thus the Lord formally instituted the Feast of Unleavened Bread, with the usual detailed description of the Land of Promise and the corresponding reference to the fruitfulness of this country. V.6. **Seven days thou shalt eat unleavened bread, and in the seventh day shall be a feast to the Lord.** Cp. chap. 12,16. on the seventh day there was to be a special assembly for the purpose of worship. V.7. **Unleavened bread shall be eaten seven days; and there shall no leavened bread be seen with thee, neither shall there be leaven seen with thee in all thy quarters.** All foods in whose preparation leaven was used were prohibited so strictly that their very presence in the house was not tolerated. V.8. **And thou shalt show thy son in that day, saying, This is done because of that which the Lord did**

unto me when I came forth out of Egypt. The use of the singular here places the duty upon every individual father and parent, for the children were not only to take part in the public services, but also to be instructed at home concerning the great miracles of the Lord. V.9. **And it shall be for a sign unto thee upon thine hand and for a memorial between thine eyes, that the Lord's Law may be in thy mouth; for with a strong hand hath the Lord brought thee out of Egypt.** These are proverbial expressions denoting that the Israelites should keep the facts of their deliverance in their memories always, as the people of many nations wore bracelets and frontlets to remind them of certain religious duties. The redemption of the Lord and His ordinance concerning it was to be accepted with believing hearts and to be fulfilled with faithful hearts, with hearts conscious of the debt of gratitude which all Israelites owed to the Lord. V.10. **Thou shalt therefore keep this ordinance in his season from year to year,** as often as these days recurred. Thus we Christians are ever mindful of the fact that we have been delivered from sin's and Satan's house of slavery through the redemption of Jesus, and that our debt of gratitude toward Him demands our purging out the old leaven of sinfulness and consecrating our lives to Him.

Concerning the first-born. — V.11. **And it shall be when the Lord shall bring thee into the land of the Canaanites, as He sware unto thee and to thy fathers, and shall give it thee,** the Lord here laying special stress upon His faithfulness, which causes Him to keep the promises of His goodness always, v.12. **that thou shalt set apart unto the Lord all that openeth the matrix, and every firstling that cometh of a beast which thou hast; the males shall**

be the Lord's. The female children and the female young were not included in this order, but the male first-born, both of man and beast, was to be offered and consecrated to the Lord. Cp. chap. 22, 29. 30; Deut. 15, 21. V.13. **And every firstling of an ass thou shalt redeem with a lamb,** clean beasts were to be substituted for the unclean; and if thou wilt not redeem it, then thou shalt break his neck, for the unredeemed animal might not be kept; **and all the first-born of man among thy children shalt thou redeem.** The Lord later provided special regulations for the redemption of the first-born sons by means of a certain sum of money, Num. 3, 46. 47; 18, 15. 16. V.14. **And it shall be when thy son asketh thee in time to come,** at some time in the future, **saying, What is this? that thou shalt say unto him, By strength of hand the Lord brought us out from Egypt, from the house of bondage;** v.15. **and it came to pass, when Pharaoh would hardly let us go, that the Lord slew all the first-born in the land of Egypt, both the first-born of man and the first-born of beast; therefore I sacrifice to the Lord all that openeth the matrix, being males; but all the first-born of my children I redeem.** The fathers of Israel are here represented as speaking collectively and as giving individual instruction to their sons, for the Lord did not want a mechanical observation of customs that were no longer understood. V.16. **And it shall be for a token upon thine hand and for frontlets between thine eyes,** they were to keep these facts in remembrance constantly; **for by strength of hand the Lord brought us forth out of Egypt.** It is well-pleasing to the Lord if His children at all times keep in mind the great acts of deliverance wrought by Him.

The first stage of the journey. — V.17. **And it came to pass, when Pharaoh had let the people go,** had dismissed them and sent them out of the country, **that God led them not through the way of the land of the Philistines, although that was near,** which would have been the shortest, the most direct route; **for God said, Lest peradventure the people repent when they see war, and they return to Egypt.** The Israelites, disheartened and weakened by a life of servitude, were at that time in no condition to cope with the warlike Philistines. V.18. **But God led the people about, through the way of the wilderness of the Red Sea,** by the southeastern route, through the desert; **and the children of Israel went up harnessed out of the land of Egypt,** they did not go in irregular troops, like fugitives, but in marching order, a provision which kept their forces together and made supervision easy. V.19. **And Moses took the bones of Joseph with him; for he had straitly sworn the children of Israel, saying, God will surely visit you in mercy; and ye shall carry up my bones away hence with you.** Gen. 50, 25. This last order of Joseph had been transmitted from generation to generation, and the vow was now remembered in all its earnestness. V.20. **And they took their journey from Succoth,** apparently nothing more than an encampment on the boundary of the desert toward Philistia, **and encamped in Etham, in the edge of the wilderness.** Instead of continuing toward the east, they turned southward, along the western shore of the Bitter Lakes, Etham being located at their southwestern end. V.21. **And the Lord,** Jehovah, the Son of God, **went before them by day in a pillar of a cloud to lead them the way, and by night in a pillar of fire to give them light, to go by**

day and night. V.22. **He took not away the pillar of the cloud by day nor the pillar of fire by night from before the people.** Thus the Lord, in a miraculous manner, gave evidence of His presence to the children of Israel and guided them on their long journey. In the same way the Lord is present in His Church at all times in the means of grace, leading His children on the right path and protecting them against all enemies.

15

Exodus 14

The Pursuing Egyptians Destroyed in the Red Sea.

Pharaoh pursues Israel. — V.1. **And the Lord spake unto Moses, saying, v.2. Speak unto the children of Israel that they turn and encamp before Pihahiroth, between Migdol and the sea, over against Baalzephon; before it ye shall encamp by the sea.** Instead of proceeding on their journey into the desert, the children of Israel were to turn back, toward the west, and pitch their tents over against Hahiroth and Baalzephon, on the west side of an arm of the Red Sea. V.3. **For Pharaoh will say of the children of Israel, They are entangled in the land,** their turning back from Etham might seem like an act of bewilderment, of uncertainty, causing them to march back and forth without definite object; **the wilderness hath shut them in;** there was no road toward Canaan on the west side of the Gulf of Suez, and so the children of Israel would be held fast in the desert. V.4. **And I will harden**

Pharaoh's heart that he shall follow after them; and I will be honored upon Pharaoh, and upon all his host, that the Egyptians may know that I am the Lord. This was the final hardening which the Lord wanted to inflict upon Pharaoh, and it would result in bringing honor and glory to the Lord as the one true, just, and mighty God. **And they,** the children of Israel, **did so;** they encamped at a place where they were apparently shut in as in a prison, a fact which caused Pharaoh to plan their capture and return to their former slavery in Egypt. V.5. **And it was told the king of Egypt that the people fled,** the report of all the events that transpired was brought to him; **and the heart of Pharaoh and of his servants was turned against the people, and they said, Why have we done this, that we have let Israel go from serving us?** What foolishness possessed us that we let these excellent workmen go? The apparent aimlessness of the journeying may have caused Pharaoh to believe that the Lord had withdrawn His hand from the people, and that he would have no difficulty in recapturing them. V.6. **And he made ready his chariot,** he had his servants hitch the horses to his own chariot, **and took his people,** his army, **with him,** all the soldiers that were available upon short notice. v.7. **And he took six hundred chosen chariots,** the pick of his supply, the flower of his army, **and all the chariots of Egypt**, whatever other wagons were available, **and captains over everyone of them,** all the necessary officers. V.8. **And the Lord hardened the heart of Pharaoh, king of Egypt, and he pursued after the children of Israel,** he was blinded in his foolishness by the apparent helplessness of his former slaves. **And the children of Israel went**

out with an high hand. It was not a case of secret flight with them, but of a bold departure in the sight of all the Egyptians. V.9. **But the Egyptians pursued after them, all the horses and chariots of Pharaoh, and his horsemen, and his army, and overtook them encamping by the sea, beside Pihahiroth, before Baalzephon.** The detailed enumeration of Pharaoh's host serves to emphasize the greatness of his destruction. It is thus that obdurate sinners deliberately close their eyes against the manifest works of God and force God, as it were, to execute justice and judgment upon them.

The great fear of the Israelites. — V.10. **And when Pharaoh drew nigh, the children of Israel lifted up their eyes, and, behold, the Egyptians marched after them; and they were sore afraid. And the children of Israel cried out unto the Lord.** As the attention of the Israelites was drawn to the pursuing host, they realized the desperate situation in which they found themselves: on the east of them, the sea; on the south, the mountains; on the northwest, the army of Pharaoh. Moreover, they lacked both the weapons and the courage for a successful stand against the armies of the tyrant. It was not a confident prayer which they sent up in this emergency, but a cry of terror. V.11. **And they said unto Moses, Because there were no graves in Egypt, hast thou taken us away to die in the wilderness? Wherefore hast thou dealt thus with us, to carry us forth out of Egypt?** This was a mixture of bitter irony and unreasoning terror; for Egypt was rich in great sepulchers and monuments. They also forgot that they had received the revelations of Moses with grateful hearts and had willingly followed his directions. V.12. **Is not this the word that**

**we did tell thee in Egypt, saying, Let us alone that we
may serve the Egyptians?** That had happened in only
one case, chap. 5, 21, whereas the Israelites had otherwise
been eager to accept the advice of Moses. **For it had been
better for us to serve the Egyptians than that we should
die in the wilderness.** These were unjust reproaches and
foreshadowed the subsequent behavior of the children of
Israel in the wilderness. V.13. **And Moses said unto the
people, Fear ye not, stand still, and see the salva tion
of the Lord which He will show to you today; for the
Egyptians whom ye have seen today ye shall see them
again no more forever.** This heroic confidence of Moses
stands out all the more splendidly by contrast with the
cringing fear of the people, as the Lord had not revealed to
him the form which His deliverance would take. V.14. **The
Lord shall fight for you, and ye shall hold your peace,**
Moses knew that the deliverance which the Lord would
bring about would be of a nature to make the Israelites
hush all their laments; they would, in fact, stand by in idle
astonishment while the Lord glorified Himself before them.
V.15. **And the Lord said unto Moses, Wherefore criest
thou unto Me?** Although Moses was outwardly silent, his
heart was praying to the Lord with anxious cries. **Speak
unto the children of Israel that they go forward;** they
were to march straight ahead. V.16. **But lift thou up
thy rod, the same shepherd's staff that had figured so
largely in Egypt, and stretch out thine hand over the
sea, and divide it.** He was not merely to cause an unusually
low ebb-tide, together with a strong wind to hold the water
back, but he was to separate, to cut apart, the waters of the
sea, the purpose of the wind afterward being merely to assist

in drying off the bottom of the sea. **And the children of Israel shall go on dry ground through the midst of the sea.** V.17. **And I, behold, I will harden the hearts of the Egyptians, and they shall follow them,** in blind obstinacy, **And I will get Me honor upon Pharaoh and upon all his host, upon his chariots, and upon his horsemen.** God's judgment upon Pharaoh was to redound to the everlasting honor of His name. V.18. **And the Egyptians shall know that I am the Lord when I have gotten Me honor upon Pharaoh, upon his chariots, and upon his horsemen.** Thus the Lord strengthens those that believe in Him in the hour of danger and tribulation by giving them the assurance that He Himself will battle for them and deliver them from all their enemies.

The Israelites delivered, the Egyptians destroyed. — V.19. **And the Angel of God,** Jehovah, the Son of God, chap. 13, 21, **which went before the camp of Israel,** who led their armies, **removed and went behind them. And the pillar of the cloud went from before their face, and stood behind them;** v.20. **and it came between the camp of the Egyptians and the camp of Israel; and it was a cloud and darkness to them** (the Egyptians), **but it gave light by night to these,** the children of Israel; in its protecting capacity the cloud revealed a double character, an effectual barrier of impenetrable darkness to the enemies, a cheering and comforting light to the believers, **so that the one came not near the other all the night.** V.21. **And Moses stretched out his hand over the sea; and the Lord caused the sea to go back by a strong east wind all that night, and made the sea dry land, and the waters were divided.** As the waters of the sea, by the miraculous power of God, were separated from each other, the strong east wind from the desert caused the moisture at the bottom to evaporate, thus making the ground dry under foot and enabling the children of Israel to march forward without difficulty. V.22. **And the children of Israel went into the midst of the sea upon the dry ground; and the waters were a wall unto them on their right hand and on their left.** It is distinctly stated that the water stood on either side, not only on the south; neither did the waters merely recede in an unusually low ebb, for they stood like walls. Thus the angel of the Lord encamps round about them that fear Him and delivers them. V.23. **And the Egyptians pursued, and went in after them to the midst of the sea, even all Pharaoh's horses, his chariots, and his horsemen,** their obstinacy making them blind toward all the dangers about them. V.24. **And it came to pass that in the morning watch,** between three o'clock in the morning and sunrise, **the Lord looked unto the host of the Egyptians through the pillar of fire and of the cloud,** by some unusual manifestation the Lord struck terror to the hearts of the Egyptians, **and troubled the host of the Egyptians,** v.25. **and took off their chariot wheels,** that they slipped from their axles, **that they drave them heavily,** with difficulty; **so that the Egyptians said, Let us flee from the face of Israel; for the Lord fighteth for them against the Egyptians.** Now at last, when it was too late, they realized the true state of affairs. V.26. **And the Lord said unto Moses, Stretch out thine hand over the sea that the waters may come again upon the Egyptians, upon their chariots, and upon their horsemen,** upon the entire host which by this time was in the bed of the sea. V.27. **And Moses stretched forth his hand over the**

sea, and the sea returned to his strength, to its usual full level everywhere, **when the morning appeared,** before the face of the morning, as dawn gave way to light; **and the Egyptians fled against it.** They had turned back to flee to the west side of the sea and were met by the waters as they were flowing together from both sides. **And the Lord overthrew the Egyptians in the midst of the sea,** He literally shook them out in utter disorder and confusion, driving them right into the face of their destruction. V.28. **And the waters returned and covered the chariots and the horsemen and all the host of Pharaoh that came into the sea after them; there remained not so much as one of them.** Cp. Ps. 136, 15. V.29. **But the children of Israel walked upon dry land in the midst of the sea; and the waters were a wall unto them on their right hand and on their left.** This statement is repeated in order to emphasize the greatness of the miracle which the Lord performed, and to set forth the climax of the punishment which had begun with the slaughtering of the first-born in Egypt. V.30. **Thus the Lord saved Israel that day out of the hand of the Egyptians; and Israel saw the Egyptians dead upon the seashore.** Thus the Lord delivered His people, not only from the slavery of Egypt, but also from their entire host, which intended to recapture them. V.31. **And Israel saw that great work which the Lord did upon the Egyptians,** they had concrete evidence before them of the manner in which God carried out His judgment upon the Egyptians; **and the people feared the Lord, and believed the Lord and His servant Moses.** The weak faith of the Israelites was strengthened in a miraculous manner, Heb. 11, 29, and they now, in consequence of the miracle, again placed full trust and confidence in the words of Moses, as the representative of God, the final praise and glory thus being the Lord's. Whereas death, destruction, judgment, condemnation is the lot of hardened sinners, of the enemies of the Church, the believers will be kept safe unto life everlasting.

16

Exodus 15

The Song of Moses and the Continuation of the Journey.

The song of triumph. — V.1. **Then sang Moses and the children of Israel this song unto the Lord,** a hymn of praise and thanksgiving for deliverance from their mighty enemies, **and spake, saying, I will sing unto the Lord, for He hath triumphed gloriously,** He has set forth His great majesty; **the horse and his rider hath He thrown into the sea,** all the host in which Pharaoh placed his trust was overcome and destroyed in a few moments by the almighty power of God. V.2. **The Lord is my Strength and Song,** the great might of Jehovah, or Jah, as the poet here abbreviates the name, is the inspiration of his song, **and He is become my Salvation;** to those that are His, He has granted deliverance from the dangers that threatened them. **He is my God,** emphatically: such a one is my God, for the true God is elevated and magnified beyond all idols; **and I will prepare Him an habitation,** I will glorify and praise

Him highly; **my father's God, and I will exalt Him.** What God had promised to the patriarchs, especially Abraham, regarding deliverance from the bondage of Egypt, had now been fulfilled, for the overthrow of Pharaoh's host marked the beginning of Israel's existence as a free people. V.3. **The Lord is a man of war,** able to wage war successfully and to subdue all enemies; **the Lord, Jehovah, is His name.** V.4. **Pharaoh's chariots and his host hath He cast into the sea; his chosen captains, the choice of his officers, also are drowned in the Red Sea,** being submerged in the water. V.5. **The depths have covered them,** the great masses of water, part of the mighty ocean; **they sank into the bottom as a stone,** without a chance of being saved. That is the first verse of this great hymn. — V.6. **Thy right hand, O Lord, is become glorious in power,** has glorified itself in strength; **Thy right hand, O Lord, hath dashed in pieces the enemy,** utterly annihilated them. V.7. **And in the greatness of Thine excellency, of Thy majesty, Thou hast overthrown them that rose up against Thee,** destroyed Thine adversaries; **Thou sentest forth Thy wrath, which consumed them as stubble.** The breath of God's glowing anger, which ate the opponents like straw, may have reference to the look of wrath which struck terror to the hearts of the Egyptians. V.8. **And with the blast of Thy nostrils the waters were gathered together,** for thus Moses regarded the strong east wind which the Lord sent, **the floods stood upright as an heap, and the depths were congealed in the heart of the sea;** for the walls of water stood up like frozen masses on either side as the Israelites marched through the sea. V.9. **The enemy said, I will pursue, I will overtake, I will divide**

the spoil; my lust shall be satisfied upon them, my soul will get its fill of them; **I will draw my sword, my hand shall destroy them.** The short sentences, hardly more than exclamations, vividly paint the certainty of victory which possessed the hearts of the Egyptians as they went forth in the overweening pride of confidence. V.10. **Thou didst blow with Thy wind, the sea covered them; they sank as lead in the mighty waters,** they sank from view like a plummet, and the rushing billows of the great sea bore witness to the glory of the Creator. Thus the second stanza of the hymn is concluded. — V.11. **Who is like unto Thee, O Lord, among the gods,** among all those to whom men apply the name gods? **Who is like Thee, glorious in holiness, fearful in praises, doing wonders?** Jehovah, who performed such great miracles, which men could contemplate. only with fear and trembling, had thereby given the guarantee that He would carry the deliverance of His people to a successful issue. V.12. **Thou stretchedst out Thy right hand, the earth swallowed them.** The miracles which the Lord had performed in Egypt and upon the host of the Egyptians showed that a similar fate awaits all the enemies of the Lord, that no man can stand before Him as His opponent. V.13. **Thou in Thy mercy hast led forth the people which Thou hast redeemed.** The deliverance out of Egypt was a proof of the fact that Israel was the Lord's people, the people of His redemption, but also that this miracle was due to His mercy alone, and not to any worthiness in them. **Thou hast guided them in Thy strength unto Thy holy habitation.** The past experience was a pledge of further mercies, and the prophet even now sees the people established in their inheritance, where the

Lord would live in their midst in the beauty of His holiness. V.14. **The people shall hear and be afraid,** be filled with restlessness and distress; that was even now the effect which the report of the mighty deliverance had upon the heathen nations**; sorrow shall take hold on the inhabitants of Palestina,** they would tremble with mournful fear. V.15. **Then the dukes of Edom shall be amazed,** will lose heart and courage; **the mighty men of Moab, trembling shall take hold upon them,** take a firm grip upon them; **all the inhabitants of Canaan shall melt away** in dread and terror. V.16. **Fear and dread shall fall upon them,** a horror which would render them helpless; **by the greatness of Thine arm they shall be as still as a stone,** mute, unable to utter a word, to raise a single objection; **till Thy people pass over, O Lord, till the people pass over which Thou hast purchased.** The final entry into the Land of Promise was assured and could not be hindered by any attempts of their enemies to render it futile. By His mighty deeds God had purchased this people for Himself, and He intended to hold His property against all adversaries. V.17. **Thou shalt bring them in, and plant them in the mountain of Thine inheritance, in the place, O Lord, which Thou hast made for Thee to dwell in, in the Sanctuary, O Lord, which Thy hands have established.** In the eyes of the prophet all these things were even now accomplished; he saw his people living in Canaan, in the place which the Lord had chosen for them; he saw the Temple of. the Lord erected in the midst of His people, as a place of worship to His holiness and mercy. V.18. **The Lord shall reign forever and ever.** The singer here rises to the greatest heights of exultation and looks even beyond the temporal kingdom of Israel in the Land of Promise, to the eternal reign of the Messiah.

The song of miriam. — V.19. **For the horse of Pharaoh went in with his chariots and with his horsemen into the sea,** the historian implying, at this point, that Pharaoh, riding forward at the head of his army, was destroyed with all his host, Ps. 136, 15, **and the Lord brought again the waters of the sea upon them; but the children of Israel went on dry land in the midst of the sea,** in the bed which the sea ordinarily filled. V.20. **And Miriam, the prophetess, the sister of Aaron,** who from now on takes her place at the side of Aaron under the leadership of Moses, although she was endowed with prophetic gifts, **took a timbrel,** a tambourine, **in her hand; and all the women went out after her with timbrels and with dances,** in a stately, solemn religious dance, with marching and singing in unison. V.21. **And Miriam answered them,** she and her company chanted their refrain at the end of every verse, or stanza, as sung by Moses and the children of Israel, **Sing ye to the Lord, for He hath triumphed gloriously,** He has exalted His majesty; **the horse and his rider hath He thrown into the sea.** Cp. v.1. All the people, men and women, were thus engaged in the hymn of praise and thanksgiving, took part in the festival in honor of Jehovah, a fine example to the believers of all times.

In the wilderness of shur. — V.22. **So Moses brought Israel from the Red Sea, and they went out into the wilderness of Shur;** they left the last fountain of fresh water behind them and marched out into the desert which extends along the eastern shore of the Gulf of Suez, the western arm of the Red Sea; **and they went three days in**

the wilderness and found no water. V.23. **And when they came to Marah,** probably the modern Hawara, thirty-three miles from the place where they had crossed the sea, **they could not drink of the waters of Marah, for they were bitter,** not merely saltish, but disagreeably repugnant; **therefore the name of it was called Marah** (bitterness). V.24. **And the people murmured against Moses, saying, What shall we drink?** So quickly did the children of Israel forget the many evidences of God's mercy in Egypt and the miraculous deliverance at the Red Sea. V.25. **And he cried unto the Lord,** for counsel and assistance; **and the Lord showed him a tree,** indicated some wood to him, **which when he had cast into the waters, the waters were made sweet,** as palatable and wholesome as the best drinking-water. In this way the Lord overlooked the weakness of His children and helped them out. **There He** (God) **made for them a statute and an ordinance, and there He proved them, v.26. and said, If thou wilt diligently hearken to the voice of the Lord, thy God, and wilt do that which is right in His sight, and wilt give ear to His commandments, and keep all His statutes, I will put none of these diseases upon thee which I have brought upon the Egyptians; for I am the Lord that healeth thee.** That was the test which the Lord proposed, namely, that the children of Israel should keep His commandments, laws, and ordinances. In that event He would prove Himself their true Physician in keeping from them the plagues which struck the Egyptians, and they could depend upon this promise as upon a definite ordinance. V.27. **And they came to Elim, where were twelve wells of water, and threescore and ten palm trees; and they encamped there by the waters.**

In this beautiful oasis the people had an opportunity to refresh themselves from the fatigue of the journey and to prepare for the continuation of the journey. Days of joy and comfort follow after periods of suffering and trial.

17

Exodus 16

Events in the Wilderness of Sin.

The murmuring about the food. — V.1. **And they took their journey from Elim, and all the congregation of the children of Israel came unto the wilderness of Sin, which is between Elim and Sinai,** on the eastern shore of the Gulf of Suez, **on the fifteenth day of the second month after their departing out of the land of Egypt.** V.2. **And the whole congregation of the children of Israel murmured against Moses and Aaron in the wilderness.** Their dissatisfied complaint was directed against both leaders, and so against the divine act of bringing them out of Egypt, that is, against Jehovah Himself. V.3. **And the children of Israel said unto them, Would to God we had died by the hand of the Lord in the land of Egypt,** in the last great plague which cut off the first-born of the Egyptians, **when we sat by the flesh-pots, and when we did eat bread to**

the full, when they, in spite of all their other afflictions, at least had their food in sufficient quantities; **for ye have brought us forth into this wilderness to kill this whole assembly with hunger,** which was an unjust accusation bordering upon insolence and, moreover, with an amount of falsehood, for they still had at least some of their cattle with them, and the congregation was by no means on the edge of starvation. V.4. **Then said the Lord unto Moses, Behold, I will rain bread from heaven for you; and the people shall go out and gather a certain rate every day,** a certain amount day after day, **that I may prove them whether they will walk in My law or no.** The Lord intended to test their faith and obedience in connection with this miraculous gift of bread. V.5. **And it shall come to pass that on the sixth day they shall prepare that which they bring in,** they should measure the portion very carefully and set it aside; **and it shall be twice as much as they gather daily.** Cp. v.22. V.6. **And Moses and Aaron said unto all the children of Israel, At even, then ye shall know that the Lord hath brought you out from the land of Egypt,** they would be given further unmistakable evidence that it was the Lord who had brought about their deliverance; v.7. **and in the morning, then ye shall see the glory of the Lord,** they would be given definite proof of His almighty power and majesty, of His glorious presence; **for that He,** God, **heareth your murmurings against the Lord,** Jehovah, the Son of God, who was the real leader of the people in its desert journey, 1 Cor. 10, 4. **And what are we, that ye murmur against us?** The persons of Moses and Aaron counted for nothing; it was as the ambassadors of Jehovah that they were here concerned; the people should realize that their complaint was directed against God. V.8. **And Moses said, This shall be when the Lord shall give you in the evening flesh to eat, and in the morning bread to the full; for that the Lord heareth your murmurings which ye murmur against Him. And what are we? Your murmurings are not against us, but against the Lord.** Thus the people were reproved for their sinful murmuring.

The Lord sends quails and manna. — V.9. **And Moses spake unto Aaron, Say unto all the congregation of the children of Israel, Come near before the Lord; for He hath heard your murmurings.** Aaron, as the spokesman of Moses, was to make this announcement, giving the people the assurance that Jehovah had heard, and was ready to grant, the prayer included in their murmuring, in spite of the fact that it indicated a sinful weakness on their part. V.10. **And it came to pass, as Aaron spake unto the whole congregation of the children of Israel, that they looked toward the wilderness, and, behold, the glory of the Lord appeared in the cloud.** This appearance confirmed the reproof and the promise given by the mouth of the Lord's ambassadors, and incidentally indicated to them that God was able to manifest Himself in their midst even in the desert wastes which now lay before them. V.11. **And the Lord spake unto Moses, saying, v.12. I have heard the murmurings of the children of Israel. Speak unto them, saying, At even ye shall eat flesh,** between the evenings, at twilight, before nightfall, **and in the morning ye shall be filled with bread; and ye shall know that I am the Lord, your God.** It would be another unmistakable proof of His almighty power. V.13. **And it came to pass that at even the quails came up, and covered the camp;**

they arose on the horizon in great masses, like a heavy cloud, their usual number being much increased by a miracle of the Lord. **And in the morning the dew lay round about the host,** all around the camp. V.14. **And when the dew that lay was gone up,** that is, the heavy fog that accompanied the precipitation, **behold, upon the face of the wilderness there lay a small round thing, as small as the hoarfrost on the ground,** like flaky kernels, Num. 11, 7. V.15. **And when the children of Israel saw it, they said one to another, What is this? For they wist** (knew) **not what it was. And Moses said unto them, This is the bread which the Lord hath given you to eat,** the miraculous, heavenly bread, of which he had spoken the evening before. V.16. **This is the thing which the Lord hath commanded, Gather of it every man according to his eating, an omer for every man,** about two and one-half quarts per person, **according to the number of your persons; take ye every man for them which are in his tents;** that was the average amount per soul, whether children or adults. V.17. **And the children of Israel did so, and gathered, some more, some less,** as every man's good fortune or his energy directed. V.18. **And when they did mete it with an omer,** the measure which the Lord had given as the standard, **he that gathered much had nothing over, and he that gathered little had no lack; they gathered every man according to his eating.** By God's miraculous arrangement the amounts gathered were just sufficient for each family and for the entire people. V.19. **And Moses said, Let no man leave of it till the morning,** in an attempt to hoard the food. V.20. **Notwithstanding they hearkened not unto Moses,** they again became guilty of stubborn disobedience; **but some of them left of it until the morning, and it bred worms and stank;** the tiny maggots that developed caused a rapid decay. **And Moses was wroth with them,** on account of their stubbornness. V.21. **And they gathered it every morning, every man according to his eating; and when the sun waxed hot, it melted.** Thus the Lord provided for His people in their need, mercifully overlooking their weakness, even as He does to this day, as His children experience time and again.

The Sabbath rest. — V.22. **And it came to pass that on the sixth day** of the week **they gathered twice as much bread, two omers for one man,** about five quarts per person; **and all the rulers of the congregation,** the princes, or leaders, of the various tribes, **came. and told Moses.** The strangeness of the happening caused them to wonder. V.23. **And he said unto them, This is that which the Lord hath said** (v.5.), **To-morrow is the rest of the holy Sabbath unto the Lord,** which up to that time had evidently not been observed. **Bake that which ye will bake today, and seethe that ye will seethe;** they were to prepare and eat their meals as usual; **and that which remaineth over lay up for you to be kept until the morning,** for use on the Sabbath-day. V.24. **And they laid it up till the morning, as Moses bade; and it did not stink, neither was there any worm therein,** which showed that the entire matter was in the hands of God's providence. V.25. **And Moses said, Eat that today; for today is a Sabbath unto the Lord; today ye shall not find it in the field,** another proof that it was not the natural manna (which in warm weather oozes out of the branches of the tarfa-tree) with which the children of Israel were dealing, but a gift from

112

heaven, sent at the direction of God. V.26. **Six days ye shall gather it; but on the seventh day, which is the Sabbath, in it there shall be none.** V.27. **And it came to pass that there went out some of the people on the seventh day for to gather,** in the same obstinate willfulness which characterized the people throughout, **and they found none.** V.28. **And the Lord said unto Moses, How long refuse ye to keep My commandments and My laws?** The people were giving a poor account of their faith in this trial of their obedience and heaping one sin upon the other. V.29. **See, for that the Lord hath given you the Sabbath, therefore He giveth you on the sixth day the bread of two days.** That was the explanation repeated, which included the reproof. **Abide ye every man in his place, let no man go out of his place on the seventh day.** That was the plain command, which permitted no evasion. V.30. **So the people rested on the seventh day;** from this time the observance of the seventh day as the Sabbath dates. V.31. **And the house of Israel called the name thereof,** of the miraculous bread, manna; **and it was like coriander seed, white,** small, round kernels of dull white or yellowish green color; **and the taste of it was like wafers made with honey.** Cp. Num. 11, 7. 8. It could be ground in a hand-mill, crushed in a mortar, cooked by baking or boiling, made into cakes or bread, and tasted like baked food. It is referred to Ps. 78, 24; 105, 40; John 6, 31–41.

Manna saved for a memorial. — V.32. **And Moses said, This is the thing which the Lord commandeth, Fill an omer of it,** a measure containing just that amount, **to be kept for your generations,** for all future times, **that they may see the bread wherewith I have fed you in the**

113

wilderness, when I brought you forth from the land of Egypt. V.33. **And Moses said unto Aaron, Take a pot, and put an omer full of manna therein, and lay it up before the Lord to be kept for your generations,** for all future descendants. V.34. **As the Lord commanded Moses, so Aaron laid it up before the testimony, to be kept.** The historian here anticipates an event of the future, for it was some time later that the Ark of the Covenant was made at God's command, the receptacle of the tables of the testimony and also of the pot of manna, chap. 25, 16.21; Heb. 9, 4. V.35. **And the children of Israel did eat manna forty years, until they came to a land inhabited; they did eat manna until they came unto the borders of the land of Canaan.** V.36. **Now, an omer is the tenth part of an ephah,** as the author adds by way of explanation, an ephah at that time measuring almost three and one-fourth pecks. This closes the account concerning the manna for the present. The entire story reminds us of the gracious providence of God, which takes care of all our needs and bids us not to worry about the morrow, Matt. 6, 34. If we seek first the kingdom of God and His righteousness, then all the things which we need for this life will be added unto us.

18

Exodus 17

Events at Rephidim.

The murmuring at Massah and Meribah. — V.1.
**And all the congregation of the children of
Israel journeyed from the wilderness of Sin,
after their journeys,** after several days' marching, on
each of which they encamped for the night, Num. 33,
12, **according to the commandment of the Lord, and
pitched in Rephidim,** on the boundary of the wilderness
of Sinai; **and there was no water for the people to drink.**
V.2. **Wherefore the people did chide with Moses and
said, Give us water that we may drink.** They deliberately
challenged Moses for an explanation; they started a quarrel,
they wrangled. **And Moses said unto them, Why chide ye
with me? Wherefore do ye tempt the Lord?** The second
question was the explanation of the first, for in attacking
Moses the people rebelled against the Lord and provoked
Him to anger. V.3. **And the people thirsted there for**

water; and the people murmured against Moses and said, Wherefore is this that thou hast brought us up out of Egypt to kill us and our children and our cattle with thirst? So this was the substance of their complaint, of their doubt as to the merciful presence of the Lord. V.4. **And Moses cried unto the Lord, saying, What shall I do unto this people? They be almost ready to stone me.** They held Moses responsible for the impending ruin, and assumed such an ugly attitude as to cause Moses to fear the worst. V.5. **And the Lord said unto Moses, Go on before the people, and take with thee of the elders of Israel; and thy rod, wherewith thou smotest the river,** the shepherd's staff which was his symbol of authority, take in thine hand and go. The solemn departure of Moses and the elders from the camp was to draw the attention of the entire army to their actions. V.6. **Behold, I will stand before thee there upon the rock in Horeb,** whose foot-hills extended down to the neighborhood of the camp; **and thou shalt smite the rock, and there shall come water out of it that the people may drink.** God assured Moses of His presence and definitely promised him a miracle. **And Moses did so in the sight of the elders of Israel.** They were witnesses to the miracle and could testify before the people as to the manner in which water had been produced. V.7. **And he called the name of the place Massah** (temptation) **and Meribah** (strife) **because of the chiding of the children of Israel, and because they tempted the Lord, saying, Is the Lord among us or not?** So that had been their real transgression, the doubts as to the presence of the Lord with their army, the pillar of cloud and of fire apparently not being sufficient any more to uphold their faith. The events here narrated were considered an example of warning throughout the time of the Old Testament as well as in the New, Ps. 95, 8; Heb. 4, 9. And as it was Christ who journeyed with His people at that time and strengthened the faith of those who noted His presence in the miracle, so it is He who gives us at all times the true spiritual water to quench the thirst of our souls.

The battle with the Amalekites. — V.8. **Then came Amalek,** the nation which had descended from Amalek, the grandson of Esau, Gen. 36, 12, **and fought with Israel in Rephidim.** V.9. **And Moses said unto Joshua, Choose us out men, and go out, fight with Amalek;** for the soldiers of the heathen nation had fallen upon the rear-guard of Israel and smitten the faint and weary, Deut. 25, 18. **Tomorrow I will stand on the top of the hill with the rod of God in mine hand,** the same staff with which he had performed so many miracles. V.10. **So Joshua,** or Hoshea, a prince of the tribe of Ephraim, Num. 13, 8. 16; Deut. 32, 44, **did as Moses had said to him, and fought with Amalek,** for these Edomites were here trying to vent their spite against the chosen people of God; **and Moses, Aaron, and Hur,** the son of Caleb, the great-grandson of Judah, 1 Chron. 2, 18–20, **went up to the top of the hill,** to assist their troops with the prayer of faith. V.11. **And it came to pass, when Moses held up his hand,** in the attitude of fervent supplication, **that Israel prevailed,** the tide of battle went in their favor; **and when he let down his hand, Amalek prevailed.** It was not a battle in which mere prowess of arms brought about the decision, but one in which the powers of the true God battled with the enemies of His Church. V.12. **But Moses' hands were heavy.** It is a test of endurance for the strongest man to hold his hands out or up for any length of time. **And they took a stone and put it under him, and he sat thereon; and Aaron and Hur stayed up his hands, the one on the one side and the other on the other side;** they supported his hands in such a way that they would not sink; **and his hands were steady until the going down of the sun,** until darkness put an end to the battle. V.13. **And Joshua discomfited,** struck down, conquered, **Amalek and his people with the edge of the sword,** without exercising pity. V.14. **And the Lord said unto Moses, Write this for a memorial in a book, and rehearse it in the ears of Joshua,** it should be revealed to Joshua and impressed upon his mind; **for I will utterly put out the remembrance of Amalek from under heaven,** the entire nation was to be annihilated, Deut.25, 19. V.15. **And Moses built an altar, and called the name of it Jehovah-nissi** (Jehovah my banner); v.16. **for he said, Because the Lord hath sworn that the Lord will have war with Amalek from generation to generation.** It was a vow with his hand upon the banner of Jehovah, the altar which he had built, that Israel should continue the war against the Amalekites until their total extinction had been accomplished. The present victory was an earnest of future victories over all the enemies. Thus all the enemies of the believers, of the Church of Christ, will eventually be conquered, but our prayers must arise to the Throne of Mercy without ceasing.

19

Exodus 18

The Visit of Jethro.

Jethro arrives with Zipporah. — V.1. **When Jethro, the priest of Midian, Moses' father-in-law,** his given name being Reuel and his official title Jethro, **heard all that God had done for Moses and for Israel, His people, and that the Lord had brought Israel out of Egypt,** v.2. **then Jethro, Moses' father-in-law, took Zipporah, Moses' wife, after he had sent her back,** which probably happened after the adventure in the inn, chap. 4, 24–26, v.3. **and her two sons; of which the name of the one was Gershom** (a stranger I am); **for he said, I have been an alien in a strange land; v.4. and the name of the other was Eliezer** (God my Helper); **for the God of my father, said he, was mine Help, and delivered me from the sword of Pharaoh.** These two sons had been born to Moses in the land of Midian while he lived with his father-in-law Reuel, chap. 2, 22; 4, 25. It seems that Moses had agreed with his wife that she should meet him when he would return with the children of Israel; for he had had, even at that time, the promise of the Lord that Israel would be delivered out of the house of bondage, and that they would worship God on Mount Horeb. As the news of the mighty deeds of God, therefore, went out into the surrounding countries, Jethro also heard it and acted accordingly. V.5. **And Jethro, Moses' father-in-law, came with his sons and his wife unto Moses into the wilderness, where he encamped at the mount of God;** for the children of Israel had now established their camp in the foot-hills of Mount Horeb. V.6. **And he said unto Moses,** sent him a message before reaching the camp, **I, thy father-in-law Jethro, am come unto thee, and thy wife and her two sons with her.** V.7. **And Moses went out to meet his father-in-law, and did obeisance, and kissed him,** he welcomed him in a manner befitting his station; **and they asked each other of their welfare,** whether peace in the best sense of the word had been granted them. **And they came into the tent.** "Notice the delicate discretion which both men observe, with all their friendship towards each other. Jethro does not rush impetuously forward; he sends word of his approach. Moses receives him with appropriate reverence, but first leads him into his tent; for whether and how he may introduce him to his people is yet to be determined." (Lange.) V.8. **And Moses told his father-in-law all that the Lord had done unto Pharaoh and to the Egyptians for Israel's sake** while they were still in bondage in Egypt, **and all the travail that had come upon them,** that had found or struck them, **by the way,** since their departure out of Egypt, **and how the Lord delivered them,** how He had shown them His salvation in every instance, given them evidence of His almighty and gracious presence. V.9. **And Jethro rejoiced for all the goodness which the Lord had done to Israel, whom He had delivered out of the hand of the Egyptians.** It was not the mere polite interest of a visitor, but the genuine, sympathetic rejoicing of a man who felt that the God of Israel was the true God. Jethro here appears as the representative of a heathen nation, of the Midianites or Kenites, the first heathen nation to show kindness to the people of God. V.10. **And Jethro said, Blessed be the Lord,** Jehovah, the true God, **who hath delivered you out of the hand of the Egyptians and out of the hand of Pharaoh, who hath delivered the people from under the hand of the Egyptians;** it had been a salvation from galling bondage. V.11. **Now I know that the Lord,** Jehovah, the God whom Moses and the children of Israel worshiped, **is greater than all gods,** having manifested Himself as being exalted above all so-called gods, the idols of the heathen; **for in the thing wherein they dealt proudly He was above them.** The Egyptians, foolishly trusting in their idols, had acted wickedly in all their dealings with the Israelites, but the Lord had shown His superiority in the plagues which He had sent, down to the final annihilation of Pharaoh's host in the Red Sea. V.12. **And Jethro, Moses' father-in-law, took a burnt offering and sacrifices for God,** the belief in whom he had so openly confessed, giving evidence of his faith by this act of sacrifice. **And Aaron came and all the elders of Israel to eat bread with Moses' father-in-law before God.** The children of Israel could enter into both religious and social fellowship with the man who had so openly confessed his belief in the true God. Eating bread before God was said of the sacrificial meal, the Lord being present as the invisible Guest. As Jethro here partook of the blessings of Israel, so heathen nations in after-years were called to the enjoyment of the Messianic hope and promises.

Jethro's advice to Moses. — V.13. **And it came to pass on the morrow that Moses sat to judge the people,** to hear cases, to adjust differences and give advice. **And the people stood by Moses from the morning unto the evening.** The number of the people being so great, there were many matters to adjust and many difficulties to untangle, and it took a great deal of Moses' time and energy. V.14. **And when Moses' father-in-law saw all that he did to the people, he said, What is this thing that thou doest to the people? Why sit test thou thyself alone, and all the people stand by thee from morning unto even?** In brief: What is the idea, what is the object of your doing all this work alone; why try to bear the great burden without assistance? V.15. **And Moses said unto his father-in-law, Because the people come unto me to inquire of God.** Moses was God's ambassador to the people, God's visible representative, and so the people came to him for divine decisions in all matters of contention, and when they needed advice. V.16. **When they have a matter, they come unto me; and I judge between one and another, and I do make them know the statutes of God and His laws.** By giving advice in all difficult matters and by rendering decisions in all disputes, Moses made known to the people the ordinances and the laws of God. V.17. **And Moses' father-in-law said unto him, The thing that thou doest is not good.** The practice which had been inaugurated by Moses was not good policy. V.18. **Thou wilt surely wear away, both thou**

and this people that is with thee. Moses would use up, and thus waste, all his strength and energy, and the people would be worn out with the chafing of suspense as they waited. **For this thing is too heavy for thee; thou art not able to perform it thyself alone.** It was a plain case of the limitation of physical strength, and Jethro's advice was good political wisdom, sound common sense. V.19. **Hearken now unto my voice, I will give thee counsel, and God shall be with thee;** Jethro knew that his advice would meet with the approval of God. **Be thou for the people to God-ward that thou mayest bring the causes unto God;** Moses was to represent the people in all cases in which they sought right and justice before God; he was to take the place of God toward the people, the visible representative of the real Ruler of Israel. V.20. **And thou shalt teach them ordinances and laws, and shalt show them, let them know, teach them, the way wherein they must walk, and the work that they must do.** Moses was to retain for himself the instruction of the people, both as to their general behavior and mode of living and as to their course in individual matters; he was to be their teacher in all questions of principle. V.21. **Moreover, thou shalt provide,** look for, select, **out of all the people able men,** men of strength of body and men of energy, **such as fear God, men of truth, hating covetousness,** distinguished for their lack of selfishness; **and place such over them to be rulers of thousands and rulers of hundreds, rulers of fifties, and rulers of tens,** the decimal system probably being taken since ten represented the average size of a family. V.22. **And let them judge the people at all seasons,** according to the degree of importance and difficulty; **and it shall be**

that every great matter they shall bring unto thee, such as were too difficult for them to decide, **but every small matter they shall judge; so shall it be easier for thyself,** he would relieve himself of some of the burden resting upon him, **and they shall bear the burden with thee,** assist Moses in the business of having charge of such a great people. V.23. **If thou shalt do this thing, and God command thee so, then thou shalt be able to endure,** to hold out under the burden resting upon him, **and all this people shall go to their place in peace,** reach their destination in safety. V.24. **So Moses hearkened to the voice of his father — in-law, and did all that he had said.** V.25. **And Moses chose able men out of all Israel, and made them heads over the people, rulers of thousands, rulers of hundreds, rulers of fifties, and rulers of tens.** This institution was only afterwards developed in greater detail, Num. 11, 16. 17. V.26. **And they judged the people at all seasons,** Moses having charged and obligated them to do their work with all considerate impartiality. **The hard causes they brought unto Moses,** as the final court of appeal, **but every small matter they judged themselves.** It is not the will of God that His servants should needlessly wear themselves out in the service of the Church. It is well-pleasing to Him that the work of the Church, both in general and in the individual congregations, be distributed according to the gifts which He has given. Thus the work will result in the benefit of all. V.27. **And Moses let his father-in-law depart; and he went his way into his own land.** He returned home a convert to the God of Israel, and it was doubtless due to his influence that at least a part of his people journeyed to Canaan with Moses' brother-in-law, Num. 10, 29.

20

Exodus 19

The Preparations for the Giving of the Law.

The arrival at Sinai and the first message. — V.1. **In the third month, when the children of Israel were gone forth out of the land of Egypt, the same day came they into the wilderness of Sinai.** The greater part of the time since the departure out of Egypt, on the fifteenth day of the first month, had apparently been spent at Elim and at Rephidim, and it was not until the third month that the great army came into the desert of Sinai proper. V.2. **For they were departed from Rephidim,** chap. 17, 1, **and were come to the desert of Sinai, and had pitched in the wilderness; and there Israel camped before the mount,** over against the mountain from which the entire range has received its name. V.3. **And Moses went up unto God,** he was on his way to the summit. **And the Lord called unto him out of the mountain, saying, Thus shalt thou say to the house of Jacob, and tell the**

children of Israel. In poetic form the Lord prepares for the statement of the covenant which He here intended to make with the entire people through the person of Moses. V.4. **Ye have seen what I did unto the Egyptians,** in punishing them with such terrible plagues, **and how I bare you on eagles' wings,** which are an image of the strong and affectionate care of God, for the eagle protects and fosters her young with great devotion, **and brought you unto myself.** The mountain on which the pillar of cloud now rested was to be considered the habitation of the Lord for the time being, the place where He intended to reveal Himself in the covenant which He was about to make with the people. V.5. **Now, therefore, if ye will obey my voice in deed and keep my covenant,** gladly enter into the relation of mercy which the Lord intended to propose, **then ye shall be a peculiar treasure unto me above all people,** a possession to be cherished and guarded most carefully, more than any other nation in the world; **for all the earth is Mine,** and the sovereign Lord of the universe, who is not a national god, has the right to manifest Himself to a single nation with unusual mercy. V.6. **And ye shall be unto Me a kingdom of priests,** kings, in order to conquer the heathen, and priests, in order to serve the living God, **and an holy nation,** a nation consecrated, set apart, for the service of Jehovah, and therefore under obligation to lead a life of sanctification before Him. **These are the words which thou shalt speak unto the children of Israel.** That was the solemn, welcoming message which the Lord sent to the people whom He had chosen. In this respect the children of Israel were a type of the New Testament Church, the chosen generation, the royal priesthood, the peculiar nation, 1 Pet. 2,

9; for Christ has made us kings and priests unto God and His Father, Rev. 1, 6. As such we should show forth the praises of Him who has called us out of darkness into His marvelous light. V.7. **And Moses came and called for the elders of the people,** he summoned or invited them, **and laid before their faces all these words which the Lord commanded him.** V.8. **And all the people** without exception **answered together,** through their elders, **and said, All that the Lord hath spoken we will do.** They solemnly vowed allegiance and obedience, they took the obligation upon themselves. **And Moses returned the words of the people unto the Lord.** V.9. **And the Lord said unto Moses, Lo, I come unto thee in a thick cloud,** whose darkness would, in a measure, conceal His glory, **that the people may hear when I speak with thee, and believe thee for ever.** The position of Moses as the receiver and the mediator of the divine revelation would thus be attested, and the revelation and the authority of the Law, as given by him, would be established. The fact that he teaches the Word of the Lord gives to every true preacher his authority to this day. **And Moses told the words of the people unto the Lord.**

The special instructions. — V.10. **And the Lord said unto Moses, Go unto the people, and sanctify them today and tomorrow, and let them wash their clothes,** v.11. **and be ready against the third day; for the third day the Lord will come down in the sight of all the people upon Mount Sinai.** The people were to be set apart, consecrated, to the Lord, the washing of the clothes being a symbol of the inner purity which should be found in every believer. They should place themselves in the proper attitude of mind to hear the terms of the covenant which the Lord would announce on the third day, when He intended to descend upon Mount Sinai in such a manner as to make His glory visible to all the children of Israel. V.12. **And thou shalt set bounds unto the people round about,** have a fence made all around the base of the mountain, **saying, Take heed to yourselves that ye go not up into the mount, or touch the border of it,** the end, or foot, of the mountain. **Whosoever toucheth the mount,** the throne of God's legislation, **shall be surely put to death.** V.13. **There shall not an hand touch it, but he shall surely be stoned or shot through;** being on the other side of the fence, such a person could not be apprehended without making him that attempted to seize him guilty likewise, therefore he should be killed from a distance with stones or darts; **whether it be beast or man, it shall not live. When the trumpet soundeth long, they shall come up to the mount,** the long-drawn blast on the horn was the signal for the representatives of the people, the elders, to approach, chap. 24, 1. V.14. **And Moses went down from the mount unto the people, and sanctified the people; and they washed their clothes,** they performed the ceremonial purifying as they had been ordered. V.15. **And he said unto the people, Be ready against the third day; come not at your wives,** all marital relations were to be suspended for the time being. All these preparations show that Israel was still a sinful, unclean people. And sinners may not appear before the face of the holy God in their natural sinfulness.

The terrifying events of the third day. — V.16. **And it came to pass on the third day in the morning that there were thunders and lightnings and a thick cloud upon the mount.** There were all the signs of an unusual, supernatural thunder-shower. The darkness indicated that the holy God is unapproachable, veiling Himself from mortals even when He discloses Himself, for it is impossible for sinners to look upon His open glory. **And the voice of the trumpet** (was) **exceeding loud, so that all the people that was in the camp trembled.** The blasts of the horn, terrifying in themselves, became doubly so since their source was the divine presence on the mountain, where the Lord had now come down with His holy angels to make known His holy will, Deut. 33, 2; Acts 7, 53; Gal. 3, 19. No wonder the people heard the sound only with great fear and trembling. V.17. **And Moses brought forth the people out of the camp to meet with God,** all of them were to be assembled before Him as His holy congregation; **and they stood at the nether part of the mount, at its foot.** V.18. **And Mount Sinai was altogether on a smoke,** the entire mountain being enveloped in smoke, **because the Lord descended upon it in fire; and the smoke thereof ascended as the smoke of a furnace,** of a great smelter, **and the whole mount quaked greatly.** The nearer the people came to the mountain, the more impressively was the scene enrolled before their eyes, and the greater their terror became. V.19. **And when the voice of the trumpet sounded long, and waxed louder and louder,** gained in intensity or strength, **Moses spake** from the foot of the mountain, asking God for His commands, **and God answered him by a voice,** an articulate sound which could be understood. V.20. **And the Lord came down upon Mount Sinai, on the top of the mount; and the Lord called Moses up to the top of the mount. And Moses went up,** in order to speak to Him alone. V.21. **And the Lord said unto Moses, Go down,**

charge the people, testify before or upon them, **lest they break through unto the Lord to gaze, and many of them perish.** To go beyond the fence and encroach upon the territory set aside for the Lord's revelation was courting death. V.22. **And let the priests also which come near to the Lord,** those who had till then had charge of the priestly functions among the people, **sanctify themselves, lest the Lord break forth upon them,** strike them down and utterly destroy them. V.23. **And Moses said unto the Lord, The people cannot come up to Mount Sinai; for Thou chargedst us, saying, Set bounds about the mount, and sanctify it.** The fence had proved its value as a barrier in preventing the people from ascending the mount. V.24. **And the Lord said unto him, Away, get thee down, and thou shalt come up, thou and Aaron with thee; but let not the priests and the people break through to come up unto the Lord, lest He break forth upon them,** strike them down in His anger. V.25. **And Moses went down to the people and spake unto them.** The entire story reminds us of the fact that we believers of the New Testament are not come unto the mount that might be touched, and that burned with fire,…but unto Mount Zion, and unto the city of the living God,…and to Jesus, the Mediator of the New Covenant, and to the blood of sprinkling, that speaketh better things than that of Abel, Heb. 12, 18–24.

21

Exodus 20

The Giving of the Ten Commandments and Other Ordinances.

The Decalog. — **V. 1. And God spake all these words, saying, v.2. I am the Lord, thy God, which have brought thee out of the land of Egypt, out of the house of bondage.** That was the Lord's solemn introduction to the legislation on Mount Sinai, a reminder of the wonderful deliverance which He had wrought when He led forth His people out of the land of Egypt, where they had virtually been slaves. Note that the Decalog, as here given, was intended for the children of Israel and applied its principles to the circumstances under which they lived, with a form of government every detail of which was fixed by the Lord. **V.3. Thou shalt have no other gods before Me,** no strange, false gods, no idols, over against Me, setting them up as rivals for the glory and power which belong to Me alone. Not that such figments of man's imagination, such works of their hands, were in truth gods in any sense of the word, but that the very thinking and fashioning of idols is forbidden by the Lord. He is supreme, He is the only God, and His will should govern all men in all situations of life; for the other nine commandments are but explanations and applications of the first. V.4. **Thou shalt not make unto thee any graven image,** a carved or sculptured idol, **or any likeness of anything,** any representation that is intended for religious worship, **that is in heaven above,** birds or stars (heavenly bodies) of any kind, **or that is in the earth beneath,** men or beasts, **or that is in the water under the earth,** and marine animals; v.5. **thou shalt not bow down thyself to them,** in the act of adoration, nor serve them, actually giving them the worship, the honor which pertains to God alone, for that is the point of the entire prohibition, that pictures and images should not be made for purposes of worship. **For I, the Lord, thy God, am a jealous God, visiting the iniquity of the fathers upon the children unto the third and fourth generation of them that hate Me,** not with the certainty of absolute fatality, but as a just punishment of those children that follow their parents and ancestors in their evil ways; v.6. **and showing mercy unto thousands of them that love Me and keep My commandments.** The Lord's holiness and righteousness demands that He visit the sinners with His punitive justice, but He takes far greater pleasure in giving proofs of His mercy and kindness: He would rather reward than punish. V.7. **Thou shalt not take the name of the Lord, thy God, in vain,** without purpose and object, in a frivolous manner; **for the Lord will not hold him guiltless that taketh His name in vain,** an

132

emphatic warning that the punishment of God will surely strike everyone who lightly and blasphemously utters the Lord's name, whether this be in thoughtless foolishness or in deliberate perjury. V.8. **Remember the Sabbath-day to keep it holy.** This commandment presupposes a knowledge of the Sabbath, but not of its formal celebration. All those that urge the keeping of the Sabbath according to the Jewish pattern with the argument that this day and this form were included in the will of God as written into the hearts of men at the beginning, overlook or ignore the facts of history as found in the Book of Exodus. The deliberate setting aside of this special day of the week and the form of observance of this day as outlined to the Jews was intended for them only. V.9. **Six days shalt thou labor and do all thy work,** perform everything connected with trade, business, or profession; v.10. **but the seventh day is the Sabbath of the Lord, thy God; in it thou shalt not do any work,** perform the labor of your ordinary occupations, **thou, nor thy son, nor thy daughter; thy manservant, nor thy maidservant, nor thy cattle, nor the stranger that is within thy gates,** the enumeration purposely being made inclusive, in order to emphasize the commandment. V.11. **For in six days the Lord made heaven and earth, the sea, and all that in them is, and rested the seventh day; wherefore the Lord blessed the Sabbath day, and hallowed it,** set it apart to the Jews for His worship. The commandment was later fixed even more definitely by the mention of specific forms of labor which were not permitted among the children of Israel, Ps. 104, 23; Num. 4, 47; Neh. 3, 15; Jer.17, 21; Amos 8, 5; Num. 15, 32 ff. Note that the simple understanding of the text demands the assumption that the Lord created the world in six ordinary days.

The commandments concerning the love of one's neighbor. — V.12. **Honor thy father and thy mother,** they are to be given the reverence due to them as the representatives of God, with heart, mouth, and hand, in thought, word, and deed. In the home, in the family, is the foundation of all social life, all governments really being dependent upon the relation of parents and children, the existence and the welfare of the nations depending upon the moral stability given them by the home in its proper form, as the promise indicates; **that thy days may be long upon the land which the Lord, thy God, giveth thee.** It is the first commandment with promise, as St. Paul writes Eph.6, 2. 3, where he changes the text to apply to all men, and not only to the Jewish nation. V.13. **Thou shalt not kill,** the duty of preserving the life which God has given to man being enjoined here in all its branches and manifestations. V.14. **Thou shalt not commit adultery,** the word here used including not only the unfaithfulness of men and women within holy marriage, but every form of impurity directed against the holiness of God's institution of wedlock. Not only is every thought, word, and deed that is sanctioned and commanded within the confines of marriage forbidden outside of these bounds, but also every form of obscenity and every kind of familiarity which is connected with the sexual development of man. V.15. **Thou shalt not steal,** the Lord here protecting the property of one's neighbor, as the condition of the dignity and peacefulness of life, not only against robbery and theft, but also against unfaithfulness, neglect, and waste. V.16. **Thou shalt not bear false witness against thy neighbor,** the object being to protect truth, not only in all public, civil relations, but also in the home, the malice of evil tongues being well known. V.17. **Thou shalt not covet thy neighbor's house, thou shalt not covet thy neighbor's wife, nor his manservant, nor his maidservant, nor his ox, nor his ass, nor anything that is thy neighbor's.** Here the thoughts of the entire second table are once more summarized with reference to the source of sin; for it is out of the heart that the evil thoughts proceed which are afterward realized in various actual sins, Matt. 15, 19. So the admirable and fitting order of the commandments, as Luther cans it, is brought to an end and the circle of injunctions completed; for it is only by the sanctification of the heart according to the Tenth Commandment that the true worship of God according to the First Commandment can be secured. It should be noted here that both the division of the Decalog as such and the distinction between the Ninth and the Tenth Commandment are matters of no material consequence. **3)** The terror of the people. — V.18. **And all the people saw the thunderings, and the lightnings, and the noise of the trumpet, and the mountain smoking.** The impression was made on all the senses, but that of sight was chiefly involved. The manifestation of God's majesty was so powerful that it effected not only a wholesome awe of the great Jehovah, but an extreme terror as well. **And when the people saw it, they removed,** they shrank back from the vicinity of the mountain, **and stood afar off.** V.19. **And they said unto Moses, Speak thou with us, and we will hear, but let not God speak with us, lest we die.** The consciousness of their own sinfulness, their freshly fear and terror, caused them to promise a ready obedience to an the words of Moses. V.20. **And Moses said unto the people,**

Fear not; for God is come to prove you, His intention was to test the disposition of their hearts, to try them out with this terrifying aspect, **that His fear may be before your faces that ye sin not.** By the Law is the knowledge of sin, and God wanted to manifest His glory in order to work in their hearts the proper, holy reverence which would keep them from faithlessness and disobedience. V.21. **And the people stood afar off,** remained standing at a distance, **and Moses,** as the mediator of the people, **drew near unto the thick darkness where God was;** in order to receive the further commands of the Lord.

The precept concerning the altar. — V.22. **And the Lord said unto Moses, Thus thou shalt say unto the children of Israel, Ye have seen that I have talked with you from heaven.** This fact proved the superiority. the authority of the Lord, His right to express His demands as He was now preparing to do. No false God would have had this power, and the incident was bound to establish Jehovah as the true God in the sight of Israel. V.23. **Ye shall not make with Me gods of silver, neither shall ye make unto you gods of gold.** The children of Israel were not to make and place on a level with Jehovah, for purposes of worship, idols of any kind, which they would then regard as their gods. The Making and worshiping of such images, every form of idolatry, was absolutely prohibited. V.24. **An altar of earth thou shalt make unto Me, and shalt sacrifice thereon thy burnt offerings and thy peace-offerings, thy sheep and thine oxen.** Such offerings were a type and figure of the heart of man, as it arose in true worship to the throne of God, for which reason also plain ground, the soil as the Lord created it, was the material which He preferred, that being found practically everywhere where the children of Israel would assemble for worship. **In all places where I record My name I will come unto thee, and I will bless thee.** God is confined neither to Temple nor to Tabernacle, but is able to reveal His glorious majesty at any place which He may choose. And wherever this takes place, those who are fortunate enough to be witnesses of such a revelation will become partakers of God's blessings. It is this fact which is of such great value to us believers of the New Testament, since we have the assurance that the presence of the Lord in the Word and in the Sacraments guarantees to us His blessings. V.25. **And if thou wilt make Me an altar of stone,** if the children of Israel should prefer such an altar, **thou shalt not build it of hewn stone; for it thou lift up thy tool upon it, thou hast polluted it,** literally: for thy sharpness thou swingest above it, and thou desecratest It. Ornamentation of the altar of the Lord under the circumstances in which the Israelites found themselves would have redounded to their own glory, and not to that of the Lord. V.26. **Neither shalt thou go up by steps unto Mine altar, that thy nakedness be not discovered thereon,** as would happen with the loose-fitting. clothes then worn. Since the consciousness of sin came to man with the feeling of shame, therefore the revealing of nakedness is equivalent to a shameless exhibition of sin, and thus not permissible in the worship of Jehovah.

22

Exodus 21

Ordinances Concerning Slaves and Various Forms of Violent Deaths.

Precepts regulating the master's relation to slaves. — V.1. **Now these are the judgments which thou shalt set before them.** These were special ordinances concerning the political commonwealth of the Jews. In the New Testament God's revelation is no longer confined to one single people, and we no longer have any state under the direct government of God. And yet, also these ordinances were recorded for our learning, especially for the purpose of teaching us various applications of the law of love. V.2. **If thou buy an Hebrew servant, as a slave, six years he shall serve in this capacity; and in the seventh he shall go out free for nothing,** the idea being that he has earned his freedom by his six years' service. V.3. **If he came in by himself,** literally, with his body, that is, unmarried, **he shall go out by himself; if he were**

married, then his wife shall go out with him. Cp. chap. 22, 3; Lev. 25, 39; Deut. 15, 12–15. V.4. **If his master have given him a wife, and she have born him sons or daughters,** the woman, of course, being a slave also, **the wife and her children shall be her master's, and he shall go out by himself.** The man could have his freedom, if he chose, but the woman would still remain the master's property, and her children as well. V.5. **And if the servant shall plainly say, I love my master, my wife, and my children, I will not go out free,** the slave preferring a continuation of his slavery in the company of his family to freedom without his loved ones, v.6. **then his master shall bring him unto the judges,** before the proper officers; **he shall also bring him to the door or unto the door-post** of his house; **and his master shall bore his ear through with an awl; and he shall serve him forever,** the opening in the ear marking the slave as such. V.7. **And if a man sell his daughter to be a maid-servant,** her position being that of housekeeper and probable concubine, **she shall not go out as the men-servants do,** that is, not be released in the seventh year, the purpose being that she meanwhile become the wife or the concubine either of the master or of his son. V.8. **If she please not her master, who hath betrothed her to himself,** that is, who had purchased her with the expectation of making her his wife or concubine, then shall he let her be redeemed by some other man who might desire her for his wife. **To sell her unto a strange nation he shall have no power, seeing he hath dealt deceitfully with her,** he has broken faith with her, for she came to him, although her father sold her for reasons of poverty, Lev. 25, 39, with the understanding that she was to occupy the position of wife or concubine. Hebrew girls were not to be sold into unconditional slavery to members of other nations. V.9. **And if he have betrothed her unto his son,** if he have purchased the girl with the intention of making her his son's wife or concubine, **he shall deal with her after the manner of daughters,** according to the rights of a daughter. That was the second possibility. V.10. **If he take him another wife,** so that he have two or more wives or concubines, **her food, her raiment, and her duty of marriage,** the special duty which marriage implies, **shall he not diminish.** She was on no account to be neglected also in case of this third possibility; the father was to use his power and authority in upholding the rights of the girl. V.11. **And if he do not these three unto her,** that is, if, in the three given instances, he does not do the right thing by her, **then shall she go out free without money.** The woman would have her freedom, and her father would have the advantage of the purchase-money. Thus was the Hebrew male or female servant protected, for the Israelites were not to forget that the lowly among their people were likewise members of God's chosen nation. The principle applies to Christian masters also, inasmuch as they will treat even the least among the believers as brethren and sisters in Christ.

Concerning murder and bodily injuries. — V.12. **He that smiteth a man,** strikes him down with deliberate intention, **so that he die, shall be surely put to death.** The reference seems to be to a murder committed in the heat of anger or in a condition of intoxication. V.13. **And if a man lie not in wait,** does not seek a man's life with deliberate intent, **but God deliver him into his hand,** God permits it to happen in that manner that a man kills another by accident,

then I will appoint thee a place whither he shall flee.
The Lord later designated certain cities as cities of refuge,
Num. 35, 11; Deut.19, 1–10. V.14. **But if a man come
presumptuously upon his neighbor, to slay him with
guile,** if he has deliberately planned the crime and carried
it out in cold blood, **thou shalt take him from Mine altar
that he may die;** in that case it would not even avail the
murderer to seek the refuge of the sanctuary. Because he has
broken down the sacred wall which protected his neighbor,
therefore it would also, in his case, not be a violation of
the altar of God to tear him away from its protection and
put him to death. V.15. **And he that smiteth his father
or his mother shall be surely put to death.** So highly
was the honor of parents esteemed in the sight of God that
the mere act of striking either of them was equivalent to
manslaughter, to cold-blooded murder, and was punished
accordingly. V.16. **And he that stealeth a man and selleth
him, or if he be found in his hand, he shall surely be
put to death.** Man-stealing, as a violent abuse of one's
neighbor's person, of his dignity as a human being, was
also placed on a plane with murder. V.17. **And he that
curseth his father or his mother shall surely be put to
death.** Since the cursing and reviling of parents flows from
the same wicked disposition of mind as striking them, v.15.
the same punishment is decreed by God. V.18. **And if men
strive together,** in a quarrel which culminates in physical
violence, **and one smite another with a stone or with his
fist,** with a clod, **and he die not, but keepeth his bed,** is
confined to his bed in consequence of the blow;v.19. **if he
rise again, and walk abroad upon his staff, then shall
he that smote him be quit,** be released from the probable

charge of manslaughter; **only he shall pay for the loss of his time, and shall cause him to be thoroughly healed;** he shall make good the loss occasioned by the enforced idleness and pay the doctor bills and the medicine. V.20. **And if a man smite his servant or his maid,** his male or his female slave, **with a rod, and he die under his hand, he shall be surely punished,** be required to give satisfaction. V.21. **Notwithstanding, if he continue a day or two** before dying, and it be shown in this way that it was not the master's intention to commit murder outright, **he shall not be punished; for he is his money,** the slave was the master's property, and in such a case it would not stand to reason that he had deliberately and purposely killed the slave. The law was intended to prevent ruthless exhibitions of temper and cold-blooded murders. V.22. **If men strive, and hurt a woman with child,** the pregnant woman interposing between the quarreling men, **so that her fruit depart from her,** that a miscarriage occurs, **and yet no mischief follow,** if the woman herself is not injured and if her ability to bear children is not impaired, **he shall be surely punished,** that is, the guilty man, **according as the woman's husband will lay upon him; and he shall pay as the judges determine;** the injured parties being awarded damages according to the merits of the case. V.23. **And if any mischief follow, then thou shalt give life for life,** v.24. **eye for eye, tooth for tooth, hand for hand, foot for foot,** v.25. **burning for burning, wound for wound, stripe for stripe.** That was the law of retaliation as it could be invoked by such as sought indemnity for injuries: the injured woman might demand expiation according to the degree of' her hurt. That was the ordinance so far as free

Israelites were concerned. V.26. **And if a man smite the eye of his servant or the eye of his maid that it perish, he shall let him go free for his eye's sake.** No distinction is made between deliberate cruelty and an unintentional blow, the effect alone being registered. V.27. **And if he smite out his man-servant's tooth or his maid-servant's tooth, he shall let him go free for his tooth's sake.** The loss, not only of some member of the body, but even of a single tooth, as a result of the master's treatment, entitled the slave to his freedom. So far as Christians are concerned, they know that they should not hurt nor harm their neighbor in his body. They will not insist upon any law of retaliation, as the granting of indemnities is a function of the government, but will keep in mind the Lord's admonition to kindness and placableness.

Ordinances for the protection of life and property. — V.28. **If an ox gore a man or a woman that they die, then the ox shall be surely stoned, and his flesh shall not be eaten,** be considered unclean; **but the owner of the ox shall be quit,** shall be considered and declared innocent of any wrongdoing. V.29. **But if the ox were wont to push with his horn in time past, and it hath been testified to his owner, and he hath not kept him in,** if the owner was fully aware that the ox was in the habit of attacking people, that he was of a mean disposition, and yet did not confine him, **but that he hath killed a man or a woman, the ox shall be stoned, and his owner also shall be put to death,** because he, by his neglect in watching the vicious animal, became the cause of the deaths. There was a possibility, however, of a man's saving his life in such a case. V.30. **If there be laid on him a sum of** money, then he shall give for the ransom of his life whatsoever is laid upon him, as a punishment for his criminal carelessness. V.31. **Whether he have gored a son or have gored a daughter, according to this judgment shall it be done unto him.** The law was justly strict and made no distinction between men and women; it was a case of paying the price of ransom or the penalty of death. V.32. **If the ox shall push a manservant or a maid-servant,** the injury resulting in death, he, the owner of the vicious brute, **shall give unto their master thirty shekels of silver,** probably the usual market price of a slave, **and the ox shall be stoned.** Thus we also, in passing judgment upon any trespass, distinguish between sins of weakness and sins of malice, between transgressions by neglect, by mistake, and by criminal intent, being very careful not to accuse anyone unjustly. V.33. **And if a man shall open a pit, or if a man shall dig a pit and not cover it, and an ox or an ass fall therein,** the result being that his neighbor is harmed in his possessions, v.34. **the owner of the pit shall make it good, and give money unto the owner of them,** restore their full value in money; and the dead beast shall be his, he may dispose of the carcass as he sees fit. V.35. **And if one man's ox hurt another's that he die, then they shall sell the live ox,** the one that did the damage, **and divide the money of it; and the dead ox also they shall divide,** both parties, in this case, bearing the loss equally, since it could rarely be determined which animal was the aggressor. V.36. **Or if it be known that the ox hath used to push in time past, and his owner hath not kept him in, he shall surely pay ox for ox; and the dead shall be his own.** In this case the owner of the mean animal would be guilty of criminal neglect, of punishable carelessness, and would therefore have to restore to his neighbor the full value of the animal which was dead through the viciousness of his ox, only the carcass being his. To this day the right understanding of the Seventh Commandment demands that full restoration be made to one's neighbor, not only in case of theft, but whenever he has suffered damage, even through the agency of a brute beast.

23

Exodus 22

Ordinances Concerning Property and General Social Relations.

Regarding property. — V.1. **If a man shall steal an ox or a sheep, and kill it or sell it, he shall restore five oxen,** five head of cattle, **for an ox and four sheep for a sheep.** The Lord wanted complete restoration to be made, the indemnity being in proportion to the transgression. V.2. **If a thief be found breaking up,** breaking through a wall, breaking into a house, Matt. 6, 20, **and be smitten that he die, there shall no blood be shed for him,** his death cannot demand the vengeance which a murder would; for the owner of the house would have to guard against every contingency, including murder. V.3. **If the sun be risen upon him, there shall be blood shed for him,** to kill a thief in broad daylight was to be considered murder. **For he,** the thief apprehended in the day, **should make full restitution,** most certainly pay back all that he stole. **If he have nothing, then he shall be sold for his theft,** for the value of the goods stolen by him. V.4. **If the theft be certainly found in his hand alive, whether it be ox or ass or sheep, he shall restore double,** the four and fivefold restitution being required only in case the stolen animals had already been slaughtered or sold. Theft being a severe offense against one's neighbor, severe measures were taken at once to keep men from this transgression. V.5. **If a man shall cause a field or vineyard to be eaten, and shall put in his beast,** if a person injures his neighbor's property by letting his cattle run loose, **and shall feed in another man's field, of the best of his own field and of the best of his own vineyard shall he make restitution;** for carelessness of this kind is inexcusable, being almost equivalent to willful damage. V.6. **If fire break out,** said of any small fire which gets beyond the control of him that started it, **and catch in thorns,** in the thornhedge at the edge of the field, which it was intended to destroy, **so that the stacks of corn,** sheaves of grain stacked after harvest, **or the standing corn or the field,** no matter what it contains, **be consumed therewith, he that kindled the fire shall surely make restitution** for his act of foolish carelessness. V.7. **If a man shall deliver unto his neighbor money or stuff to keep, entrusts any valuables to him for safe-keeping, and It be stolen out of the man's house; If the thief be found, let him pay double.** V.8. **If the thief be not found, then the master of the house shall be brought unto the judges, to the proper officials of the government, to see whether he have put his hand unto his neighbor's goods.** The object of the investigation was to give the lord of the house an opportunity to clear himself of suspicion, as though he had been guilty of appropriating his neighbor's property, which he was to guard as he did his own. V.9. **For all manner of trespass,** in the case of any accusation alleging a crime, **whether It be for ox, for ass, for sheep, for raiment, or for any manner of lost thing, which another challengeth to be his, the cause of both parties shall come before the judges,** before the officials having the jurisdiction of the case; **and whom the judges shall condemn,** declare to be in the wrong, **he shall pay double unto his neighbor.** This is the general rule for all cases of contested property. V.10. **If a man deliver unto his neighbor an ass or an ox or a sheep or any beast to keep, and it die or be hurt or driven away, no man seeing it,** the fact that no witnesses were near making the matter very complicated, v.11. **then shall an oath of the Lord be between them both,** the one suspected being given an opportunity to declare his innocence under oath, **that he hath not put his hand unto his neighbor's goods; and the owner of it shall accept thereof, and he,** the man to whom the animals had been entrusted, **shall not make it good.** V.12. **And If It be stolen from him, he shall make restitution unto the owner thereof.** In the case of animals, unlike that of money and valuables, the guardian of the property was also expected to act as watchman, his failure in this respect costing him dearly. V.13. **If It be torn In pieces, then let him bring it for witness, and he shall not make good that which was torn,** for the fact that he produced the torn animal proved that he had watched and even driven off the attacking predatory beast. V.14. **And if a man borrow aught of his neighbor,** some work animal, which he then uses, **and it be hurt or die, the owner thereof** being not with it, he shall surely make it good; for in this case neglect might be assumed. V.15. But if the owner thereof be with it, be present when some accident befalls his animal, he, the borrower, shall not make it good; if it be an hired thing, it came for his hire, he paid for the use of the animal and cannot be held responsible for the accident. Fairness and justice was to govern all the relations of the children of Israel toward one another.

Regarding various social relations. — V.16. And if a man entice a maid that is not betrothed, and lie with her, thus seducing her and robbing her of her honor and virginity, he shall surely endow her to be his wife. The crime could be expiated at least in a measure by his marrying the girl and by giving dowry money to her father. V.17. If her father utterly refuse to give her unto him, he shall pay, weigh out, money according to the dowry of virgins. This procedure, in a way, reinstated the girl as a virgin, and she was afterwards not barred from marrying. The transgressor thus made good his crime as far as possible and showed his repentance. In the case of a betrothed virgin the punishment inflicted upon the seducer was death, Deut. 22, 23. 24. V.18. Thou shalt not suffer a witch to live; every one, man or woman, actually guilty of witchcraft, was to be put to death. The sorceress is merely named because women were more addicted to this practice than men. V.19. Whosoever lieth with a beast, in sexual intercourse, shall surely be put to death. Cp. Lev. 18, 23; 20, 15; Deut. 27, 21. This vice was placed on the same level with pederasty or sodomy, Lev. 20, 13. V.20. He that sacrifceth unto any god, save unto the Lord only, he shall be utterly destroyed. Since the government of the children of Israel was a theocracy, under the direct rule of Jehovah, the idolater forfeited his life. At the present time it would be wrong for a government to punish sorcery, idolatry, heresy, with death or in any form whatsoever, unless social damage has been done; for the state is concerned with outward matters only. But so far as the Christian congregations are concerned, they cannot tolerate offenders of this kind in their midst, for the trespasses named are deadly sins, which absolutely drive out faith. V.21. **Thou shalt neither vex a stranger nor oppress him,** in no manner make life miserable for him, either by open persecution or by constant nagging; **for ye were strangers in the land of Egypt,** and the memory of those years of oppression was intended to foster in their hearts true kindness. The word "stranger" apparently applies to non-Canaanitish strangers only; for the Canaanites were to be extirpated. V.22. **Ye shall not afflict any widow or fatherless child.** To humble widows and orphans by acts of unkindness is to challenge the Lord, who is the special Protector of the desolate. V.23. **If thou afflict them in any wise, and they cry at all unto Me, I will surely hear their cry; v.24. and My wrath shall wax hot, and I will kill you with the sword; and your wives shall be widows and your children fatherless.** In the wars which the Lord would bring upon them as an act of retaliation and revenge, their own loved ones, by their death, would be left as helpless as those whom the Israelites oppressed and humbled in the first place. V.25. **If thou lend money to any of My people that is poor by thee,** to any members of the Jewish nation that were in such need as to be compelled to borrow for the necessaries of life, **thou shalt not be to him as an usurer, neither shalt thou lay upon him**

usury, take interest in such a case. V.26. **If thou at all take thy neighbor's raiment to pledge, take his garment as security, thou shalt deliver it unto him by that the sun goeth down;** v.27. **for that is his covering only, it is his raiment for his skin,** it serves to cover and protect his body against the inclemencies of the weather; **wherein shall he sleep?** The upper garment of the Oriental served him as a cover in which he wrapped himself at night. **And it shall come to pass, when he crieth unto Me, that I will hear; for I am gracious,** His divine favor rests upon such as are in need. We Christians also know that it pleases the Lord if we have compassion upon the widow and the fatherless, and that any oppression of the poor and needy will bring upon us His punishment. V.28. **Thou shalt not revile the gods,** that is, Elohim, the one true God, they shall not blaspheme, **nor curse the ruler of thy people,** who is a representative of the Lord on earth. V.29. **Thou shalt not delay to offer the first of thy ripe fruits and of thy liquors,** literally, "Of thy fullness or plenty and of thy drop [of oil and wine] thou shalt not delay"; for.the Lord wanted the first-fruits of the field, of the vineyard, and of the olive-orchard. **The first-born of thy sons shalt thou give unto Me.** Cp. chap. 13, 2. 12. V.30. **Likewise shalt thou do with thine oxen and with thy sheep: seven days it shall be with his dam; on the eighth day thou shalt give it Me** as a sacrifice. V.31. **And ye shall be holy men unto Me,** set apart as a peculiar nation; **neither shall ye eat any flesh that is torn of beasts in the field; ye shall cast it to the dogs.** As a people that was consecrated to the Lord in the first-born they should abstain from the eating of unclean meat, to which that belonged which had been tom by beasts of prey. Christians will also abstain from all practices which will defile the heart and the mind and be glad to offer to the Lord of their income from all sources.

24

Exodus 23

Directions Concerning Worship and the Continuation of the Journey.

Further ordinances regarding social relations. — V.1. **Thou shalt not raise a false report,** undertake to testify of a promise or agreement which was not heard with your own ears. **Put not thine hand with the wicked to be an unrighteous witness,** to charge your neighbor with any form of wickedness, to involve him in quarrels before court. Testimony should never be given in favor of some criminal act. V.2. **Thou shalt not follow a multitude to do evil; neither shalt thou speak in a cause to decline after many to wrest judgment.** The thought of the first half of the sentence is emphasized in the second part; for to yield to the hasty judgment of the multitude merely because of the great numbers that hold an opinion, if this means deviating from the way of truth and of justice, is sharply condemned by the Lord. A witness in any case should speak the full truth to the best of his knowledge. V.3. **Neither shalt thou countenance a poor man in his cause.** To pretend to be moved by sympathy for the poor in favoring them in each and every suit is an affectation; God wanted His people to stand on the side of justice, regardless of consequences. V.4. **If thou meet thine enemy's ox or his ass going astray, thou shalt surely bring it back to him again;** for difficulties and differences with any person should not set aside the love for him as a neighbor, and for this reason the command is made emphatic. V.5. **If thou see the ass of him that hateth thee lying under his burden,** borne down to the ground by the greatness of the load upon him, **and wouldest forbear to help him, thou shalt surely help with him,** literally: "Wouldest thou hold back from helping?" Surely no man's feeling of revenge would reach the point of permitting a dumb beast to suffer. There is only one thing to do in such an extremity: relieve the beast of its load, help him to arise, assist his master in saving the burden. That such conduct requires self-denial is implied, but the Lord wants such self-denial to be practiced. V.6. **Thou shalt not wrest the Judgment of thy poor,** of the poor dependent upon thee, **in his cause.** This ordinance supplements v.3, bidding the mighty beware of violating their position and the rights of those that are defenseless before them, since the Lord is their Protector. V.7. **Keep thee far from a false matter; and the innocent and the righteous slay thou not; for I will not justify the wicked.** This is said to the selfish, unrighteous judge, whose perversion of justice may, under circumstances, bring death to an innocent, righteous man. The form of the threat is particularly effective in setting forth the certain condemnation of the wicked judge. V.8. **And thou shalt take no gift,** no judge should ever accept a bribe, even in the form of an innocent-looking present; **for the gift blindeth the wise,** acts as a hood before the eyes of him who otherwise may see well in any case brought to his attention**, and perverteth the words of the righteous,** making right wrong and causing the judge to render false decisions. V.9. **Also thou shalt not oppress a stranger,** an injunction which in this connection refers chiefly to court cases; **for ye know the heart of a stranger,** just how he feels in the midst of humiliation and oppression, **seeing ye were strangers in the land of Egypt.** So much the Christians will also heed, especially such as are in positions of authority, where they must judge, render decisions, set forth the truth, that they be strictly impartial, not permitting themselves to be influenced by the social status of any persons with whom they have dealings, but frankly reproving the evil and acknowledging the good.

The holy periods and feasts. — V.10. **And six years thou shalt sow thy land, and shalt gather in the fruits thereof,** whatever it yields under careful cultivation; v.11. **but the seventh year thou shalt let it rest and lie still,** let it remain unused, make no attempt to cultivate it**, that the poor of thy people may eat,** namely, that produced by the land without cultivation, the so-called volunteer grain; **and what they leave the beasts of the field shall eat.** This fallowing of the land would give it an opportunity to recuperate. **In like manner thou shalt deal with thy vineyard and with thy oliveyard.** There also the fruits were not to be gathered, but left for the poor and needy, for the beasts of the field, and for the fowls of the air. This was the so-called Sabbath of Years, analogous to the Sabbath of the Week. V.12. **Six days thou shalt do thy work, and on the seventh day thou shalt rest,** mainly by desisting from work, **that thine ox and thine ass may rest, and the son of thy handmaid and the stranger may be refreshed.** So the slaves and the strangers, as well as the domestic animals, were to be given a breathing spell once a week, the Sabbath thus serving not only religious, but also humanitarian ends. V.13. **And in all things that I have said unto you be circumspect,** be on your guard, watch most carefully; **and make no mention of the name of other gods,** the very reference to them being prohibited, **neither let it be heard out of thy mouth.** Jehovah was to be adored exclusively in the midst of Israel. V.14. **Three times thou shalt keep a feast unto Me in the year.** This is the enumeration of the great Jewish festivals, as it is repeatedly found in the ordinances given through Moses in the wilderness. V.15. **Thou shalt keep the Feast of Unleavened Bread,** in connection with the Passover; **(thou shalt eat unleavened bread seven days, as I commanded thee,** chap. 12, **in the time appointed of the month Abib,** from the fourteenth to the twenty-first; **for in it thou camest out from Egypt,** it was the festival in commemoration of the deliverance from the bondage of Egypt; **and none shall appear before Me empty,** that is, with empty hands, everyone being expected to bring sacrificial gifts to the Lord;) v.16. **and the Feast of Harvest,** afterwards known as the Feast of Weeks, or Pentecost, **the first-fruits of thy labors, which thou hast sown in the field,** the festival of the grain harvest; **and the Feast of Ingathering,** afterwards known as the Feast of Tabernacles, **which is in the end of the year,** in the fall of the year, in October, **when thou hast gathered in**

thy labors out of the field, not only the grain, but also the fruits, the three great products being usually mentioned as corn, wine, and oil. V.17. **Three times in the year all thy males shall appear before the Lord God.** So it was specifically ordered that on the above-mentioned feasts the men of the congregation were obliged to appear before the Lord, a fact which excludes neither women, 1 Sam. 1, 3, nor children, Luke 2, 41 ff. V.18. **Thou shalt not offer the blood of My sacrifice,** that of the Passover, which, in a most particular sense, belonged to the Lord, **with leavened bread**; neither shall the fat of My sacrifice (or feast) **remain until the morning.** This is a reference to the institution of the Passover and of the Feast of Unleavened Bread, for the Lord had decreed that leaven and leavened bread should not be found in the houses of the Israelites when this great sacrifice was made, and also that no part of the Passover lamb was to remain till the morning. V.19. **The first of the first-fruits of thy land thou shalt bring into the house of the Lord, thy God.** This refers to the festivals in general, for not only were the firstlings of the barley sheaves offered at Passover and two pentecostal loaves during the Feast of Weeks, but the people were expected in general to bring gifts of first-fruits to the Lord. **Thou shalt not seethe a kid in his mother's milk,** this practice being prohibited as unnatural and tending to make the feasting the central feature, especially in connection with the great festivals. The Old Testament Sabbath and festivals with their ordinances are no longer binding upon the Christians of the New Testament; yet God expects also us to thank and to praise, to serve and obey Him in true faith and love.

Concerning the continuation of the journey. — V.20.

157

Behold, I send an Angel before thee to keep thee in the way and to bring thee into the place which I have prepared. This special guiding and protecting Angel was the Son of God Himself, for in Him Jehovah was revealed; in Him, as the Angel of the face of God, the innermost essence of God was manifested. Under His almighty guidance their journey would prosper. V.21. **Beware of Him, and obey His voice, provoke Him not,** do not embitter Him; **for He will not pardon your transgressions; for My name is in Him.** The salvation of the children of Israel would depend upon their obedience, implicit, cheerful obedience. V.22. **But if thou shalt indeed obey His voice, and do all that I speak,** as the Lord's word and His word would be identical, **then I will be an enemy unto thine enemies and an adversary unto thine adversaries;** all those that bore or showed ill will to the children of Israel the Lord would requite in kind. V.23. **For Mine Angel shall go before thee, and bring thee in unto the Amorites, and the Hittites, and the Perizzites, and the Canaanites, and the Hivites, and the Jebusites; and I will cut them off,** destroy, annihilate, extirpate them. V.24. **Thou shalt not bow down to their gods, nor serve them, nor do after their works,** in no manner become guilty of false worship, of idolatry; **but thou shalt utterly overthrow them,** the destruction of the heathen tribes of Canaan being expressly commanded here, **and quite break down their images,** break in pieces, smash the carved pillars used for idolatrous purposes. V.25. **And ye shall serve the Lord, your God, and He shall bless thy bread and thy water; and I will take sickness away from the midst of thee.** Bread and water are symbols of welfare, and well-being and health were to be the reward of faithfulness. V.26. **There shall nothing cast their young nor be barren in thy land;** the population of men as well as of domestic animals was not to be diminished by epidemics of miscarriages and by barrenness. **The number of thy days I will fulfill;** for a long life, under the blessing of God, is a reward of His goodness and mercy. V.27. **I will send My fear before thee,** causing all the heathen to be filled with apprehension and dread, **and I will destroy all the people to whom thou shalt come, and I will make all thine enemies turn their backs upon thee,** in flight, without having so much as begun a battle. V.28. **And I will send hornets before thee,** a figurative expression to denote the utmost terror, caused probably by some severe epidemic which the Lord sent to frighten the Canaanites, **which shall drive out the Hivite, the Canaanite, and the Hittite from before thee.** V.29. **I will not drive them out from before thee in one year,** as the Lord could very easily have done, **lest the land become desolate, and the beast of the field multiply against thee,** their numbers as yet not being great enough to occupy the entire country. Cp. Deut. 7, 22; Lev. 26, 22; Josh. 13, 1–7. V.30. **By little and little I will drive them out from before thee, until thou be increased and inherit the land;** while the heathen nations as such would be destroyed, individuals would still be found throughout the country until such a time as the growing number of the Israelites would crowd them out. V.31. **And I will set thy bounds from the Red Sea,** on the south, **even unto the sea of the Philistines,** the Mediterranean, on the west, **and from the desert** of Arabia, on the southeast, **unto the river,** the Euphrates, on the north, these being the ideal boundaries of the Promised Land;

for I will deliver the inhabitants of the land into your hand, and thou shalt drive them out before thee. V.32. **Thou shalt make no covenant with them,** be inveigled into forming an alliance with them, **nor with their gods,** the idols which they had made for themselves. V.33. **They shall not dwell in thy land, lest they make thee sin against Me;** if they would remain in the land, their presence and their idolatrous customs would be a continual temptation to Israel, as the Lord well knew; **for if thou serve their gods, it will surely be a snare unto thee.** Even so, the intercourse of Christians with the children of this world all too often proves a snare to them, and they are lured into the idolatrous customs of the unbelievers. It is to our greatest advantage not to provoke the Lord at any time, lest He take His gracious presence from us. It is only by staying with Him that we are safe forever.

25

Exodus 24

The Formal Covenant.

Moses summoned by God. — V.1. **And he said unto Moses, Come up unto the Lord, thou and Aaron, Nadab and Abihu, and seventy of the elders of Israel; and worship ye afar off.** The emphatic position of the word "Moses" in the Hebrew text shows that this command was given to Moses directly, not addressed to the people, as the Ten Commandments had been. Nadab and Abihu were sons of Aaron, and the seventy elders represented the people. In drawing near to the Lord these men were commanded to bow down, to worship, but only from a distance, Moses alone, as the prophet of Jehovah, being permitted to go to the top of the mountain. V.2. **And Moses alone shall come near the Lord; but they shall not come nigh; neither shall the people go up with him.** Both Aaron and his sons, representing the priests, and the seventy elders, the government representatives of the popular assembly, were excluded from the intimate privileges of the prophet of the Lord. V.3. **And Moses,** who had been in the darkness at the foot of the mountain, at some distance from the people, **came and told the people all the words of the Lord, and all the judgments,** all the ordinances recorded in the preceding chapters; **and all the people answered with one voice and said, All the words which the Lord hath said will we do.** Under the influence of the awe-inspiring manifestation of Jehovah which they had witnessed they voiced their unanimous consent, their unconditional agreement. V.4. **And Moses wrote all the words of the Lord,** he recorded all the laws and ordinances which had been given till now, that none might be overlooked or forgotten, **and rose up early in the morning, and builded an altar under the hill,** at the foot of the mountain, **and twelve pillars, according to the twelve tribes of Israel.** The altar indicated the presence of Jehovah, while the twelve pillars symbolized the twelve tribes of Israel, representing their presence. V.5. **And he sent young men of the children of Israel,** chiefly because they possessed the necessary strength and agility to perform the work quickly, **which offered burnt offerings, and sacrificed peace offerings of oxen unto the Lord,** true offerings of salvation, which symbolized the gracious regard of the Lord for the people of His choice, the union effected by His mercy. V.6. **And Moses took half of the blood, and put it in basins,** saving it for a ceremony shortly to be performed; **and half of the blood he sprinkled on the altar,** he poured it out before the Lord with one swift movement. V.7. **And he took the book of the covenant, and read in the audience of the people,** as containing the terms of the covenant on God's side; it was called out with a loud voice, so all could hear. **And they said, All that the Lord hath said will we do and be obedient;** having had another opportunity to hear the ordinances, they willingly consented to all the terms. V.8. **And Moses took the blood,** which had been kept in the basins, **and sprinkled it on the people, and said, Behold the blood of the covenant which the Lord hath made with you concerning all these words.** The significance of this solemn ceremony was that the people, through the blood of the sacrifice as it was sprinkled upon them, were received into the full fellowship with God, just as the blood poured out at the altar signified the complete surrender of the people to God. But the surrender of the people in general, as they voiced their consent to the Lord's ordinances, preceded their obedience in particular, the order which is observed to this day. We Christians are brought into true fellowship with God, not by the sacrificial blood of mere animals, but through the precious blood of Christ, as of a lamb without blemish and without spot.

The elders appear before God; Moses remains. — V.9. **Then went up Moses and Aaron, Nadab and Abihu, and seventy of the elders of Israel,** representing the prophetic, the priestly, and the political element of the children of Israel, according to God command, v. 1; v.10. **and they saw the God of Israel,** who revealed Himself to them in some form which gave them an idea of His divine essence; **and there was under His feet as it were a paved work of a sapphire stone,** a brilliant formation of sapphire blue, **and as it were the body of heaven in his clearness.** It was a vision of the covenant God of Israel, of Him who had first revealed Himself to the patriarchs, in all the beauty of His grace and faithfulness. Thus the fellowship, the alliance, of the children of Israel with the majestic God was perfected. V.11. **And upon the nobles of the children of Israel He laid not His hand,** the Lord did not harm them, although they, sinful people as they were, stood in the presence of God's holiness and justice; **also they saw God, and did eat and drink,** they held a feast in the presence of the vision, thus testifying to the complete and strong fellowship that obtained between them and the Lord of the covenant. It was a foretaste of the precious and wonderful blessings with which the Lord intended to satisfy the souls of His people forever. V.12. **And the Lord said unto Moses, Come up to Me into the mount and be there.** Moses is here summoned to a private interview and to a long stay on the mountain. **And I will give thee tables of stone, and a Law, and commandments which I have written,** a codex prepared by the hand of God Himself, **that thou mayest teach them.** V.13. **And Moses rose up and his minister,** his servant, **Joshua,** chap. 17, 9; 32, 17; 33, 11; **and Moses went up into the mount of God,** to the summit of Sinai. V.14. **And he said unto the elders,** who were still at the side, or at the foot of the mountain where the glory of the Lord had been revealed to them, **Tarry ye here for us until we come again unto you; and, behold, Aaron and Hur are with you. If any man have any matters to do,** any difficult matter which requires adjustment, **let him come unto them;** he appointed them as chief magistrates to act during his absence. V.15. **And Moses went up into the mount, and a cloud covered the mount,** blotting out all the brilliance and clearness which the elders had witnessed.

164

V.16. **And the glory of the Lord abode upon Mount Sinai, and the cloud covered it six days,** thus increasing the impression of awe which the people felt in consequence of all these marvelous happenings. **And the seventh day He called unto Moses out of the midst of the cloud,** summoning him into His very presence. V.17. **And the sight of the glory of the Lord was like devouring fire on the top of the mount in the eyes of the children of Israel.** "Into this fiery radiance Moses enters, through the fiery flame of the unapproachable justice of God, through the lightnings of the flaming sword of the cherubim, in order to receive the fiery Law." (Lange.) V.18. **And Moses went into the midst of the cloud, and gat him up into the mount. And Moses was in the mount forty days and forty nights.** But we are reminded of the fact that our Lord, unless approached in and through Christ, is a consuming fire, Heb. 12, 29.

26

Exodus 25

The Order to Prepare the Tabernacle and Its Appointments.

Offerings of the Israelites requested. — V.1. **And the Lord spake unto Moses, saying,** v.2. **Speak unto the children of Israel that they bring Me an offering;** according to the Hebrew text, a gift which one lifts off, takes away from the rest of his property and reaches out and up to God; **of every man that giveth it willingly with his heart,** literally, "from the side of every man whom his heart impels," **ye shall take My offering;** truly a fine description of the eager willingness which should characterize all the gifts of the believers in the interest of the kingdom of God on earth. V.3. **And this is the offering which ye shall take of them: gold and silver and brass,** iron not being included, probably on account of its tendency to rust, v.4. **and blue,** a hyacinth colored or dark-blue purple, **and purple,** that is, the purple proper, of a brilliant dark-red, **and scarlet,** or crimson purple, dyed with the color prepared from the coccus insect, **and. fine linen,** a silklike, snow-white muslin, **and goats' hair,** v.5. **and rams' skins dyed red, and badgers' skins,** probably the skins of a marine animal found in the Red Sea, which were used both for sandal-leather and for tent coverings, **and shittim wood,** that of the Arabian acacia, which is very light and yet very strong and durable, v.6. **oil for the light,** as it was required to burn in the great candelabrum, **spices,** sweet-smelling ingredients, **for anointing oil and for sweet incense,** the odor of which was pleasant, v.7. **onyx stones, and stones to be set in the ephod,** in rows or clusters on one of the ornamental garments of the high priest, **and in the breastplate,** chap. 28, 6 ff. V.8. **And let them make Me a sanctuary,** a tabernacle, or building, set apart or consecrated for holy uses, **that I may dwell among them.** V.9. **According to all that I show thee, after the pattern of the Tabernacle,** the tent of God's dwelling, **and the pattern of all the instruments thereof, even so shall ye make it.** The Lord laid before Moses sketches, plans, or models, which gave him an adequate and correct idea of the great tent with all its equipment, a type, or figure, of heavenly things, Acts 7, 44; Heb. 8, 5, as well as of the blessings of the New Testament, Heb. 9.

The Ark of the Tabernacle. — V.10. **And they shall make an ark of shittim wood,** a chest made of acacia **wood; two cubits and a half shall be the length thereof** (a cubit being between 18 and 21 inches), **and a cubit and a half the breadth thereof, and a cubit and a half the height thereof.** V.11. **And thou shalt overlay it with pure gold, within and without shalt thou overlay it,**

and shalt make upon it a crown of gold round about, evidently an ornamental molding at the top. V.12. **And thou shalt cast four rings of gold for it, and put them in the four corners thereof,** on the four ornamental feet on which the cheat stood; **and two rings shall be in the one side of it, and two rings in the other side of it,** firmly fastened, in order to bear a strain. V.13. **And thou shalt make staves of shittim wood,** long poles of acacia wood, and overlay them with gold. V.14. **And thou shalt put the staves into the rings by the sides of the ark, that the ark may be borne with them,** lifted up and carried along readily. V.15. **The staves shall be in the rings of the ark; they shall not be taken from it,** for the bearers of the ark were not to touch the chest itself, Num. 4, 15. V.16. **And thou shalt put into the ark the testimony which I shall give thee,** the tables of stone on which God intended to write the Ten Commandments, as the words through which He would permanently testify to His people. V.17. **And thou shalt make a mercy-seat,** a lid, or covering, of the ark, **of pure gold; two cubits and a half shall be the length thereof, and a cubit and a half the breadth thereof.** This mercy seat, or lid of expiation, received its name from the fact that the guilt of the people, by virtue of the blood sprinkled against it on the great Day of Atonement, was expiated, their sin was covered. V.18. **And thou shalt make two cherubim of gold, of beaten work shalt thou make them,** enchased and rounded with a hammer, the figures thus being not massive. but hollow, **in the two ends of the mercy seat.** V.19. **And make one cherub on the one end and the other cherub on the other end; even of the mercy-seat shall ye make the cherubim on the**

two ends thereof, fastened to the solid gold of the ark's lid in such a manner as to form a structural unit. V.20. **And the cherubim shall stretch forth their wings on high, covering the mercy-seat with their wings,** their wings overshadowing the entire lid, **and their faces shall look one to another; toward the mercy-seat shall the faces of the cherubim be.** The figures, probably formed like those of men, with the wings added, and standing upright on the cover, were to face each other with outstretched wings, but with their eyes directed to the lid on which they stood. V.21. **And thou shalt put the mercy-seat above upon the ark; and in the ark thou shalt put the testimony,** the two tables of stone with their engraving, **that I shall give thee.** V.22. **And there I will meet with thee, and I will commune with thee from above the mercy-seat, from between the two cherubim which are upon the Ark of the Testimony, of all things which I give thee in commandment unto the children of Israel.** According to this statement the mercy-seat became the throne of God in the midst of His people, the footstool of the Most High, the place where He not only bore witness to His people, but where He also dispensed His mercy, by virtue of the greater expiation by blood which was foreshadowed in the rites connected with the lid of expiation. For the covering of the ark was a type of Christ, who is the true Mercy-seat, Rom. 3, 25; Heb. 4, 16. Through His own blood Christ has wrought a perfect expiation and redemption for us, and He now stands as our Mediator between God, whose throne is above the cherubim, and sinful men. It is our privilege, by faith in Him, to come boldly unto the Throne of Grace, that we may obtain mercy and find grace to help in time of need, Heb. 4, 16.

The table for the showbread. — V.23. **Thou shalt also make a table of shittim wood; two cubits shall be the length thereof, and a cubit the breadth thereof,** that being the size of the plate, **and a cubit and a half the height thereof.** V.24. **And thou shalt overlay it with pure gold, and make thereto a crown of gold round about,** heavy cross-pieces, or molding, connecting the legs of the table. V.25. **And thou shalt make unto it a border of an handbreadth round about,** a heavy molding at the edge of the plate, **and thou shalt make a golden crown to the border thereof round about,** a special rim which stood up above the plate of the table, to prevent the objects on the table from rolling or sliding off. V.26. **And thou shalt make for it four rings of gold,** doubtless cast like those of the ark, **and put the rings in the four corners that are on the four feet thereof.** V.27. **Over against the border,** next to the heavy molding at the top, **shall the rings be for places of the staves to bear the table,** containers for the poles which were used in moving the table. V.28. **And thou shalt make the staves of shittim wood,** the same material from which those of the ark were made, **and overlay them with gold, that the table may be borne with them.** V.29. **And thou shalt make the dishes thereof,** the large plates for the showbread, and spoons thereof, the small vessels for the incense, Num. 7, 14, **and covers thereof, and bowls thereof,** pitchers and goblets for the drink-offering, **to cover withal,** that is, formed so as to make pouring possible; **of pure gold shalt thou make them.** V.30. **And thou shalt set upon the table showbread before Me alway,** the bread of the face of the Lord, twelve cakes made of fine flour, set forth in two heaps of six each. These vessels and sacrifices

170

were to remind Israel of the fruits of good works which all believers were to work always. The covenant people of the New Testament will also offer the sacrifices of heart, lips, and hands as a sweet savor unto the Lord.

The candlestick and the holy vessels. — V.31. **And thou shalt make a candlestick of pure gold; of beaten work shall the candlestick be made,** of chased work, rounded with the hammer, apparently not solid, but hollow inside; **his shaft,** the base with its feet, **and his branches,** the heavy middle trunk of the candlestick, **his bowls,** the calyxshaped burners, **his knops,** the knobs, or apple. like ornaments beneath the calyces; **and his flowers,** the blossom-shaped ornaments on the branches, **shall be of the same,** of pure gold. V.32. **And six branches shall come out of the sides of It, three branches of the candlestick out of the one side and three branches of the candlestick out of the other side,** the hollow central shaft thus being the trunk, and the three branches on either side, standing in a horizontal line, lifting their burners at even distances, forming a luminous tree. V.33. **Three bowls made like unto almonds,** like the blossoms of the almond-tree, **with a knop and a flower in one branch,** in each individual branch; **and three bowls made like almonds in the other branch, with a knop and a flower; so in the six branches that come out of the candlestick.** v.34. **And in the candlestick, in the central shaft, shall be four bowls made like unto almonds, with their knops and their flowers,** one apparently at each whorl of branches, and one at the top. V.35. **And there shall be a knop under two branches of the same, and a knop under two branches of the same, and a knop under two branches of the**

same, the branches thus extending out from the middle shaft immediately above each set of knobs, **according to the six branches that proceed out of the candlestick. V.36. Their knops and their branches shall be of the same,** shall be a continuation of the main shaft, form a unit with the trunk, not merely be attached on the outside; **all it shall be one beaten work of pure gold. V.37. And thou shalt make the seven lamps thereof; and they shall light the lamps thereof,** set them in place in the bowls, **that they may give light over against it,** that is, toward the east and north from the Most Holy Place, especially in the neighborhood of the altar of incense and the table of the showbread. V.38. **And the tongs thereof, the snuffers, and the snu1f-dishes thereof,** the shears, or pincers, for trimming the wicks, or the small dishes for holding the trimmings, **shall be of pure gold. V.39. Of a talent of pure gold shall he make it,** the artisan entrusted with the work, **with all these vessels.** It was a costly and heavy candlestick, for a talent is about 118 pounds Troy. V.40. **And look that thou make them after their pattern, which was showed thee in the mount.** Moses had seen the picture, or model, and he was to have an exact copy made. The golden candlestick, which is here described in such detail, was to remind Israel of the high calling which the believers have in this world. And in the same way the Christians are never to lose sight of the fact that the Lord expects them to be the light of the world, that they should let their light shine before men in word and work.

27

Exodus 26

A Detailed Description of the Tabernacle.

The covering of the tent. — V.1. **Moreover, thou shalt make the Tabernacle with ten curtains,** long pieces, or strips, corresponding to the canvas of modern tents, **of fine twined linen,** the silky byssus cloth, **and blue, and purple, and scarlet,** chap. 25, 4; **with cherubim of cunning work shalt thou make them.** The work was to be that of an artist in weaving, the meaning evidently being that the white, shiny byssus threads were to be woven with similar fine yarns of hyacinth, purple, and crimson, to form figures of cherubim, the appearance of the cloth afterward being that of a heavy damask. V.2. **The length of one curtain shall be eight and twenty cubits and the breadth of one curtain four cubits; and everyone of the curtains shall have one measure,** be exactly of the same size. V.3. **The five curtains shall be coupled together one to another,** five strips should be sewed together side by side to form a large piece twenty-eight cubits long and twenty cubits wide; **and other five curtains shall be coupled one to another.** V.4. **And thou shalt make loops of blue,** of hyacinth-colored material, **upon the edge of the one curtain from the selvage in the coupling,** along the seam where they were to be attached to each other; **and likewise shalt thou make in the uttermost edge of another curtain, in the coupling of the second,** at the place where the two should be joined together. V.5. **Fifty loops shalt thou make in the one curtain, and fifty loops shalt thou make in the edge of the curtain that is in the coupling of the second,** where it is attached to the first; **that the loops may take hold one of another,** be placed so exactly as to be just opposite one another by pairs. V.6. **And thou shalt make fifty taches of gold,** clasps to hold the loops together, **and couple the curtains together with the taches; and it shall be one tabernacle,** these fine curtains forming the inner covering. V.7. **And thou shalt make curtains of goats' hair to be a covering upon the Tabernacle,** the outside covering, or tent proper; **eleven curtains shalt thou make.** V.8. **The length of one curtain shall be thirty cubits and the breadth of one curtain four cubits; and the eleven curtains shall be all of one measure,** of the same size. V.9. **And thou shalt couple five curtain. by themselves and six curtains by themselves,** just as it was done in the case of the fine inner covering, the extra length and width serving for the protection of the cherubim cloths, **and shalt double the sixth curtain in the forefront of the Tabernacle,** which consequently formed a projection or gable over the entrance. V.10. **And thou shalt make fifty loops on the edge of the**

one (large) **curtain that is outmost in the coupling,** along the edge where the curtains were to be attached to each other, **and fifty loops in the edge of the curtain which coupleth the second,** the loops likewise being just opposite one another by pairs. V.11. **And thou shalt make fifty taches of brass,** copper or brass clasps, **and put the taches into the loops, and couple the tent together,** this covering being the tent proper, **that it may be one.** V.12. **And the remnant that remaineth of the curtains of the tent,** after the covering of the roof had been provided for, **the half curtain that remaineth, shall hang over the back side of the Tabernacle,** to form its rear wall. V.13. **And a cubit on the one side and a cubit on the other side of that which remaineth in the length of the curtains of the tent,** there being a total difference of two cubits between the inner and the outer covering, **it shall hang over the sides of the Tabernacle on this side and on that side, to cover it.** Thus the north, the south, and the west side of the Tabernacle received its tent-covering. V.14. **And thou shalt make a covering for the tent,** a protecting curtain, **of rams' skins dyed red,** of a tawny color, **and a covering above of badgers' skins,** of leather made from the skins of some marine animal, probably of the sea-cow. These outer coverings served to shield the tent against wind and weather. Just as God made the Tabernacle His dwelling in the midst of His people in the Old Testament, so His presence is with us to this day in His Word and Sacraments.

The framework of the Tabernacle. — V.15. **And thou shalt make boards for the Tabernacle of shittim wood standing up,** planks of acacia wood that were durable, such as could stand up under the strain of the wind and the frequent handling. V.16. **Ten cubits shall be the length of a board, and a cubit and a half shall be the breadth of one board.** V.17. **Two tenons shall there be in one board, set in order one against another,** each set of tenons, or small projections, fitting exactly into the corresponding sockets in the base below; **thus shalt thou make for all the boards of the Tabernacle.** V.18. **And thou shalt make the boards for the Tabernacle, twenty boards on the south side southward,** the entire length of the Tabernacle thus being thirty cubits. V.19. **And thou shalt make forty sockets of silver under the twenty boards,** these silver feet, or bases, serving to hold the planks upright: **two sockets under one board for his two tenons and two sockets under another board for his two tenons.** V.20. **And for the second side of the Tabernacle on the north side there shall be twenty boards;** v.21. **and their forty sockets of silver: two sockets under one board and two sockets under another board,** the north and the south wall of the Tabernacle thus being constructed in exactly the same manner. V.22. **And for the sides of the Tabernacle westward thou shalt make six boards,** for the wall proper. V.23. **And two boards shalt thou make for the corners of the Tabernacle in the two sides,** in such a way as to form a right angle. V.24. **And they shall be coupled together beneath, and they shall be coupled together above the head of it unto one ring,** the two planks being dovetailed, or mortised, together at right angles. **Thus shall it be for them both,** in this way they should be constructed; **they shall be for the two corners,** forming the two rear corners. V.25. **And they shall be eight boards** in the west wall, **and their sockets of silver, sixteen sockets: two sockets**

under one board and two sockets under another board. V.26. And thou shalt make bars of shittim wood, crossbars extending along the walls of the Tabernacle: **five for the boards of the one side of the Tabernacle,** v.27. **and five bars for the boards of the other side of the Tabernacle, and five bars for the boards of the side of the Tabernacle, for the two sides westward.** So the north, the south, and the west wall were each to have five rows of connecting bars, which evidently were passed, through large rings. V.28. **And the middle bar in the midst of the boards shall reach from end to end,** passing through the entire length of the framework to give solidity to the structure. V.29. **And thou shalt overlay the boards with gold, and make their rings of gold for places for the bars; and thou shalt overlay the bars with gold.** V.30. **And thou shalt rear up the Tabernacle according to the fashion thereof which was showed thee in the mount.** This setting up of the Tabernacle included not only an exact copying of the model which Moses had seen on the mountain, but the tent was to agree also with the object and with the significance of the dwelling as the home of God in the midst of His people. This rectangular building, thirty cubits long, ten cubits wide, and ten cubits high, was the sanctuary of Israel for more than four hundred years, and serves. as the type of the more perfect tabernacle of heaven, into which Jesus has entered as our Mediator, Heb. 9, 6–10.

The veil and the position. of the appointments. — V.31. **And thou shalt make a veil of blue and purple and scarlet, and fine twined linen of cunning work,** tapestry, or damask, made according to the highest skill of the weaver's art, of byssus and the other costly materials named here; **with cherubim shall it be made,** showing figures of cherubim. V.32. **And thou shalt hang it upon four pillars of shittim wood overlaid with gold; their hooks,** to which the veil should be fastened, **shall be of gold, upon the four sockets of silver.** These were four single upright posts inside the Tabernacle, held in an upright position by their heavy silver bases. V.33. **And thou shalt hang up the veil under the taches,** that is, directly under the seams where the couplings of the goats' hair coverings came together, ten cubits from the west wall, **that thou mayest bring in thither within the veil the Ark of the Testimony,** the only piece of furniture which was permitted in this part of the Tabernacle; **and the veil shall divide unto you between the Holy Place,** the eastern end of the Tabernacle, **and the Most Holy,** its western end. V.34. **And thou shalt put the mercy-seat,** chap. 25, 17, **upon the Ark of the Testimony in the Most Holy Place.** V.35. **And thou shalt set the table** for the showbread, the so-called table of *prothesis,* **without the veil,** on its east side, **and the candlestick over against,** opposite, **the table on the side of the Tabernacle toward the south; and thou shalt put the table on the north side** of the tent. V.36. **And thou shalt make an hanging,** a heavy curtain, **for the door of the tent,** the entrance to the Holy Place, **of blue, and purple, and scarlet, and fine twined linen,** the fine materials which were used throughout, **wrought with needlework,** that is, woven in stripes or squares and in various geometrical figures formed by them. V.37. **And thou shalt make for the hanging five pillars of shittim wood,** acacia posts from which the door-curtain might be suspended, **and overlay them with gold, and their hooks shall be of gold; and**

thou shalt cast five sockets of brass, or bronze, **for them,**
these bases being heavy enough to hold the pillars upright.
The double curtain of the Tabernacle indicated that there
was as yet no free access to God's throne of grace. But Christ,
having entered into the Most Holy Place of heaven through
the veil of His flesh, has found an eternal redemption for us,
by virtue of which we may now freely enter into the presence
of God, assured in advance of His mercy. Heb.10, 20; 9, 11
ff.

28

Exodus 27

Further Account of the Tabernacle and Its Court.

The altar. — V.1. **And thou shalt make an altar of shittim wood, five cubits long and five cubits broad; the altar shall be foursquare,** a form which gave it great solidity; **and the height thereof shall be three cubits.** V.2. **And thou shalt make the horns of it upon the four corners thereof,** hornlike projections which were firmly attached to the altar, as though growing out of it. They are often mentioned, and their significance appears from the fact that the blood of the sin-offering was put upon them, and that people fleeing for their life took hold of them for their protection, Lev. 4, 7; 1 Kings 1, 50. **His horns shall be of the same,** that is, made of acacia wood, like the body of the altar; **and thou shalt overlay it with brass.** V.3. **And thou shalt make his pans to receive his ashes,** the vessels which were used in removing the ashes of the fat, **and his shovels, and his basins,** or bowls, used for sprinkling the blood of the sacrifices, **and his flesh-hooks,** the great prongs for spearing the meat, **and his fire-pans,** in which the live coals for the kindling of the fires were carried: **all the vessels thereof thou shalt make of brass,** of copper or one of its common alloys. V.4. **And thou shalt make for it a grate of network of brass,** probably for the purpose of catching such pieces of the sacrifices as fell from the altar; **and upon the net shalt thou make four brazen rings in the four corners thereof,** as sockets for the poles with which the altar was carried. V.5. **And thou shalt put it under the compass of the altar beneath,** the projecting ledge, or shelf, on which the priest stepped when engaged in sacrificing or when replenishing the fire, **that the net may be even to the midst of the altar.** V.6. **And thou shalt make staves for the altar, staves of shittim wood, and overlay them with brass,** with the same metal of which all the instruments and dishes of the altar were made. V.7. **And the staves shall be put into the rings, and the staves shall be put upon the two sides of the altar to bear it.** V.8. **Hollow with boards shalt thou make it; as it was showed thee in the mount, so shall they make it.** It is probable that the hollow space inside the altar was always filled with earth, chap. 20, 24, the place for the fire being in the center of this square and far enough from the wooden walls to obviate the danger of setting these afire. This altar was always in plain sight before all the children of Israel, reminding them of the fact that an expiation of sins was needed. The altar of the Christians is the cross of Christ, on which He bare our sins, that we, being dead to sins, should live unto righteousness, 1 Pet. 2, 24; Heb. 13, 10.

The court of the Tabernacle. — V.9. **And thou shalt**

make the court of the Tabernacle, an enclosed yard to mark the space set aside for formal worship; **for the south side southward there shall be hangings for the court of fine twined linen,** curtains made of byssus, **of an hundred cubits long for one side;** v.10. **and the twenty pillars thereof,** the posts between which the curtains were suspended, **and their twenty sockets shall be of brass; the hooks of the pillars and their fillets,** the rods connecting the several posts, **shall be of silver. V.11. And likewise for the north side in length there shall be hangings of an hundred cubits long, and his twenty pillars and their twenty sockets of brass; the hooks of the pillars and their fillets of silver,** corresponding exactly to the enclosure on the south side of the court. V.12. **And for the breadth of the court on the west side shall be hangings of fifty cubits; their pillars ten and their sockets ten.** This was on the side of the court in the rear of the Tabernacle, behind the Most Holy Place. V.13. **And the breadth of the court on the east side eastward,** where the entrance was, **shall be fifty cubits. V.14. The hangings of one side of the gate shall be fifteen cubits; their pillars three and their sockets three. V.15. And on the other side shall be hangings fifteen cubits; their pillars three and their sockets three.** The entire length of the byssus curtains, which formed the enclosure of the court, thus amounted to one hundred and eighty cubits. V.16. **And for the gate of the court,** the great and only entrance, toward the east, **shall be an hanging of twenty cubits, of blue, and purple, and scarlet, and fine twined linen, wrought with needlework,** the same material and workmanship as that used for the door-curtain of the Holy Place; and their pillars shall be four and their sockets four. V.17. **All the pillars round about the court shall be filleted with silver,** the connecting rods were to be of this precious metal; **their hooks shall be of silver and their sockets of brass,** of copper or one of its common alloys, brass or bronze. V.18. **The length of the court shall be an hundred cubits and the breadth fifty everywhere,** wherever one chose to measure, **and the height five cubits of fine twined linen, and their sockets of brass.** V.19. **All the vessels of the Tabernacle in all the service thereof,** as they were employed in sacrificial worship, **and all the pins thereof,** the pegs to which the ropes of the Tabernacle were fastened, **and all the pins of the court,** the pegs which held the guy ropes of the posts, **shall be of brass.** V.20. **And thou shalt command the children of Israel that they bring thee pure oil olive beaten for the light to cause the lamp to burn always.** The oil used in the Tabernacle was not that pressed out of olives by stamping with the feet or by means of an oil-press, but that which flowed from the ripe olives after they were cut or bruised. This oil was pure and clear, and therefore served well for burning in the Holy Place. V.21. **In the Tabernacle of the Congregation without the veil, which is before the testimony,** before the Ark of the Covenant, **Aaron and his sons shall order it from evening to morning before the Lord,** the lamps burned from the time of the evening sacrifice till the next morning. The Tabernacle is here for the first time called the "tent of meeting," because the Lord met with the representatives of the people when He communicated with them from the mercy-seat. **It shall be a statute forever unto their generations on the behalf of the children of Israel.** This refers both to the furnishing of the oil on the part of the people and to the lighting of the lamps on the part of the priests. Just as the children of Israel were to be reminded that their light was not to be quenched as long as they remained in the covenant of the Lord, so we Christians should remember that the light of our faith should ever be visible in good works.

29

Exodus 28

The Vestment of the High Priest.

The materials and the ephod. — V.1. **And take thou unto thee Aaron, thy brother, and his sons with him, from among the children of Israel,** a man out of their own midst, **that he may minister unto Me in the priest's office,** as the high priest of the people, **even Aaron, Nadab and Abihu, Eleazar and Ithamar, Aaron's sons,** who were Aaron's assistants in the capacity of priests. V.2. **And thou shalt make holy garments for Aaron, thy brother,** such as were separated from all ordinary use and to be employed in the service of the Tabernacle only, **for glory and for beauty,** expressive of the high dignity and excellence of the office. V.3. **And thou shalt speak unto all that are wise-hearted, whom I have filled with the spirit of wisdom** (to the natural skill of the craftsman was added special artistic understanding and ability for this particular work), **that they may make Aaron's garments**

to consecrate him, that he may minister unto Me in the priest's office. For consecration the garments were to serve, to set Aaron apart in the functions of his office, and for the service of the priest's work, all this latter being designated by a single verb in the Hebrew. V.4. **And these are the garments which they shall make: a breastplate, and an ephod, and a robe, and a broidered coat, a miter, and a girdle,** all these garments being described in this connection and in later ordinances. **And they shall make holy garments for Aaron, thy brother, and his sons, that he may minister unto Me in the priest's office.** V.5. **And they shall take gold, and blue, and purple, and scarlet, and fine linen.** In addition to the fine materials which were used in making the precious hangings of the Tabernacle, the artisans were to weave gold threads into the cloth for the priest's garments. V.6. **And they shall make the ephod of gold, of blue, and of purple, of scarlet, and fine twined linen, with cunning work,** a masterpiece of the weaver's art. V.7. **It shall have the two shoulder-pieces thereof joined at the two edges thereof; and so it shall be joined together,** thus forming a kind of vest, but with the two parts distinct. V.8. **And the curious girdle of the ephod,** the girdle of the fastening, **which is upon it,** firmly attached to it, **shall be of the same, according to the work thereof; even of gold, of blue, and purple, and scarlet, and fine twined linen,** the ephod with its girdle forming practically a single garment, for the girdle was crossed over the stomach and carried around the waist, to hold the ephod firmly in place. V.9. **And thou shalt take two onyx stones, and grave on them the names of the children of Israel;** v.10. **six of their names on**

one stone, and the other six names of the rest on the other stone, according to their birth, according to their respective ages, as the twelve sons of Jacob succeeded one another. V.11. **With the work of an engraver in stone, like the engravings of a signet, thou shalt engrave the two stones with the names of the children of Israel,** the ancestors of the twelve tribes; **thou shalt make them to be set in ouches of gold,** in settings which held them firmly all around. V.12. **And thou shalt put the two stones upon the shoulders of the ephod for stones of memorial unto the children of Israel; and Aaron shall bear their names before the Lord upon his two shoulders for a memorial.** The two stones with the names of the tribes of Israel engraved upon them, in their golden setting, which was continued in the form of a buckle, or clasp, were to bring the remembrance of the people before the Lord whenever the high priest wore this garment. The entire paragraph is typical, foreshadowing the office of our great High Priest, Jesus Christ. Clothed with incomparable dignity and glory, Christ performed the work of sacrifice for us, and, by virtue of His atonement, brings our names into remembrance before God, commends us to the Lord's grace.

The breastplate. — V.13. **And thou shalt make ouches of gold,** clasps or buckles; v.14. **and two chains of pure gold at the ends,** attached to the clasps; **of wreathen work shalt thou make them,** by braiding gold wire, **and fasten the wreathen chains to the ouches,** so that the buckles, which probably had the form of rosettes, were firmly attached to the braided chains, the entire ornament being intended for holding the breastplate. V.15. **And thou shalt make the breastplate of judgment,** that being its full technical name,

187

with cunning work, with the highest artistic workmanship; **after the work of the ephod thou shalt make it; of gold, of blue, and of purple, and of scarlet, and of fine twined linen shalt thou make it.** V.16. **Foursquare it shall be being doubled,** folded together to form a sort of pocket; **a span shall be the length thereof, and a span shall be the breadth thereof,** a span being half a cubit. V.17. **And thou shalt set in it settings of stones,** fill its outer side with rows of precious gems, **even four rows of stones. The first row shall be a sardius, a topaz, and a carbuncle; this shall be the first row.** V.18. **And the second row shall be an emerald, a sapphire, and a diamond.** V.19. **And the third row a ligure, an agate, and an amethyst.** V.20. **And the fourth row a beryl, and an onyx, and a jasper** (or a chrysolite, a beryl, and a jasper); **they shall be set in gold in their inclosings,** that is, in their settings. The modern names pretty accurately reproduce the Hebrew names, and may be accepted as fairly exact. The settings of the stones seem to have been ornamental clasps, which were of value also in fastening the stones to the heavy cloth of the breastplate. "The twelve precious stones denote the variety, manifoldness, and totality of the natural and gracious gifts bestowed on the people of God, and united in the one spirit of heavenly preciousness." V.21. **And the stones shall be with the names of the children of Israel, twelve, according to their names, like the engravings of a signet; everyone with his name shall they be according to the twelve tribes,** corresponding both in number and in names. V.22. **And thou shalt make upon the breastplate chains at the ends of wreathen work of pure gold.** Cp. v.14. V.23. **And thou shalt make upon the breastplate two rings of**

188

gold, and shalt put the two rings on the two ends of the breastplate, evidently above. V.24. And thou shalt put the two wreathen chains of gold, the braids of gold wire, in the two rings which are on the ends of the breastplate. V.25. And the other two ends of the two wreathen chains thou shalt fasten in the two ouches, in the clasps connected with the onyx stones on the shoulders, and put them on the shoulder-pieces of the ephod before it. V.26. And thou shalt make two rings of gold, and thou shalt put them upon the two ends of the breastplate in the border thereof, which is in the side of the ephod inward, on the lower edge, on the rear, or inner, side, facing the ephod. V.27. And two other rings of gold thou shalt make, and shalt put them on the two sides of the ephod underneath, toward the forepart thereof, over against the other coupling thereof, above the curious girdle of the ephod. The description indicates that these rings were placed on the shoulder-pieces of the ephod in the center below, where it was held together above the girdle. V.28. And they shall bind the breastplate by the rings thereof, that is, the lower rings, unto the rings of the ephod with a lace of blue, with threads of the hyacinth material which was used in the weaving of the cloth, that it may be above the curious girdle of the ephod, and that the breastplate be not loosed from the ephod. It was not only to be prevented from moving up and down, but also from sliding back and forth as it was worn, and from falling forward as the high priest stooped over. V.29. And Aaron shall bear the names of the children of Israel in the breastplate of judgment, of judicial sentence, upon his heart, when he goeth in unto the Holy Place, for a memorial before the Lord continually, v.12. V.30. **And thou shalt put in the breastplate of judgment,** in the pocket formed by its fold, **the Urim and the Thummim** (light and perfection; or revelation and truth); **and they shall be upon Aaron's heart when he goeth in before the Lord; and Aaron shall bear the judgment of the children of Israel upon his heart before the Lord continually,** that is, the sentence of salvation, or righteousness, and the sentence of judgment; as the high priest he was the mediator between God and the people. Every high priest appearing before the Lord with the Urim and Thummim thereby became the advocate of the people, and usually received from the Lord such illumination as served to protect the children of Israel in their promised rights, Num. 27, 21. Christ is our High Priest. He is our Advocate with the Father; He reveals to us God's light and truth, God's gracious and good will toward us, by which we receive counsel and comfort in dark days. The Word of the Lord is a lamp unto our feet and a light upon our path.

The garments proper. — V.31. **And thou shalt make the robe of the ephod,** the robe of office, on which the ephod was fastened, **all of blue,** of the hyacinth-colored material which reminded them of the heavenly origin and character of the high-priestly office. This outer garment reached to the knees, leaving the skirts of the inner garment in plain sight. V.32. **And there shall be an hole in the top of it, in the midst thereof; it shall have a binding of woven work,** a sort of tape or heavy border, **round about the hole of it, as it were the hole of an habergeon,** of a linen shirt worn by soldiers, **that it be not rent.** V.33. **And beneath, upon the hem of it, thou shalt make pomegranates,** ornaments of that shape, **of blue, and of purple, and of scarlet, round**

about the hem thereof; and bells of gold between them round about, which gave forth a musical tinkle as the high priest walked and the skirts of this garment swung back and forth. V.34. **A golden bell and a pomegranate, a golden bell and a pomegranate, upon the hem of the robe round about,** the two ornaments fastened alternately. V.35. **And it shall be upon Aaron to minister; and his sound shall be heard when he goeth in unto the Holy Place before the Lord, and when he cometh out, that he die not.** For as the pomegranates symbolized the sweet odor and the refreshing taste of the Word of God, Prov. 25, 11, so the golden bells symbolized the beautiful sound of the revelation and proclamation of God. The high priest, therefore, as the representative of the congregation and the bearer of the divine testimony, was not to undertake the work of his office without this official vestment, under penalty of death. V.36. **And thou shalt make a plate of pure gold, and grave upon it, like the engravings of a signet, HOLINESS TO THE LORD.** This was the high priest's badge of office, a very important part of his priestly insignia, the crown of holiness, chap. 39, 30. V.37. **And thou shalt put it on a blue lace, that it may be upon the miter; upon the forefront of the miter it shall be,** held in place by a hyacinth-colored string. V.38. **And it shall be upon Aaron's forehead, that Aaron may bear the iniquity of the holy things, which the children of Israel shall hallow in all their holy gifts.** The main function of the high priest's office was to expiate sins, also such transgressions as were connected with the sacrifices of the people. **And it shall be always upon his forehead, that they may be accepted before the Lord.** Even so the expiation made by our great High Priest, Jesus Christ, removes from us all transgressions, including even that guilt of weakness which is connected with our Christian profession and worship. V.39. **And thou shalt embroider the coat of fine linen,** the tunic proper, of white byssus, reaching to the ankles; **and thou shalt make the miter,** the high turban or headdress, **of fine linen,** of byssus; **and thou shalt make the girdle of needlework,** woven out of the same precious materials from which the ephod was made. V.40. **And for Aaron's sons,** as members of the order of priests, **thou shalt make coats, and thou shalt make for them girdles, and bonnets shalt thou make for them,** caps instead of the more elaborate turban of Aaron, **for glory and for beauty,** to signify both the great dignity and the peculiar excellence of Jehovah's worship. The garments of the ordinary priests were pure white with the exception of the girdle; for the color of purity was exceptionally appropriate in the case of the priests, who were continually engaged in making offerings in behalf of the people. V.41. **And thou shalt put them upon Aaron, thy brother, and his sons with him,** each one was to receive the garments intended for his special office; **and shalt anoint them, and consecrate them,** the application of oil signified the setting apart, the transmitting of the rights and duties, the inducting into office, **and sanctify them, that they may minister unto Me in the priest's office.** V.42. **And thou shalt make them linen breeches to cover their nakedness,** cp. chap. 20, 26; **from the loins even unto the thighs they shall reach,** for these parts must be kept covered on account of both natural or hereditary and acquired guilt. Not only every act of shamelessness, but even everything that called attention to sexual matters was to be avoided in the sanctuary. V.43. **And they shall be upon Aaron and upon his sons when they come in unto the Tabernacle of the Congregation, or when they come near unto the altar to minister in the Holy Place,** in their work of offering sacrifices, **that they bear not iniquity, and die. It shall be a statute forever unto him and his seed after him.** Cp. Lev. 8. All believers of the New Testament have the rank of priests before God, and their garments have been made white by the blood of the Lamb.

30

Exodus 29

Of the Consecration of the Priests and Some Sacrifices.

O rder of consecration. — V.1. **And this is the thing that thou shalt do unto them to hallow them, to minister unto Me in the priest's office;** this was the order of consecration which was to be in force for all times in the Jewish Church: **Take one young bullock and two rams without blemish,** free from sickness and any physical defects, v.2. **and unleavened bread, and cakes unleavened, tempered with oil,** olive-oil being mixed in when the dough was prepared, **and wafers unleavened,** very thin, cracker like sacrificial cakes, **anointed with oil; of wheaten flour shalt thou make them,** a specification which should be noted very carefully. V.3. **And thou shalt put them into one basket, and bring them in the basket, with the bullock and the two rams,** the meal-offering, or bloodless offering, being represented as well as the burnt offering. V.4. **And Aaron and his**

sons thou shalt bring unto the door of the Tabernacle of the Congregation, apparently inside the entrance of the court, **and shalt wash them with water,** the external cleansing symbolizing the inner purification; for only he that is hallowed inwardly is fit for holy service. V.5. **And thou shalt take the garments,** which the Lord had described in detail chap. 28, **and put upon Aaron the coat,** the long robe of white byssus, **and the robe of the ephod,** the hyacinth-colored garment that reached to the knees, **and the ephod, and the breastplate, and gird him with the curious girdle of the ephod; v.6. and thou shalt put the miter upon his head, and put the holy crown,** the diadem of holiness inscribed to the Lord, **upon the miter,** chap. 28, 36. V.7. **Then shalt thou take the anointing oil, and pour it upon his head, and anoint him,** this form of induction into office being used not only in the case of the high priest, but also in that of prophets and kings. The oil was a symbol of the Holy Spirit, who alone is able to sanctify man and prepare him properly for the service of the Sanctuary. V.8. **And thou shalt bring his sons, and put coats upon them,** the characteristic white byssus garments of the common priests. V.9. **And thou shalt gird them with girdles, Aaron and his sons;** for in this one article of dress the likeness between the ordinary priests and the high priest was shown, both classes using an embroidered girdle wrought in the four colors of the Sanctuary, **and put the bonnets on them,** bind the miter on Aaron and the caps on his sons. **And the priest's office shall be theirs for a perpetual statute. And thou shalt consecrate Aaron and his sons,** literally, fill their hands, invest them with the dignity and the obligations of their office. V.10. **And thou shalt**

cause a bullock, the sacrificial animal mentioned above, **to be brought before the Tabernacle of the Congregation; and Aaron and his sons shall put their hands upon the head of the bullock,** in a gesture symbolizing the transfer of their own sins and guilt to the sacrificial animal, for, indeed, it was necessary that their own sins be expiated before they could offer sacrifice for the sins of the people. V.11. **And thou shalt kill the bullock before the Lord, by the door of the Tabernacle of the Congregation,** inside the entrance of the court. V.12. **And thou shalt take of the blood of the bullock, and put it upon the horns of the altar with thy finger,** smear it upon these peculiar projections of the large altar before the Holy Place, **and pour all the blood beside the bottom of the altar,** the blood of the animal thus offered to the Lord taking, in a symbolic manner, the place of the sinner's blood. V.13. **And thou shalt take all the fat that covereth the inwards,** that is found in the abdominal cavity, **and the caul that is above the liver,** the fatty gathering between the liver and the duodenum, **and the two kidneys, and the fat that is upon them, and burn them upon the altar,** the rich bloom of life falling to Jehovah as His part. V.14. **But the flesh of the bullock, and his skin, and his dung shalt thou burn with fire without the camp; it is a sin-offering;** the complete destruction probably represented the sinner's complete break with his past life. V.15. **Thou shalt also take one ram; and Aaron and his sons shall put their hands upon the head of the ram,** as in the case of the bullock, v.10. V.16. **And thou shalt slay the ram, and thou shalt take his blood, and sprinkle it round about upon the altar,** as a token of complete surrender to the Lord. V.17. **And**

thou shalt cut the ram in pieces, dissect it according to the rules of the craft, **and wash the inwards of him and his legs,** that is, the thighs, **and put them unto his pieces, and unto his head,** the head forming the center of the pile. V.18. **And thou shalt burn the whole ram upon the altar,** after the removal of the skin and the unclean parts; **it is a burnt offering unto the Lord; it is a sweet savor, an offering made by fire unto the Lord.** An odor of pleasantness was this fire-offering unto Jehovah, because it signified that the priests were dedicating themselves with body and soul to the service of the Lord. V.19. **And thou shalt take the other ram; and Aaron and his sons shall put their hands upon the head of the ram,** as before. V.20. **Then shalt thou kill the ram, and take of his blood, and put it upon the tip of the right ear of Aaron and upon the tip of the right ear of his sons,** that is, upon the ear-lap, next to the opening, **and upon the thumb of their right hand and upon the great toe of their right foot,** the gestures conveying the duties of obedience, of willing work, and of a walk according to the precepts of God's holy Law, **and sprinkle the blood upon the altar round about.** V.21. **And thou shalt take of the blood that is upon the altar, and of the anointing oil, and sprinkle it upon Aaron, and upon his garments, and upon his sons, and upon the garments of his sons with him; and he shall be hallowed, and his garments, and his sons, and his sons' garments with him.** V.22. **Also thou shalt take of the ram the fat and the rump,** the heavy tail of fat which is a characteristic of the sheep referred to, **and the fat that covereth the inwards,** the fat of the abdominal net, **and the caul above the liver, and the two kidneys, and the fat that is upon them, and the**

right shoulder, "these parts representing the vigor of life, its comfort, and its conscientiousness," and the shoulder-piece being included here, though it otherwise belonged to the priests, for a special reason; **for it is a ram of consecration.** The priests here voluntarily returned to Jehovah a part of the emoluments belonging to them. V.23. **And one loaf of bread and one cake of oiled bread and one wafer out of the basket of the unleavened bread that is before the Lord,** vv.2 and 3; Lev. 8, 26; v.24. **and thou shalt put all in the hands of Aaron and in the hands of his sons, and shalt wave them for a wave-offering before the Lord,** moving them up and down, and back and forth, in token of their voluntary surrender to the Lord. V.25. **And thou, Moses, shalt receive them of their hands,** the gifts of Israel and of Israel's priests, **and burn them upon the altar for a burnt offering, for a sweet savor before the Lord; it is an offering made by fire unto the Lord,** this sacrifice indicating an important part of the priests' work. V.26. **And thou shalt take the breast of the ram of Aaron's consecration,** of the sacrifice of fullness, **and wave it for a wave-offering before the Lord; and it shall be thy part,** as the prince and leader of the people. V.27. **And thou shalt sanctify the breast of the wave-offering, and the shoulder of the heave-offering,** the former being merely moved back and forth in the gesture of giving, while the latter was also lifted up high to indicate the willing surrender to Jehovah, **which is waved, and which is heaved up, of the ram of the consecration, even of that which is for Aaron, and of that which is for his sons;** for it seems that all the rest of the body went with the thigh, as the priests' part. V.28. **And it shall be Aaron's and**

his sons' by a statute forever from the children of Israel; for it is an heave-offering; and it shall be an heave-offering from the children of Israel of the sacrifice of their peace-offerings, even their heave-offering unto the Lord. These parts were taken from the peace-offerings and the heave-offerings of the children of Israel, lifted off to be given to the priests. This signified in general that the priests were to be nourished from the sacrifices of Israel, even as the Lord has now ordained that they who preach the Gospel should live of the Gospel. V.29. **And the holy garments of Aaron shall be his sons' after him, to be anointed therein, and to be consecrated in them,** the office of high priest being hereditary in Aaron's family. V.30. **And that son that is priest in his stead shall put them on seven days,** just as it was done in the consecration of Aaron, Lev. 8, 35, **when he cometh into the Tabernacle of the Congregation to minister in the Holy Place.** Aaron was a type of the true High Priest, Jesus Christ, who was anointed with the Holy Ghost without measure, as the true Mediator between God and sinful mankind. The sons of Aaron are types of the believers of the New Testament, who have been made priests before God and the Father and serve Him in holiness and righteousness, as it pleases Him.

The portion of the priests. — V.31. **And thou shalt take the ram of the consecration, and seethe his flesh in the Holy Place;** it was sacred food intended to nourish them during the week of consecration. V.32. **And Aaron and his sons shall eat the flesh of the ram, and the bread that is in the basket, by the door of the Tabernacle of the Congregation,** that being their official place of abode when they were engaged in their work. V.33. **And they shall eat**

those things wherewith the atonement was made, the parts of the daily offerings of consecration, which also served for expiation, **to consecrate and to sanctify them. But a stranger shall not eat thereof, because they are holy,** set apart for the worship of the Lord. V.34. **And if aught of the flesh of the consecrations or of the bread remain unto the morning,** the priests finding themselves unable to eat all, **then thou shalt burn the remainder with fire; it shall not be eaten, because it is holy.** Once being set aside for the Lord's use, it should not be returned to profane use. V.35. **And thus shalt thou do unto Aaron and to his sons according to all things which I have commanded thee: seven days shalt thou consecrate them.** Moses was held responsible for the proper and complete execution of God's orders. V.36. **And thou shalt offer every day a bullock for a sin-offering for atonement, as on the first day,** vv. 10 and 11; **and thou shalt cleanse the altar when thou hast made an atonement for it;** the altar was also included in the rites of expiation and dedication; **and thou shalt anoint it, to sanctify it.** V.37. **Seven days thou shalt make an atonement for the altar and sanctify it; and it shall be an altar most holy; whatsoever toucheth the altar shall be holy,** set apart and dedicated to the Lord. Thus was the altar, in a symbolic sense, cleansed from defilement, and placed exclusively in the service of Jehovah, designed for permanent use in His service.

The daily burnt offering. — V.38. **Now this is that which thou shalt offer upon the altar: two lambs of the first year day by day continually.** This sacrifice is here ordered, because it was to be made daily just as soon as the Tabernacle should be finished and dedicated. V.39.

The one lamb thou shalt offer in the morning; and the other lamb thou shalt offer at even, literally, between the evenings, at twilight, which the Jews later explained as referring to the time between noon and sundown, for which reason their evening worship took place about three o'clock in the afternoon. V.40. **And with the one lamb a tenth deal** (about two and one half quarts) **of flour mingled with the fourth part of an hin** (about one quart) **of beaten oil,** of the fine oil which was not forcibly pressed out of the olives, but allowed to flow out freely after they had been crushed or cut; **and the fourth part of an hin of wine for a drink-offering.** V.41. **And the other lamb thou shalt offer at even, and shalt do thereto according to the meat-offering of the morning and according to the drink-offering thereof, for a sweet savor, an offering made by fire unto the Lord.** This daily sacrifice signified that the life of the entire people was surrendered to Jehovah day by day. V.42. **This shall be a continual burnt offering throughout your generations at the door of the Tabernacle of the congregation before the Lord, where I will meet you to speak there unto thee.** At the altar of burnt offering the Lord wanted to give evidence of His presence with His people; there He would meet them by dealing with their representatives in person. V.43. **And there I will meet with the children of Israel, and the Tabernacle** (or rather, Israel) **shall be sanctified by My glory.** V.44. **And I will sanctify the Tabernacle of the Congregation and the altar; I will sanctify also both Aaron and his sons to minister to Me in the priest's office.** V.45. **And I will dwell among the children of Israel and will be their God.** This gracious promise is all the more beautiful by reason of the fact that the Lord did not confine His presence in their midst to the Most Holy Place, but gave them the assurance that He would also look upon their daily burnt offering in mercy, thereby always emphasizing anew the covenant made with them. V.46. **And they shall know that I am the Lord, their God, that brought them forth out of the land of Egypt, that I may dwell among them. I am the Lord, their God.** As the Lord lived in the midst of His people of old in the Sanctuary dedicated to His name, so He dwells in the midst of His believers at the present time in His Word and Sacraments.

31

Exodus 30

Ordinances Concerning Public Worship.

The altar of incense. — V.1. **And thou shalt make an altar to burn incense upon; of shittim wood shalt thou make it,** of the same Arabian acacia wood which was to be used for all the wooden appointments. V.2. **A cubit shall be the length thereof, and a cubit the breadth thereof; foursquare shall it be; and two cubits shall be the height thereof; the horns thereof shall be of the same.** It was also ornamented with small. hornlike projections, the symbols of power. V.3. **And thou shalt overlay it with pure gold, the top thereof,** that is, its plate, **and the sides thereof round about, and the horns thereof; and thou shalt make unto it a crown of gold round about,** a heavy, decorated molding of gold, similar to that on the ark and on the table of showbread. Since the entire altar was so completely covered with gold, it was often designated simply as the golden altar, chap. 39, 38; 40,

5. 26; Num. 4, 11. V.4. **And two golden rings shalt thou make to it under the crown of it, by the two corners thereof, upon the two sides of it shalt thou make it,** rings set solidly into the material of the altar; **and they shall be for places for the staves to bear it withal. V.5. And thou shalt make the staves,** the carrying poles, **of shittim wood, and overlay them with gold.** V.6. **And thou shalt put it before the veil that is by the Ark of the Testimony,** so that it occupied a position between the large candlestick and the table of showbread, **before the mercy-seat that is over the testimony, where I will meet with thee.** The altar of incense was thus brought into a direct and intimate relation to the mercy-seat, so close to the Most Holy Place that it could be considered as a part of its equipment in the wider sense, 1 Kings 6, 22; Heb. 9, 4. V.7. **And Aaron shall burn thereon sweet incense every morning; when he dresseth the lamps, he shall burn incense upon it,** that is, when he trims and cleans the lamps of the large candlestick. V.8. **And when Aaron lighteth the lamps at even,** putting back the lamps in place at the time of the evening sacrifice, chap. 29, 41, **he shall burn incense upon it, a perpetual incense before the Lord throughout your generations,** as regularly as the sacrifice of burnt offering was made, chap. 29, 42. V.9. **Ye shall offer no strange incense thereon,** such as was not ordered for that purpose by Jehovah nor such as was not made according to His precept, **nor burnt sacrifice, nor meat-offering,** the unbloody sacrifices of baked or fried cakes; **neither shall ye pour drink-offering thereon.** V.10. **And Aaron shall make an atonement upon the horns of it once in a year with the blood of the sin-offering of atonements; once in the year shall he**

make atonement upon it throughout your generations, namely, on the great Day of Atonement; **it is most holy unto the Lord.** The altar of incense thus served a double purpose: it was in use daily for the offering of incense, the aromatic substance whose odor was pleasant to the Lord, since it signified the prayer of the saints; and it served on the great Day of Atonement for the dedication of the blood of expiation, before the high priest entered the Most Holy Place. We Christians also let our prayers rise to the Lord like incense, that is, in the name of Jesus Christ the Savior, knowing that they are pleasing to the Lord for His sake.

The church tax. — V.11. **And the Lord spake unto Moses, saying,** v.12. **When thou takest the sum of the children of Israel after their number,** whenever a census of the people was taken, **then shall they give every man a ransom for his soul unto the Lord, when thou numberest them,** a sum of money by which they were to redeem themselves from the personal service which they really owed to the Lord in the house of worship; **that there be no plague among them when thou numberest them.** The refusal or the neglect to pay this assessment would make a person liable to the punishment of God. V.13. **This they shall give, everyone that passeth among them that are numbered,** everyone that is included in the census, **half a shekel after the shekel of the Sanctuary; (a shekel is twenty gerahs;) an half shekel shall be the offering of the Lord.** Every male Israelite was to be enrolled in the army of Jehovah after he had reached the age of twenty years and be obliged to pay this assessment of half a shekel standard weight, that is, about 32 cents annually. This tax was used for the maintenance of the sacrificial service, since the expenses connected with the Jewish form of worship must have been quite large. The payment of this fee distinguished the people of the Lord from the heathen that knew nothing of Him. V.14. **Every one that passeth among them that are numbered, from twenty years old and above, shall give an offering unto the Lord.** V.15. **The rich shall not give more,** as they might have felt tempted to do, in order to display their wealth, **and the poor shall not give less than half a shekel,** for even the poorest could afford that much for the Lord, **when they give an offering unto the Lord to make an atonement for your souls.** Free-will offerings were acceptable at all other times, and were made in large quantities for the purpose of building the Tabernacle, but here the sum was definitely fixed. V.16. **And thou shalt take the atonement money of the children of Israel, and shalt appoint it for the service of the Tabernacle of the Congregation,** for the perpetual service of God in the building devoted to His worship; **that it may be a memorial unto the children of Israel before the Lord to make an atonement for your souls.** They were ever to be reminded of the fact that they owed their souls to the Lord, that they were in His debt to the extent of their souls: in this sense the assessment was a ransom, money paid in atonement. To this day the Christians give evidence of the thankfulness of their hearts to God for the perfect atonement which was assured to them through Jesus Christ, also through their gifts and sacrifices.

The laver. — V.17. **And the Lord spake unto Moses, saying,** v.18. **Thou shalt also make a laver of brass,** of copper or one of its chief alloys, **and his foot also of brass, to wash withal; and thou shalt put it between the**

Tabernacle of the Congregation and the altar, between the altar of burnt offerings in the court and the entrance to the Holy Place, **and thou shalt put water therein.** For this laver, or great wash-basin, the Israelitish women brought their metal mirrors, chap. 38, 8, glad to contribute what they could for this sacred purpose. V.19. **For Aaron and his sons shall wash their hands and their feet thereat;** v.20. **when they go into the Tabernacle of the Congregation,** before entering the Holy Place, **they shall wash with water, that they die not; or when they come near to the altar to minister, to burn offering made by fire unto the Lord;** v.21. **so they shall wash their hands and their feet, that they die not; and it shall be a statute forever to them, even to him** (Aaron) **and to his seed throughout their generations.** The description indicates that the basin was a reservoir for water rather than a basin in which the priests performed their ablutions. No priest was to touch holy things with unclean, defiled hands. All this symbolized the inward purification effected by the Lord, even as we Christians have a never-failing fountain which cleanses us from all sin and impurity, the blood of Jesus Christ, the Son of God.

The oil of ointment. — V.22. **Moreover, the Lord spake unto Moses, saying,** v.23. **Take thou also unto thee principal spices, of pure myrrh five hundred shekels** (about fifteen pounds), **and of sweet cinnamon half so much, even two hundred and fifty shekels, and of sweet calamus two hundred and fifty shekels,** v.24. **and of cassia five hundred shekels, after the shekel of the Sanctuary,** the standard of weight among the children of Israel at that time, **and of oil olive an hin,** a little more than a gallon;

207

v.25. **and thou shalt make it an oil of holy ointment, an ointment compound after the art of the apothecary,** the man skilled in the preparing of spices and ointments. **It shall be an holy anointing oil.** The myrrh gum as it is found in the Arabian desert was to be mixed with costly, sweet-smelling spices, some of the finest products of the land; for this holy anointing oil was to excel in richness. "It might be said of the myrrh that it denotes that fine, higher kind of pain which enables one to overcome natural pain; cinnamon denotes the warmest feeling of light and life; the bitterness of calamus might also be noticed; but the significance of the cassia is difficult to determine." (Lange.) V.26. **And thou shalt anoint the Tabernacle of the Congregation therewith, and the Ark of the Testimony,** v.27. **and the table** (of showbread) **and all his vessels, and the candlestick and his vessels, and the altar of incense,** v.28. **and the altar of burnt offering with all his vessels,** all the instruments used in its service, **and the laver and his foot.** V.29. **And thou shalt sanctify them,** set them apart for the worship of the Lord, **that they may be most holy; whatsoever toucheth them shall be holy,** consecrated to the Lord. The oil of ointment was declared to be holy, because the recipe for its making was given by the Lord and because it was used for holy purposes. V.30. **And thou shalt anoint Aaron and his sons, and consecrate them, that they may minister unto Me in the priest's office.** V.31. **And thou shalt speak unto the children of Israel, saying, This shall be an holy anointing oil unto Me throughout your generations,** reserved for use in the Sanctuary and its service. V.32. **Upon man's flesh shall it not be poured,** that is, it was not to be used for ordinary anointing of the body, **neither shall ye make any other like it,** after the composition of it, they were not to compound their oil for private use in these proportions; **it is holy, and it shall be holy unto you.** V.33. **Whosoever compoundeth any like it, or whosoever putteth any of it upon a stranger,** upon a layman, as contrasted with a priest, **shall even be cut off from his people.** The oil of ointment was a symbol of the Holy Ghost, who alone is able effectually to prepare a person for the service of the Lord, for the working of truly good works.

The holy incense. — V.34. **And the Lord said unto Moses, Take unto thee sweet spices, stacte,** a sweet-smelling gum similar to myrrh, **and onycha,** the pulverized shell of a mollusk, **and galbanum,** a bitter resin gained from a shrub of the desert, which strengthens the odor of the incense; **these sweet spices with pure frankincense,** which to this day is gathered from a small tree in.Arabia Felix and the surrounding country; **of each shall there be a like weight,** the ingredients were to be mixed in equal parts. V.35. **And thou shalt make it a perfume, a confection after the art of the apothecary,** as in the case of the ointment, **tempered together,** carefully cleaned from all impurities, **pure,** without strange admixtures, **and holy; v.36. and thou shalt beat some of it very small,** literally, pound it into powder, **and put it before the testimony in the Tabernacle of the Congregation, where I will meet with thee,** before the Ark of the Covenant in the Most Holy Place. **It shall be unto you most holy.** V.37. **And as for the perfume,** this holy incense, **which thou shalt make, ye shall not make to yourselves according to the composition thereof; it shall be unto thee holy for the**

Lord. V.38. Whosoever shall make like unto that, to smell thereto, to enjoy its pleasant odor, **shall even be cut off from his people.** That which was consecrated to the Lord was not to be made common by profane use. Thus also prayer, which was symbolized by the incense, is never to be made in the spirit of levity, though it may now be sent up to the throne of God anywhere and at any time.

32

Exodus 31

The Chief Artisans. The Sabbath Ordinance Repeated.

The master craftsmen engaged. — V.1. **And the Lord spake unto Moses, saying,** v.2. **See, I have called by name Bezaleel, the son of Uri, the son of Hur, of the tribe of Judah,** the grandson of the influential man in his tribe, one of Moses' right-hand men, chap. 17, 10; 24, 14; v.3. **and I have filled him with the spirit of God in wisdom, and in understanding, and in knowledge, and in all manner of workmanship,** in every craft connected with the art of building and equipping the Tabernacle, v.4. **to devise cunning works,** to execute artistic designs, **to work in gold and in silver and in brass,** the precious and costly metals which were used for the various parts of the equipment, v.5. **and in cutting of stones, to set them,** the work of the jeweler and the silversmith, **and in carving of timber,** another branch of artistic achievement, **to work in all manner of workmanship.** In this man technical knowledge was united with practical ability; he could not only devise and plan artistic work in all its details, but he could also supervise its proper execution. His natural talents had been sanctified by the influence of the Lord and consecrated to His service, a combination which, even now, makes the best church architects and the most excellent artists. V.6. **And I, behold, I have given with him Aholiab, the son of Ahisamach, of the tribe of Dan; and in the hearts of all that are wise-hearted I have put wisdom, that they may make all that I have commanded thee,** Aholiab being a master not only in metal, stone, and woodwork, but also an artist in fancy weaving: v.7. **the Tabernacle of the Congregation, and the Ark of the Testimony, and the mercy-seat that is thereupon, and all the furniture,** the sacred vessels, **of the Tabernacle,** v.8. **and the table and his furniture, and the pure candlestick with all his furniture,** the instruments and vessels needed for keeping it in order, **and the altar of incense,** v.9. **and the altar of burnt offering with all his furniture, and the laver and his foot,** v.10. **and the cloths of service,** the special garments of the high priest which he alone wore in the service of the Tabernacle and Temple, **and the holy garments for Aaron, the priest,** which he had in common with the ordinary priests, **and the garments of his sons, to minister in the priest's office,** v.11. **and the anointing oil, and sweet incense for the Holy Place; according to all that I have commanded thee shall they do.** The entire work was entrusted to the Jewish artisans under the leadership of these two masters, for it was necessary that the workmanship throughout be of the very best. It is well-pleasing to the Lord if work done in His service is performed with painstaking care, as being really worth while.

Concerning the celebration of the Sabbath. — V.12. **And the Lord spake unto Moses, saying,** v.13. **Speak thou also unto the children of Israel, saying, Verily, My Sabbaths ye shall keep; for it is a sign between Me and you throughout your generations, that ye may know that I am the Lord that doth sanctify you.** Through the rest of the Sabbath-day the children of Israel were to remain conscious of the fact that it was Jehovah that sanctified them, the Sabbath being the day especially consecrated to His service. V.14. **Ye shall keep the Sabbath therefore,** observe it most religiously; **for it is holy unto you. Everyone that defileth it shall surely be put to death,** the desecration or profanation of the day consisting chiefly in not observing the rest enjoined by the Lord; **for whosoever doeth any work therein, that soul shall be cut off from among his people,** the breaking of the Sabbath being a capital crime. V.15. **Six days may work be done; but in the seventh is the Sabbath of rest,** a day devoted entirely to rest from physical labor, **holy to the Lord; whosoever doeth any work in the Sabbath-day, he shall surely be put to death.** V.16. **Wherefore the children of Israel shall keep the Sabbath to observe the Sabbath throughout their generations,** their resting should make the day a real Sabbath, **for a perpetual covenant.** V.17. **It is a sign between Me and the children of Israel forever,** the public symbol and expression of the relation between Jehovah and Israel; **for in six days the Lord made heaven and earth, and on the seventh day He rested and was refreshed.** As the text expressly notes, this phase of the

Third Commandment, according to which one special day was set apart for total rest, concerned only the children of Israel. For the believers of the New Testament the observance of the Third Commandment consists in this, that we gladly hear and learn the Word of God. He that despises preaching and God's Word destroys himself by starving his soul. V.18. **And He** (God) **gave unto Moses, when He had made an end of communing with him upon Mount Sinai, two tables of testimony, tables of stone, written with the finger of God.** In what manner this engraving was done is not revealed, the fact alone being stated. The Decalog is the word and will of the Lord, of which He Himself says that heaven and earth will pass away before one tittle of this will is invalidated. The ministry of the New Testament is written with the Spirit of the living God, not in tables of stone, but in the fleshy tables of the heart, 2 Cor. 3, 3.

33

Exodus 32

The Idolatry of the People.

The golden calf. — V.1. **And when the people saw that Moses delayed to come down out of the mount,** the text implies that they had waited for his return in vain, and therefore foolishly concluded that he had forsaken them, **the people gathered themselves together unto Aaron,** not in the spirit of an orderly congregation, but of a mob bent on violence, **and said unto him, Up, make us gods which shall go before us! For as for this Moses,** as they now contemptuously called him, **the man that brought us up out of the land of Egypt, we wot** (know) **not what is become of him.** They had given up all hopes regarding the leadership of Moses, and therefore proposed to establish their own gods, fashioned according to the ideas of their perverted mind. V.2. **And Aaron said unto them, Break off the golden earrings which are in the ears of your wives, of your sons, and of your daughters,** the heavy ring pendants worn according to Oriental fashion, **and bring them unto me.** If Aaron, as some commentators state, made this demand in a spirit of cunning, thinking that the great sacrifice which this involved would keep the people from carrying out their plan, he found himself badly in error. V.3. **And all the people brake off the golden earrings which were in their ears, and brought them unto Aaron.** Swept along by a wave of mob activity, the people showed a fanatical readiness to part with the possessions which they prized most highly. It is the same tendency which may be observed in the case of the many cults and heresies of our days, which spread with such alarming rapidity and command such great resources. V.4. **And he received them at their hand, and fashioned it with a graving-tool after he had made it a molten calf.** After melting the golden rings, Aaron cast a rough figure of a young ox, or bullock, and then finished the outline with the tools of an engraver. It may not have been a work of art, but it served its purpose. **And they said, These be thy gods, O Israel, which brought thee up out of the land of Egypt.** In these words the people proclaimed the idol as god and rejected the true and only God. V.5. **And when Aaron saw it, he built an altar before it; and Aaron made proclamation and said, To-morrow is a feast to the Lord.** The name of Jehovah was introduced to cover up the evil, the implication being that he, Aaron, at least, had erected this figure in honor of Jehovah, the true God. St. Paul expressly calls the children of Israel idolaters in speaking of this incident, 1 Cor. 10, 7. V.6. **And they rose up early on the morrow, and offered burnt offerings,** in honor of the false god, **and brought peace-offerings; and the people sat down to eat and to drink,** in a joyful sacrificial meal, **and rose up to play,** in merry festive games, in wilful abandon. The worship of the golden calf is a picture of the idolatry of our days, for these are the gods of the world, mammon, gold, money, luxury, eating, drinking, lascivious merriment. It is the very height of hypocrisy if Christians take part in the idolatrous ways of the world and then try to cover their sin with a sanctimonious behavior.

Moses intercedes for the people. — V.7. **And the Lord said unto Moses, Go, get thee down; for thy people, which thou broughtest out of the land of Egypt, have corrupted themselves.** The omniscient, omnipresent God saw the transgression of the people and stated this fact to Moses as the representative and the mediator of Israel. V.8. **They have turned aside quickly out of the way which I commanded them,** their guilt was increased by the great hurry which they displayed in choosing the ways of idolatry; **they have made them a molten calf, and have worshiped it, and have sacrificed thereunto, and said, These be thy gods, O Israel, which have brought thee up out of the land of Egypt.** With the children of Israel engaged in wilful idolatry, it was impossible for the work on the mountain to continue, and the indignation of the Lord breaks forth like a flood. V.9. **And the Lord said unto Moses, I have seen this people,** have observed it very closely, **and, behold, it is a stiff-necked people,** as rigid of neck as an unwilling draught-animal, chap. 33, 3. 5; 34, 9; Deut. 9, 6. V.10. **Now, therefore, let Me alone, that My wrath may wax hot against them, and that I may consume them** in revenge and punishment; **and I will make of thee a great nation;** of the entire people only Moses and his family were to remain, as the stock, or nucleus, of a new nation. It was an expression of just anger, a threat of righteous punishment. V.11. **And Moses besought the Lord, his God,** he showed himself the real priestly advocate of the people. The prospect of being the progenitor of a great nation held no allurements for him, as he began to plead for his people, **and said, Lord, why doth Thy wrath wax hot against Thy people which Thou hast brought forth out of the land of Egypt with great power and with a mighty hand?** Note how skilfully Moses parries the Lord's statement in v.7. as he reminds Him that it was His, Jehovah's, great power, His mighty hand, that had effected the deliverance out of the land of Egypt. V.12. **Wherefore should the Egyptians speak and say, For mischief did He bring them out,** that is, for misfortune, for their destruction, **to slay them in the mountains, and to consume them from the face of the earth?** This was an appeal to the honor of the Lord. **Turn from Thy fierce wrath, and repent of this evil against Thy people. V.13. Remember Abraham, Isaac, and Israel, Thy servants, to whom Thou swarest by Thine own self, and saidst unto them, I will multiply your seed as the stars of heaven, and all this land that I have spoken of will I give unto your seed, and they shall inherit; it forever.** This was a reminder of the faithfulness and truth, the trust in which had sustained the patriarchs during the long years when they were strangers in the land of Canaan. Note also that Moses omits all reference to himself; he does not think of urging his own work as a consideration to influence the Lord. V.14. **And the Lord repented of the evil which He thought to do unto His people,** although, as it seems, He did make known His change of mind at this time, as vv.30–34 indicate.

As Moses here acted in the capacity of advocate for the sinful people, so Jesus, at once the propitiation for our sins and our Advocate with God, pleads for us with His heavenly Father.

The wrath of Moses. — V.15. **And Moses turned and went down from the mount, and the two tables of testimony were in his hand. The tables were written on both their sides; on the one side and on the other were they written,** engraved, or chiseled, in the stone by the finger of God. V.16. **And the tables were the work of God,** hewn or fashioned by God Himself, **and the writing was the writing of God, graven upon the tables.** V.17. **And when. Joshua heard the noise of the people as they shouted, he said unto Moses, There is a noise of war in the camp.** It was characteristic of the soldier that his thoughts were engaged with matters of war. V.18. **And he** (Moses) **said, It is not the voice of them that shout for mastery, neither is it the voice of them that cry for being overcome,** it was neither the triumphant shout of the victors nor the answering moans of the conquered, **but the noise of them that sing do I hear,** the sound of antiphonal songs which the people shouted as they frolicked in their idolatrous dance. V.19. **And it came to pass, as soon as he came nigh unto the camp,** so that he could distinguish things clearly, **that he saw the calf and the dancing,** for the riotous celebration was now at its height; **and Moses' anger waxed hot, and he cast the tables out of his hands, and brake them beneath the mount,** at its foot, where it merged into the plain. His action symbolized the fact that Israel had broken the covenant of the Lord. V.20. **And he took the calf which they had made, and burned it in the fire, and ground it to powder, and strewed it upon** the water, and made the children of Israel drink of it. So he not only demonstrated to them the nothingness of their god, but even had them drink down, devour, the idol, thus humbling them and putting them to shame openly for some time. V.21. **And Moses said unto Aaron, What did this people unto thee,** what kind of sorcery, what means of persuasion did they employ, **that thou hast brought so great a sin upon them?** It was a sharp question, a direct accusation. making Aaron the moral author of the sin and the seducer of the people. V.22. **And Aaron said, Let not the anger of my lord wax hot. Thou knowest the people, that they are set on mischief.** It is always the sinner's convenient excuse to blame the transgression on some one else's wickedness. V.23. **For they said unto me, Make us gods which shall go before us; for as for this man Moses, the man that brought us up out of the land of Egypt, we wot not what is become of him.** V.24. **And I said unto them, Whosoever hath any gold, let them break it off. So they gave it me; then I cast it into the fire, and there came out this calf.** He speaks of the calf as almost an accidental image produced by the fire without his design, without his knowledge and will. Thus Aaron added to his first sin the second of attempting to evade the accusation and casting the blame on others, whose spiritual knowledge did not equal his own. True repentance will not make use of such schemes. Cp. Deut. 9, 20.

The slaughter of the idolaters. — V.25. **And when Moses saw that the people were naked;** they had stripped themselves of their ornaments and had also neglected to keep the camp properly protected; **(for Aaron had made them naked unto their shame among their enemies,** he had given them free reign in their festivities, a fact which caused the camp to be unprotected and exposed the children of Israel to derision in more than one respect;) v.26. **then Moses stood in the gate of the camp and said, Who is on the Lord's side;** who will take the Lord's part? **Let him come unto me. And all the sons of Levi gathered themselves together unto him.** They were the first to turn from their sin in true repentance and to show their willingness to make amends for their sin. V.27. **And he said unto them, Thus saith the Lord God of Israel, Put every man his sword by his side, and go in and out from gate to gate throughout the camp,** that is, passing through the length of the camp twice, going and returning, **and slay every man his brother, and every man his companion, and every man his neighbor.** No matter how close the relationship, there was to be indiscriminate slaughter: all those whom it would strike should die. V.28. **And the children of Levi did according to the word of Moses; and there fell of the people that day about three thousand men.** V.29. **For Moses had said,** before the men of Levi went forth to the slaughter, **Consecrate yourselves today to the Lord, even every man upon his son and upon his brother, that He may bestow upon you a blessing this day.** They were to dedicate themselves to the Lord by this implicit and unquestioning obedience, which disregarded the ties of even the closest relationship in order to secure the blessing of the Lord. For the Christians also it often becomes necessary to deny the nearest relatives, namely, when the alternative is Christ or the world. Obedience toward our Lord must always be the first consideration.

Moses again intercedes for the people. — V.30. **And it**

came to pass on the morrow that Moses said unto the people, Ye have sinned a great sin; and now I will go up unto the Lord; peradventure I shall make an atonement for your sin. He indicates that their crime may still be covered by means of an expiation, and states his willingness to make an effort to obtain this atonement. V.31. **And Moses returned unto the Lord and said, Oh, this people have sinned a great sin, and have made them gods of gold!** It was a flagrant case of idolatry in a form which the Lord had expressly condemned, chap. 20, 23. V.32. **Yet, now, if Thou wilt forgive their sin-.** The greatness of his love for the people, on the one hand, and his awe of God, on the other, does not permit him to finish the sentence. It was a most profound appeal for mercy. **And if not, blot me, I pray Thee, out of Thy book which Thou hast written,** out of the book of life. Here is a case of magnanimous nobleness equaled only by Paul, Rom. 9, 3, and surpassed only by Christ in His unexcelled devotion, in His incomprehensible sacrifice. V.33. **And the Lord said unto Moses, Whosoever hath sinned against Me, him will I blot out of My book.** He would not accept the sacrifice offered by Moses, He would not offer up the just for the unjust in this case. V.34. **Therefore go now, lead the people unto the place of which I have spoken unto thee,** all of which indicated that He would spare the people at this time. **Behold, Mine Angel shall go before thee,** the Son of God Himself accompanied the army on its march; **nevertheless in the day when I visit I will visit their sin upon them.** The time would come when their period of grace would be at an end, when the Lord's revenge would strike them, when His judicial visitation would be upon them. V.35. **And the Lord plagued the people because they made the calf, which Aaron made.** The punishment meted out by the children of Levi was sufficient for the time being. God has patience with the sinners, with those that reject the Savior, for the sake of that very Redeemer. But when the sinners persist in refusing the grace offered to them, and despise the patience of God, death and destruction will finally come upon them.

34

Exodus 33

The Lord's Anger over the People. His Kindness to Moses.

The sorrow of the people over their sins. — V.1. **And the Lord said unto Moses, Depart, and go up hence, thou and the people which thou hast brought up out of the land of Egypt, unto the land which I sware unto Abraham, to Isaac, and to Jacob, saying, Unto thy seed will I give it.** The intercession of Moses in behalf of the children of Israel had been successful: the Lord, in accordance with the promise given to the patriarchs, did not destroy the people, did not even withdraw the special Messianic feature of the promise, although His pardon, for the present, was limited. V.2. **And I will send an angel before thee,** cp. chap. 32, 34; **and I will drive out the Canaanite, the Amorite, and the Hittite, and the Perizzite, the Hivite, and the Jebusite:** v.3. **unto a land flowing with milk and honey,** distinguished for its extraordinary fruitfulness; **for I will not go up in the**

**midst of thee; for thou art a stiff-necked people; lest
I consume thee in the way.** Because they had shown
themselves a people with a rigid neck, chap. 32, 9, as
incorrigible as a stubborn draught-animal, therefore the
Lord, for the time being, withdrew His presence from their
midst. His purpose was to lead the people to a proper
estimate of their guilt and thus to full repentance; for as
it was, their willful transgressions continually challenged
destruction. This announcement had the desired effect.
V.4. **And when the people heard these evil tidings, they
mourned,** they showed their deep sorrow by putting on the
garments of mourning; **and no man did put on him his
ornaments.** The repentance was general and sincere. V.5.
**For the Lord had said unto Moses, Say unto the children
of Israel, Ye are a stiff-necked people: I will come up
into the midst of thee in a moment and consume thee;**
that had been the Lord's intention when His anger first flared
up, chap. 32, 10; **therefore now put off thy ornaments
from thee, that I may know what to do unto thee.** The
Lord demanded this evidence of sincere repentance; for
if they had refused and He had appeared in their midst
for as much as a moment, their total destruction would
have resulted. V.6. **And the children of Israel stripped
themselves of their ornaments by the Mount Horeb.**
From this time on, from Mount Horeb onwards, the children
of Israel discarded rings, bracelets, and all other jewelry, as
in a period of mourning, to remind themselves always of
the guilt which they had loaded upon themselves through
similar ornaments at Mount Horeb. V.7. **And Moses
took the tabernacle,** his own tent, **and pitched it without
the camp, afar off from the camp, and called it the**

Tabernacle of the Congregation, the "tent of meeting." Until matters were adjusted between the Lord and the people and the building of the Sanctuary could be undertaken, his own tent had to serve the purpose. The people were to become more deeply conscious of their guilt and of their separation from Jehovah, and yet Moses wanted to keep the way open for the renewal of the covenant, by giving the people an opportunity to keep in touch with Jehovah. **And it came to pass that everyone which sought the Lord went out unto the Tabernacle of the Congregation which was without the camp.** This was the first step in bringing the penitent people to a new life, that individuals went out to consult with Jehovah, instead of following their own ideas and opinions. V.8. **And it came to pass, when Moses went out unto the Tabernacle, that all the people rose up, and stood every man at his tent door and looked after Moses until he was gone into the Tabernacle.** This was a second sign of repentance, the expression of reverence with which the people accompanied the going of Moses into the tent of meeting. V.9. **And it came to pass, as Moses entered into the Tabernacle, the cloudy pillar,** which served to show the way by day, **descended and stood at the door of the Tabernacle; and the Lord,** who was present in the pillar, **talked with Moses.** V.10. **And all the people saw the cloudy pillar stand at the Tabernacle door,** in the place which was afterward occupied by the altar of burnt offering. **And all the people rose up and worshiped, every man in his tent door.** That was the third proof of their sincerity and of their desire to enter into the former relations with Jehovah once more. V.11. **And the Lord spake unto Moses face to face, as a man speaketh unto his friend.** It was not a

226

communicating from a distance, nor through any mediating person or agency, but the perfect intercourse of God with the friend of God, although not in the full revelation of His glory. **And he** (Moses) **turned again into the camp,** after having communicated with God; **but his servant Joshua, the son of Nun, a young man, departed not out of the Tabernacle.** To him, as an unmarried man, was entrusted the care of the Sanctuary by day and by night. We learn here that unfaithfulness, idolatry, excludes a person from the intercourse, from the fellowship with God, and that it is the will of God that all transgressors should turn to Him in sincere and earnest repentance.

The Lord promises his gracious presence. — V.12. **And Moses said unto the Lord, See, Thou sayest unto me, Bring up this people; and Thou hast not let me know whom Thou wilt send with me.** The people having given such unmistakable evidences of a real change of heart, Moses thought the time opportune to intercede once more and, if possible, to have the mercy of the Lord turn back to His people, as of old. **Yet Thou hast said, I know thee by name, and thou hast also found grace in My sight.** Upon this promise Moses bases his assurance in making his plea, just as we Christians come before Him with all boldness, trusting in the grace belonging to us in Christ Jesus. V.13. **Now, therefore, I pray Thee, if I have found grace in Thy sight, show me now Thy way that I may know Thee, that I may find grace in Thy sight; and consider that this nation is Thy people.** Moses wanted to know how the Lord intended to lead His people, what intentions He had with regard to their further journey, just in what way the Angel of the Lord would assume the leadership, incidentally reminding the Lord that the children of Israel were His people, His commonwealth. By the granting of this prayer the fact of his having found mercy in God's sight would be confirmed. V.14. **And he said, My presence shall go with thee, and I will give thee rest.** The face of Jehovah, the Angel of the Presence, the Son of God Himself, was to be the Leader of the people. Under His leadership the people were to reach the Land of Promise and there settle down to a life of peace and plenty, Deut. 3, 20. Thus the Lord heard the prayer of His servant. V.15. **And he said unto Him, If Thy presence go not with me, carry us not up hence.** It would be better to remain in the wilderness, to die in the desert, than to attempt a continuance of the journey without the presence of Jehovah. V.16. **For wherein shall it be known here that I and Thy people have found grace in Thy sight? Is it not in that Thou goest with us?** The presence of the Lord would be a sign, a guarantee, to Moses and the people that the Lord had really forgiven their great sin and turned back to them in mercy. **So shall we be separated, I and Thy people, from all the people that are upon the face of the earth.** The visible guidance of God would be a sign to all men that Israel was the nation of God's choice. V.17. **And the Lord said unto Moses, I will do this thing also that thou hast spoken; for thou hast found grace in My sight, and I know thee by name.** The boldness of faith shown by Moses vanquished even the Lord, and He yielded to this request, because He cherished Moses with an extraordinary love. V.18. **And he said, I beseech Thee, show me Thy glory.** The success of Moses made him so bold that he desired to see the revelation of God in the totality of His attributes, as Isaiah saw it in the vision, chap. 6. V.19. **And he said, I will make all My goodness pass before thee,** He would reveal Himself in the greatness of His excellence, **and I will proclaim the name of the Lord before thee,** He would call out, explain to Him, Jehovah's name; **and will be gracious to whom I will be gracious, and will show mercy on whom I will show mercy.** The entire revelation, as promised to Moses, was an act of God's free grace and mercy, upon which no man, not even Moses, could lay claim. V.20. **And He said, Thou canst not see My face,** Moses could not endure to look upon the full revelation of God's glory; **for there shall no man see Me and live.** No mortal, sinful man could survive a glance into the face of the holy God. It is only after we have become partakers of the divine nature, 2 Pet. 1, 4, and have entered into the state of glorification, Phil. 3, 21, that we shall see Him face to face, as He is, 1 John 3, 2. V.21. **And the Lord said, Behold, there is a place by Me, and thou shalt stand upon a rock;** v.22. **and it shall come to pass, while My glory passeth by, that I will put thee in a clift of the rock, and will cover thee with My hand while I pass by;** v.23. **and I will take away Mine hand, and thou shalt see My back parts; but My face shall not be seen.** While standing in the cave or in the cleft of the rock, under the protecting power of the Lord, Moses was to see the afterglow, the reflection, of the Lord's glory, which would enable him to form some conception of the surpassing beauty and excellence of the divine majesty, as he would see it later, in the life of glorification. For us Christians it is a matter of great comfort that the Son of God, our Savior Jesus Christ, protects us from wrath and judgment, and will finally bring us to the home above, where we shall see His glory, world without end.

35

Exodus 34

Moses Witnesses the Lord's Glory.

The glorious vision. — V.1. **And the Lord said unto Moses, Hew thee two tables of stone like unto the first,** which the Lord Himself had fashioned: **and I will write upon these tables the words that were in the first tables, which thou brakest.** Moses was familiar with the form and workmanship of the original tables, and could therefore make the second set after that pattern. V.2. **And be ready in the morning, and come up in the morning unto Mount Sinai, and present thyself there to Me in the top of the mount.** The covenant relation between God and the people having been restored by the Lord's pardon, the giving of the covenant ordinances could now be resumed. V.3. **And no man shall come up with thee, neither let any man be seen throughout all the mount; neither let the flocks nor herds feed before the mount,** that is. anywhere in its neighborhood. The entire mountain was again shut off to the people, as before the giving of the Law. chap. 19, 12. 13. 20–23. V.4. **And he hewed two tables of stone like unto the first. And Moses rose up early in the morning, and went up unto Mount Sinai, as the Lord had commanded him, and took in his hand the two tables of stone,** all ready for the engraving by the hand of God. V.5. **And the Lord descended in the cloud,** in the pillar in which His glory usually was hidden, **and stood with him there,** outside the cloud, **and proclaimed the name of the Lord,** called out and explained the name Jehovah. All this while He covered Moses with His hand. as the latter stood in the cleft of the rock. V.6. **And the Lord passed by before him and proclaimed,** delivered His great sermon on the name of the Lord, as Luther says. **The LORD, the LORD God, merciful and gracious, long-suffering, and abundant in goodness and truth,** v.7. **keeping mercy for thousands, forgiving iniquity and transgression and sin.** That is the one side of the Lord's essence: Jehovah, the mighty God. the same yesterday and today and forever. whose loving-kindness is shown in compassion on the miserable. in grace toward the repentant sinners, in patience toward human weakness. in truth and faithfulness in the keeping of His gracious promises. But the other side is also brought out: **And that will by no means clear the guilty; visiting the iniquity of the fathers upon the children and upon the children's children unto the third and to the fourth generation.** To those that reject His mercy the Lord proves Himself a stern Judge, who does not let the least offense go unpunished, but avenges the insults to His holiness not only upon the fathers. but also upon the children that follow in the footsteps of their wicked parents. and that down to the great-grandchildren. Cp. chap. 20, 5. This proclamation of the goodness, the mercy, the grace, the truth and faithfulness of God continues throughout the period of the New Testament; it is a testimony of the living God, who, however, states, on the other hand, as well: He who rejects His grace will receive everlasting condemnation. V.8. **And Moses made haste, and bowed his head toward the earth, and worshiped,** overcome by the glory of the vision. What he saw is not described in detail, for it is beyond human understanding, even as Paul heard words which no man can utter. God here gave to Moses a taste of the future glory which will be revealed to all those who remain faithful to the end. V.9. **And he said, If now I have found grace in Thy sight, O Lord, let my Lord, I pray thee, go among us;** he pleaded for the personal presence of God in the midst of the people; **for it is a stilf-necked people; and pardon our iniquity and our sin, and take us for Thine inheritance.** Note that Moses includes himself with the people, placing himself under their guilt, in order to make his prayer all the more fervent. The Lord should once more regard Israel as His peculiar people, to consider and to treat them as His own. He wanted to make assurance doubly sure, for the sake of the Messianic promise. Such clinging trust should be found in the Christians at all times, for that is the power which vanquished even the Lord.

The gracious promise. — V.10. **And He said, Behold, I make a covenant,** in the place of or in addition to that which had been broken by Israel's idolatry: **Before all the people,** in their presence, in their sight, **I will do marvels, such as have not been done in all the earth nor in any nation,** namely, in bringing His people safely into the Land

233

of Promise. **And all the people among which thou art shall see the work of the Lord; for it is a terrible thing that I will do with thee,** a thing which would strike fear and terror to the hearts of all enemies and adversaries, as the majesty of the mighty God would sweep them away. V.11. **Observe thou** (Israel) **that which I command thee this day: behold, I drive out before thee the Amorite, and the Canaanite, and the Hittite, and the Perizzite, and the Hivite, and the Jebusite.** V.12. **Take heed to thyself, lest thou make a covenant with the inhabitants of the land whither thou goest, lest it be for a snare in the midst of thee.** All intimate alliances were absolutely forbidden at the outset, because the danger of introducing heathen abominations and thus repeating the offense of Mount Horeb was too great. V.13. **But ye shall destroy their altars,** which were devoted to the worship of false gods, **break their images,** the statues or pillars erected in honor of their idols, **and cut down their groves,** the pillarlike tree-trunks devoted to the service of Asherah or Astarte, whose voluptuous worship was found throughout Canaan. V.14. **For thou shalt worship no other god,** idols to which the divine name was applied by the heathen; **for the Lord, whose name is Jealous, is a jealous God,** having revealed Himself as such in the recent transgression of the people; v.15. **lest thou make a covenant with the inhabitants of the land, and they go a-whoring after their gods,** idolatry being considered throughout Scriptures as spiritual adultery, **and do sacrifice unto their gods, and one call,** that is, invite, **thee** to the idolatrous feast, **and thou eat of his sacrifice;** v.16. **and thou take of their daughters unto thy sons, and their daughters go**

a-whoring after their gods, and make thy sons go a-whoring after their gods, the husbands being led into idolatry, into spiritual unfaithfulness, by their wives. V.17. **Thou shalt make thee no molten gods,** idols cast out of any metal. While the participation in sacrificial meals of the heathen and intermarriages with heathen women only led to idolatry, the making of images was in itself a transgression of the First Commandment and a breaking of God's covenant. That is the distinct command of the Lord, that he who has forgiveness of sins should fear God and guard against backsliding, also by avoiding social intimacy with the godless world.

The second festivals. — V.18. **The Feast of Unleavened Bread shalt thou keep.** Cp. chap. 23, 15. **Seven days thou shalt eat unleavened bread, as I commanded thee, in the time of the month Abib**; **for in the month Abib thou camest out from Egypt.** Because of the defection of the Israelites the Lord here repents the ordinances regarding the chief festival days and seasons. V.19. **All that openeth the matrix is Mine,** all the firstborn sons of the children of Israel; **and every firstling among thy cattle, whether ox or sheep, that is male.** This precept is here stated on account of its close connection with the Passover and its significance. V.20. **But the firstling of an ass thou shalt redeem with a lamb,** ransom by the payment of a lamb or a kid; **and if thou redeem him not, then shalt thou break his neck. All the first-born of thy sons thou shalt redeem. And none shall appear before Me empty.** Cp. chap. 23, 15. V.21. **Six days thou shalt work, but on the seventh day thou shalt rest,** cp. chap. 20, 9; 23, 12; **in earing time and in harvest thou shalt rest,** these two seasons being mentioned since they were the busiest season for the farmer, when he would be inclined to use also the Sabbath for work. V.22. **And thou shalt observe the Feast of Weeks, of the first-fruits of wheat harvest,** namely, Pentecost, **and the Feast of Ingathering at the year's end,** the Feast of Tabernacles at the end of the season. V.23. **Thrice in the year shall all your men-children,** all the males, the men, **appear before the Lord God, the God of Israel.** On these three great festivals the attendance of all Israelites was commanded; they were obliged to meet, first at the Sanctuary, and later in the Temple. V.24. **For I will cast out the nations before thee, and enlarge thy borders,** cp. chap. 23, 31; **neither shall any man desire thy land when thou shalt go up to appear before the Lord, thy God, thrice in the year;** the Lord promised to keep away all enemies at these times, so that they would not take advantage of the men's absence to invade the country. V.25. **Thou shalt not offer the blood of My sacrifice,** of the Passover lamb, **with leaven; neither shall the sacrifice of the Feast of the Passover be left unto the morning;** it should either be eaten to the last fragment, or the remainder burned with fire, chap. 12, 10. V.26. **The first of the first-fruits of thy land thou shalt bring unto the house of the Lord, thy God,** this being the most prominent rite of the Feast of Unleavened Bread. **Thou shalt not seethe a kid in his mother's milk.** Cp. chap. 23, 19. V.27. **And the Lord said unto Moses, Write thou these words,** the ordinances were to be preserved in writing; **for after the tenor of these words I have made a covenant with thee and with Israel.** The first covenant had hereby been renewed or reinstituted. V.28. **And he** (Moses) **was there with the**

Lord forty days and forty nights, as he had been the first time, chap. 24, 18; **he did neither eat bread, nor drink water,** being miraculously sustained by the Lord. **And He** (God) **wrote upon the tables the words of the covenant, the Ten Commandments,** the Decalog. The true hallowing of God's name in the New Testament consists in this, that we gladly hear and learn the Word of God, and help to uphold the ministry in our midst and to spread the Gospel-news.

The shining face of Moses. — V.29. **And it came to pass, when Moses came down from Mount Sinai with the two tables of testimony in Moses' hand, when he came down from the mount, that Moses wist** (knew) **not that the skin of his face shone while He** (God) **talked with him.** This wonderful brilliancy was caused by the vision of God on Mount Sinai. A reflection of the divine glory lingered in the face of Moses for some time after his return from the mountain. V.30. **And when Aaron and all the children of Israel saw Moses, behold, the skin of his face shone; and they were afraid to come nigh him.** Even the reflection of the glory of the Lord is too much for sinners. V.31. **And Moses called unto them,** encouraged first the leaders of the people to hear the precepts of the Lord; **and Aaron and all the rulers of the congregation returned unto him. And Moses talked with them.** V.32. **And afterward all the children of Israel came nigh,** having been inspired with some measure of courage by the action of the rulers; **and he gave them in commandment all that the Lord had spoken with him in Mount Sinai,** all the people thus hearing Jehovah's precepts, with which He had again established the covenant. V.33. **And till Moses had done speaking with them,** while he was laying the ordinances of the Lord before them, **he put a veil on his face.** V.34. **But when Moses went in before the Lord to speak with Him,** in the tent and afterwards in the Tabernacle, **he took the veil off until he came out. And he came out and spake unto the children of Israel that which he was commanded;** he transmitted to them the Lord's commandments. V.35. **And the children of Israel saw the face of Moses, that the skin of Moses' face shone,** the splendor being renewed whenever Moses appeared before the Lord. **And Moses put the veil upon his face again, until he went in to speak with Him.** This splendor of Moses' face symbolized the glory of the Mosaic office, 2 Cor. 3, 5 if. Since the Law was the Word of God, it also had a glory. But the glory of the New Testament office, that of the Gospel, exceeds it in beauty. For the Law is the letter that killeth, but the Gospel is the spirit that maketh alive. And the glory of the Old Testament passed away, while the glory of the Gospel remains forever. All fear and terror is driven out of the heart by the comforting assurances of the Gospel, by its promises of life and salvation.

36

Exodus 35

Preparations for Building the Tabernacle.

The call for voluntary offerings. — V.1. **And Moses gathered all the congregation of the children of Israel together,** in a solemn assembly, **and said unto them, These are the words which the Lord hath commanded that ye should do them.** It was the formal, impressive statement of God's precept. V.2. **Six days shall work be done.** These words contain not only a permission, but a command: the people were to be engaged in the labor of their calling during the week, and none to be found needlessly idle. Cp. 2 Thess. 3, 12. **But on the seventh day there shall be to you an holy day, a Sabbath of rest to the Lord; whosoever doeth work therein,** performs the labor of his station or calling, **shall be put to death.** The government of Israel being theocratic, under the immediate direction of the Lord, the rulers were charged to execute the Sabbath-breaker. V.3. **Ye shall**

239

kindle no fire throughout your habitations upon the Sabbath-day. This ordinance made the Sabbath precept, chap.20, 9–11; 31, 13–17, more severe, and prepared for the work connected with the building of the Tabernacle. V.4. **And Moses spake unto all the congregation of the children of Israel, saying, This is the thing which the Lord commanded, saying, v. 5 Take ye from among you an offering,** a gift presented to the Lord by willingly lifting up the hands containing the sacrifice, **unto the Lord; whosoever is of a willing heart, let him bring it, an offering of the Lord; gold, and silver, and brass,** copper or some of its standard alloys, v.6. **and blue, and purple, and scarlet, and fine linen,** the expensive materials of hyacinth, purple, and crimson, and of white, shining byssus, to be used in the weaving of the sacred paraments, **and goats' hair,** of the long-haired Oriental goats, v.7. **and rams' skins dyed red** (or tawny), **and badgers' skins,** those of the sea-cow of the Indian Ocean and its branches, **and shittim (** acacia) **wood, v.8. and oil for the light, and spices for anointing oil, and for the sweet incense,** chap. 30, 22–38, v.9. **and onyx stones, and stones to be set for the ephod, and for the breastplate.** This list includes all the materials which were used for the Tabernacle and its appointments. V.10. **And every wise-hearted among you shall come and make all that the Lord hath commanded;** all the artistic talent among the children of Israel was pressed into service; v.11. **the Tabernacle, his tent, and his covering, his taches** (loops), **and his boards, his bars, his pillars, and his sockets, v.12. the ark, and the staves** (carrying-poles) **thereof, with the mercy-seat, and the veil of the covering,** given this designation because it hid the ark

240

with its mercy-seat from the eyes of all but the high priest, v.13. **the table, and his staves, and all his vessels, and the showbread,** v.14. **the candlestick also for the light, and his furniture,** the instruments needed for keeping it in good order, **and his lamps, with the oil for the light,** v.15. **and the incense altar, and his staves, and the anointing oil, and the sweet incense, and the hanging for the door at the entering in of the Tabernacle,** at the eastern door, which led into the Holy Place, v.16. **the altar of burnt offering, with his brazen grate,** chap. 27, 1–4, **his staves, and all his vessels, the laver and his foot,** v.17. **the hangings of the court,** the curtains which formed its enclosure, **his pillars, and their sockets, and the hanging for the door of the court,** made of the same materials as the Tabernacle curtains, v.18. **the pins of the Tabernacle,** the pegs for holding the guy-ropes, **and the pins of the court, and their cords** (ropes), v.19. **the cloths of service, to do service in the Holy Place, the holy garments for Aaron, the priest, and the garments of his sons, to minister in the priest's office.** All these appointments, these various articles of equipment, had been ordered by the Lord, and were to be made in accordance with His will.

The willing offerings. — V.20. **And all the congregation of the children of Israel departed from the presence of Moses.** They hurried from the meeting-place to their tents with a spontaneous, joyful willingness. V.21. **And they came, everyone whose heart stirred him up,** who felt lifted up, moved thereto, **and everyone whom his spirit made willing, and they brought the Lord's offering to the work of the Tabernacle of the Congregation, and for all his service, and for the holy garments.** V.22. **And**

they came, both men and women, the women almost getting ahead of the men in the joyful, spirited rivalry, **as many as were willing-hearted, and brought bracelets, and earrings, and rings,** such as were worn on the fingers, **and tablets,** small golden globules which were worn in strings at the wrist or around the neck, **all jewels of gold,** ornaments of every kind; **and every man that offered, offered an offering of gold unto the Lord,** whatever he had consecrated to the Lord by the gesture of weaving, or moving back and forth. V.23. **And every man with whom was found blue, and purple, and scarlet, and fine linen, and goats' hair, and red skins of rams, and badgers' skins** (cp. vv. 6. 7), **brought them.** V.24. **Every one that did offer an offering of silver and brass brought the Lord's offering,** he took or lifted his gift from his property and dedicated it for the service of the Lord; **and every man with whom was found shittim wood for any work of the service, brought it.** V.25. **And all the women that were wise hearted,** that had artistic talent, **did spin with their hands, and brought that which they had spun, both of blue, and of purple, and of scarlet, and of fine linen** (cp. v. 6). V.26. **And all the women whose heart stirred them up in wisdom spun goats' hair** for the outer covering of the Tabernacle. V.27. **And the rulers brought onyx stones, and stones to be set, for the ephod and for the breastplate;** v.28. **and spice, and oil for the light, and for the anointing oil, and for the sweet incense.** V.29. **The children of Israel brought a willing offering unto the Lord, every man and woman whose heart made them willing,** urged them on, **to bring for all manner of work which the Lord had commanded to be made by**

the hand of Moses. It was a scene altogether different from that which had taken place some two months before, when the people had been swayed by their idolatrous passions.

The master artisans. — V.30. **And Moses said unto the children of Israel, See, the Lord hath called by name: Bezaleel, the son of Uri, the son of Hur, of the tribe of Judah;** v.31. **and He hath filled him with the Spirit of God,** his natural talent and love of the work being increased and intensified by the Lord Himself, **in wisdom,** to devise and plan ornaments, **in understanding,** to make the pattern applicable to the work in hand, **and in knowledge,** practical sense, **and in all manner of workmanship,** the various branches of the fine arts coming into consideration in the building of the Tabernacle and in the preparation of its appointments; v.32. **and to devise curious works,** skilful designs, **to work in gold, and in silver, and in brass,** v.33. **and in the cutting of stones, to set them, and in carving of wood, to make any manner of cunning work,** that pertaining to every branch of art. V.34. **And He hath put in his heart that he may teach,** God had given him the ability to instruct others, to give them directions for making the individual parts and vessels, **both he and Aholiab, the son of Ahisamach, of the tribe of Dan.** V.35. **Them hath He filled with wisdom of heart, to work all manner of work, of the engraver, and of the cunning** (skilful) **workman,** the artistic craftsman, **and of the embroiderer,** the weaver, **in blue, and in purple, in scarlet, and in fine linen, and of the weaver,** one skilled both in weaving and in plaiting or braiding, **even of them that do any work, and of those that devise cunning work;** these two men ranked above all others in artistic ability combined with practical

243

sense. It is a combination of gifts which has often been placed in the service of the Lord in times past and deserves to be cultivated today.

37

Exodus 36

The Making of the Tabernacle.

The gifts exceed the needs. — V.1. **Then wrought Bezaleel and Aholiab and every wise-hearted man in whom the Lord put wisdom and understanding to know how to work all manner of work for the service of the sanctuary, according to all that the Lord had commanded.** That was their calling, and in this calling they proved themselves willing. V.2. **And Moses called Bezaleel and Aholiab and every wise-hearted man in whose heart the Lord had put wisdom, even every one whose heart stirred him up to come unto the work to do it,** to offer his talents for the service of the Lord; v.3. **and they received of Moses all the offering which the children of Israel had brought for the work of the service of the Sanctuary, to make it withal.** That was the first great collection of gold, metals, and all other materials of which the artists stood in need for the work entrusted to them. **And they brought yet unto him free offerings every morning.** The enthusiasm was no mere straw-fire, but it lasted in a steady glow. V.4. **And all the wise men that wrought all the work of the Sanctuary,** the artists engaged in their labor of love, **came every man from his work which they made,** after they had carefully estimated the amount of material needed; v.5. **and they spake unto Moses, saying, The people bring much more than enough for the service of the work which the Lord commanded to make.** The material offered by the people was far in excess of the needs of the work. V.6. **And Moses gave commandment, and they caused it to be proclaimed throughout the camp, saying, Let neither man nor woman make any more work for the offering of the Sanctuary.** Moses did not even wait to summon a meeting, but had a crier pass through the camp with a message restraining the eagerness of the people. **So the people were restrained from bringing.** V.7. **For the stuff they had was sufficient for all the work to make it, and too much;** even with a lavish use of material there would be some remaining. The willingness of the children of Israel at this time is a shining example to the believers of the New Testament and a spur to many so-called Christians, who are very often unwilling to offer to the Lord even their surplus.

The curtains of the Tabernacle. — V.8. **And every wise-hearted man among them,** all the artists appointed to the work, **that wrought the work of the Tabernacle, made ten curtains of fine twined linen, and blue, and purple, and scarlet; with cherubim of cunning work made he them,** the figures of the cherubim were skillfully woven into the cloth, as it was made on the loom with the four kinds of yarn, or thread, mentioned throughout the narrative. V.9. **The length of one curtain** of the inner wall of the tent **was twenty and eight cubits and the breadth of one curtain four cubits; the curtains were all of one size.** V.10. **And he coupled the five curtains one unto another; and the other five curtains he coupled one unto another,** the inner tent thus consisting of two large pieces, each twenty by twenty-eight cubits in size. V.11. **And he made loops of blue on the edge of one curtain from the selvage in the coupling; likewise he made in the uttermost side of another curtain, in the coupling of the second.** Cp. chap. 26. V.12. **Fifty loops made he in one curtain, and fifty loops made he in the edge of the curtain which was in the coupling of the second; the loops held one curtain to another.** V.13. **And he made fifty taches of gold,** froglike clasps, **and coupled the curtains one unto another with the taches; so it became one tabernacle,** a single tent curtain for the inside covering. V.14. **And he made curtains of goats' hair,** evidently woven from the hair as it was spun into threads, **for the tent over the Tabernacle; eleven curtains he made them.** V.15. **The length of one curtain was thirty cubits, and four cubits was the breadth of one curtain. The eleven curtains were of one size.** V.16. **And he coupled five curtains by themselves and six curtains by themselves.** The five and six strips, respectively, as sewed together, formed two pieces of unequal size, which formed the tent proper. V.17. **And he made fifty loops upon the uttermost edge of the curtain in the coupling, and fifty loops made he upon the edge of the curtain which coupleth the second.** V.18. **And he**

made fifty taches of brass, clasps of copper or bronze, **to couple the tent together, that it might be one.** V.19. **And he made a covering for the tent of rams' skins dyed red, and a covering of badgers' skins above that.** Cp. chap. 26, 1–14. The leather coverings were intended to serve for a protection against the weather. **4)**

The framework and the veils. — V.20. **And he made boards** (planks) **for the Tabernacle of shittim wood, standing up,** strong and durable. V.21. **The length of a board was ten cubits and the breadth of a board one cubit and a half.** V.22. **One board had two tenons, equally distant one from another. Thus did he make for all the boards of the Tabernacle.** V.23. **And he made boards for the Tabernacle; twenty boards for the south side southward;** v.24. **and forty sockets of silver he made under the twenty boards: two sockets under one board for his two tenons and two sockets under another board for his two tenons.** The tenons, fitting exactly in the sockets of the bases, held the planks upright. V.25. **And for the other side of the Tabernacle, which is toward the north corner, he made twenty boards,** v.26. **and their forty sockets of silver: two sockets under one board and two sockets under another board.** V.27. **And for the sides of the Tabernacle westward he made six boards,** of the regular width. V.28. **And two boards made he for the corners of the Tabernacle in the two sides,** the planks on the northwest and southwest corners, respectively, being apparently only one half cubit in width, as they were dovetailed to the first planks on the north and the south side to form a solid corner. V.29. **And they were coupled beneath, and coupled together at the head** thereof, to one ring. Thus he did to both of them in both the corners. V.30. And there were eight boards all told, on the west side; and their sockets were sixteen sockets of silver, under every board two sockets. V.31. And he made bars of shittim wood, cross-bars of acacia wood to lock the planks in place: five for the boards of the one side of the Tabernacle, v.32. and five bars for the boards of the other side of the Tabernacle, and five bars for the boards of the Tabernacle for the sides westward. V.33. And he made the middle bar to shoot through the boards from the one end to the other, thus making the walls solid. 5) V.34. And he overlaid the boards with gold, and made their rings of gold to be places for the bars, and overlaid the bars with gold. Cp. chap. 26, 15–30. V.35. And he made a veil of blue, and purple, and scarlet, and fine twined linen; with cherubim made he it of cunning work, the four kinds of thread woven into a damask cloth with figures of cherubim. V.36. And he made thereunto four pillars of shittim wood, for the entrance of the Most Holy Place, and overlaid them with gold; their hooks, to which the curtain was fastened, were of gold; and he cast for them four sockets of silver, heavy bases to hold the pillars upright. V.37. And he made an hanging for the Tabernacle door, the door leading to the Holy Place, of blue, and purple, and scarlet, and fine twined linen, of needlework, woven in geometrical figures. V.38. And the five pillars of it with their hooks, from which this outer screen was suspended; and he overlaid their chapiters, their heads, or capitals, and their fillets, the rods connecting them, with gold; but their five sockets were of brass, of less costly metal than those of the inner curtain. Cp. chap. 26, 31–37. Thus the directions of the Lord, as given to Moses, were followed with the most painstaking exactness, as the Lord had commanded Moses.

38

Exodus 37

The Appointments of the Tabernacle.

The ark. — V.1. **And Bezaleel made the ark of shittim wood,** the light, but strong wood of the Arabian acacia; **two cubits and a half was the length of it, and a cubit and a half the breadth of it, and a cubit and a half the height of it;** v.2. **and he overlaid it with pure gold within and without, and made a crown,** a molding, **of gold to it round about.** V.3. **And he cast for it four rings of gold, to be set by** (on or at) **the four corners of it: even two rings upon the one side of it and two rings upon the other side of it.** V.4. **And he made staves of shittim wood and overlaid them with gold.** V.5. **And he put the staves into the rings by the sides of the ark to bear the ark.** V.6. **And he made the mercy-seat,** the lid, or covering, of the ark, **of pure gold; two cubits and a half was the length thereof and one cubit and a half the breadth thereof.** V.7. **And he made** two cherubim of gold, beaten out of one piece made he them, enchased and fashioned with a hammer, on the two ends of the mercy-seat: v.8. one cherub on the end on this side and another cherub on the other end on that side, one at the north end, the other at the south end of the lid; out of the mercy-seat made he the cherubim on the two ends thereof, not merely set on top, but so firmly attached to the covering of the ark as to be an integral part of it. V.9. And the cherubim spread out their wings on high, and covered with their wings over the mercy-seat, with their faces to another, even to the mercy-seatward were the faces of the cherubim; they were facing toward each other, and bending forward over the ark. Cp. chap. 25, 10–22.

The table of the showbread. — V.10. And he made the table of shittim wood; two cubits was the length thereof, and a cubit the breadth thereof, and a cubit and a half the height thereof. V.11. And he overlaid it with pure gold, and made thereunto a crown of gold round about, heavy crosspieces connecting the legs of the table. V.12. Also he made thereunto a border of an handbreadth round about, a heavy molding just beneath the edge of the plate; and made a crown of gold for the border thereof round about, a rim which stood up above the plate of the table. V.13. And he cast for it four rings of gold, and put the rings upon the four corners that were in the four feet thereof. V.14. Over against the border were the rings, next to the heavy molding at the top, the places for the staves to bear the table. V.15. And he made the staves of shittim wood, and overlaid them with gold, to bear the table. V.16. And he made the vessels which were upon the table, his dishes, the showbread plates, **and his spoons,** the small incense vessels, **and his bowls, and his covers to cover withal,** pitchers and goblets for the drink-offering, **of pure gold.** Cp. chap. 25, 23–30.

The candlestick. — V.17. **And he made the candlestick of pure gold; of beaten work made he the candlestick,** of chased workmanship; **his shaft,** the base, **and his branch,** the heavy upright holder, **his bowls, his knops, and his flowers, were of the same;** v.18. **and six branches going out of the sides thereof; three branches of the candlestick out of the one side thereof and three branches of the candlestick out of the other side thereof;** v.19. **three bowls made after the fashion of almonds,** shaped like the blossoms of the almond-tree, **in one branch, a knop and a flower; and three bowls made like almonds in another branch, a knop and a flower; so throughout the six branches going out of the candlestick.** V.20. **And in the candlestick,** in the shaft itself, **were four bowls made like almonds, his knops, and his flowers;** v.21. **and a knop under two branches of the same, and a knop under two branches of the same, and a knop under two branches of the same, according to the six branches going out of it,** the knobs thus serving as ornaments at the branching of the arms. V.22. **Their knops and their branches were of the same; all of it was one beaten work of pure gold.** V.23. **And he made his seven lamps,** which were set into the bowls, **and his snuffers and his snuff-dishes,** the shears and pincers for trimming the wicks and the small plates for the trimmings, **of pure gold.** V.24. **Of a talent of pure gold made he it, and all the vessels thereof,** their value, by a rough estimate, being some $30,000. Cp. chap. 25, 31–40.

The altar of incense. — V.25. **And he made the incense altar of shittim wood; the length of it was a cubit, and the breadth of it a cubit; it was foursquare; and two cubits was the height of it; the horns thereof were of the same.** V.26. **And he overlaid it with pure gold, both the top,** the plate, **of it, and the sides thereof round about, and the horns of it; also he made unto it a crown of gold round about,** a heavy, decorated molding. V.27. **And he made two rings of gold for it under the crown thereof,** next to the heavy molding, **by the two corners of it, upon the two sides thereof, to be places for the staves to bear it withal.** Thus was the "golden altar" finished. V.28. **And he made the staves of shittim wood and overlaid them with gold.** Cp. chap. 30, 1–10. V.29. **And he made the holy anointing oil and the pure incense of sweet spices according to the work of the apothecary.** Cp. chap. 30, 22–28.

39

Exodus 38

The Appointments of the Court.

The altar of burnt offering. — V.1. **And he made the altar of burnt offering of shittim wood; five cubits was the length thereof and five cubits the breadth thereof (it was foursquare) and three cubits the height thereof.** There is no top or plate mentioned, and it is probable that the hollow frame-work was filled with earth or stones whenever the altar was in position. V.2. **And he made the horns thereof on the four corners of it; the horns thereof were of the same,** made of acacia wood; **and he overlaid it with brass.** V.3. **And he made all the vessels of the altar, the pots, and the shovels, and the basins,** bowls used for sprinkling and pouring the blood of the sacrifices, **and the flesh-hooks,** for spearing the meat in the caldrons, 1 Sam. 2, 13, **and the fire-pans,** for carrying the live coals used in kindling the fires; **all the vessels thereof made he of brass,** of copper or one of its alloys. V.4. **And he made for the altar a brazen grate of network under the compass thereof beneath unto the midst of it.** V.5. **And he cast four rings for the four ends of the grate of brass, to be places for the staves.** V.6. **And he made the staves of shittim wood and overlaid them with brass.** V.7. **And he put the staves into the rings on the sides of the altar to bear it withal. He made the altar hollow with boards.** Cp. chap. 27, 1–8. V.8. **And he made the laver of brass and the foot of it of brass, of the looking-glasses of the women assembling, which assembled at the door of the Tabernacle of the congregation.** These were women that served in the court of the Tabernacle, probably by washing and polishing the articles used in the sacred worship. They freely scarified their metal mirrors, otherwise thought indispensable pieces of furniture, for the Sanctuary of the Lord. The laver was a reservoir for the water used in the Sanctuary and in the court, and its base may have contained wash-basins for the prescribed ablutions. Cp. chap. 30, 17–21.

The great enclosure. — V.9. **And he made the court; on the south side southward the hangings of the court were of fine twined linen,** curtains of byssus, **an hundred cubits;** v.10. **their pillars were twenty, and their brazen sockets twenty; the hooks of the pillars and their fillets were of silver.** While the posts themselves were of bronze, the hooks and the connecting rods from which the curtains were suspended were of silver. V.11. **And for the north side the hangings were an hundred cubits, their pillars were twenty, and their sockets of brass twenty; the hooks of the pillars and their fillets of silver.** V.12. **And for the west side,** in the rear of the Tabernacle, **were hangings** of fifty cubits, their pillars ten, and their sockets ten; the hooks of the pillars and their fillets of silver. v.13. And for the east side eastward fifty cubits. V.14. The hangings of the one side of the gate were fifteen cubits; their pillars three, and their sockets three. V.15. And for the other side of the court gate, the large entrance to the sacred enclosure, on this hand and that hand, were hangings of fifteen cubits; their pillars three and their sockets three. This section of the enclosure toward the east was just like the curtains on the north, south, and west sides. V.16. All the hangings of the court round about were of fine twined linen. V.17. And the sockets for the pillars, the bases, were of brass, the hooks of the pillars and their fillets of silver, and the overlaying of their chapiters, the capitals of the posts only, of silver; and all the pillars of the court were filleted with silver, their connecting rods were made of silver. V.18. And the hanging for the gate of the court was needlework, woven in geometrical figures like the screen before the Holy Place, of blue, and purple, and scarlet, and fine twined linen; and twenty cubits was the length of this curtain, for that was the width of the gate, and the height in the breadth was five cubits, answerable to, agreeing with, the hangings of the court. V.19. And their pillars were four and their sockets of brass four; their hooks of silver and the overlaying of their chapiters and their fillets of silver. V.20. And all the pins of the Tabernacle and of the court round about were of brass, the pegs for holding the guy-ropes. Cp. chap. 27, 9–19.

The summary of gold, silver, and brass. — V.21. This is the sum of the Tabernacle, even of the Tabernacle

of Testimony, as it was counted, the enumeration, the summary of the mustered things, the appointments of the Sanctuary, **according to the commandment of Moses, for the service of the Levites, by the hand of Ithamar, son to Aaron, the priest.** The duty of counting the amount of metal used was committed to the Levites under the direction of Ithamar. V.22. **And Bezaleel,** as the master artisan, **the son of Uri, the son of Hur, of the tribe of Judah, made all that the Lord commanded Moses.** V.23. **And with him was Aholiab, son of Ahisamach, of the tribe of Dan, an engraver, and a cunning** (skilful) **workman, and an embroiderer in blue, and in purple, and in scarlet, and fine linen,** an artist in all the various crafts that came into consideration. V.24. **All the gold that was occupied** (employed, made use of) **for the work in all the work of the Holy Place, even the gold of the offering,** the gifts which the people brought voluntarily, **was twenty and nine talents, and seven hundred and thirty shekels, after the shekel of the Sanctuary,** that is, standard weight. This was 87,730 shekels in gold, or more than $600,000, accepting the lowest estimate, according to which a gold shekel was worth $7.20. If its value is taken at 9.60, as some scholars do, the value of the gold used in preparing the Tabernacle was almost $850,000. V.25. **And the silver of them that were numbered of the congregation was an hundred talents and a thousand seven hundred and threescore and fifteen shekels, after the shekel of the Sanctuary; v.26. a bekah for every man, that is, half a shekel, after the shekel of the Sanctuary, for everyone that went to be numbered, from twenty years old and upward, for six hundred thousand and three thousand**

and five hundred and fifty men. So the standard which was afterward fixed served as a guide in estimating the value of the voluntary contributions, the total amount being 301,775 shekels of silver, or almost $200,000. V.27. **And of the hundred talents of silver were cast the sockets of the Sanctuary and the sockets of the veil and hundred sockets of the hundred talents, a talent for a socket,** that is, almost 118 pounds Troy. V.28. **And of the thousand seven hundred seventy and five shekels he made hooks for the pillars, and overlaid their chapiters, and filleted them.** V.29. **And the brass of the offering was seventy talents and two thousand and four hundred shekels.** V.30. **And therewith he made,** that is, he made out of the copper which was offered or out of its alloy, bronze, **the sockets to the door of the Tabernacle of the Congregation,** the pillars of the entrance to the Holy Place having bronze bases, **and the brazen altar, and the brazen grate for it, and all the vessels of the altar,** v.31. **and the sockets of the court round about, and the sockets of the court gate, and all the pins of the Tabernacle, and all the pins of the court round about.** The example of the children of Israel in sacrificing for their Sanctuary may well inspire enthusiasm of the right kind in the hearts of the believers of the New Testament, making them willing to contribute for the building and the spreading of the Kingdom.

40

Exodus 39

The Priestly Vestments.

T he ephod and its girdle. — V.1. **And of the blue and purple and scarlet,** the fine woven fabrics which they had made, **they made cloths of service, to do service in the Holy Place, and made the holy garments for Aaron, as the Lord commanded Moses.** This included all the vestments and paraments in use in the Tabernacle. V.2. **And he made the ephod of gold, blue, and purple, and scarlet, and fine twined linen,** the fine, damasklike cloth being interwoven with threads of gold. V.3. **And they did beat the gold into thin plates,** gold, being highly malleable, yielding readily to this treatment, **and cut it into wires,** thin threads, **to work it in the blue, and in the purple, and in the scarlet, and in the fine linen with cunning work.** V.4. **They made shoulder-pieces for it to couple it together; by the two edges was it coupled together,** the effect being that of a stole, or vest. V.5. **And the curious**

girdle of his ephod, that was upon it, was of the same, according to the work thereof, of the same material and workmanship; **of gold, blue, and purple, and scarlet, and fine twined linen, as the Lord commanded Moses.** V.6. **And they wrought onyx stones,** cut and polished them, **inclosed in ouches of gold,** that is, in settings which were continued as clasps, or buckles, **graven, as signets are graven, with the names of the children of Israel.** V.7. **And he put them on the shoulders of the ephod that they should be stones for a memorial to the children of Israel,** to keep their names in remembrance before the Lord, **as the Lord commanded Moses.** Cp. chap. 28,6–12.

The breastplate and its fastenings. — V.8. **And he made the breastplate of cunning work,** a production of the highest artistic skill, **like the work of the ephod; of gold, blue, and purple, and scarlet, and fine twined linen.** V.9. **It was foursquare,** half a cubit either way; **they made the breastplate double,** the material forming a sort of pocket; **a span was the length thereof and a span the breadth thereof, being doubled.** V.10. **And they set in it four rows of stones,** precious gems. **The first row was a sardius, a topaz, and a carbuncle; this was the first row.** V.11. **And the second row, an emerald, a sapphire, and a diamond.** V.12. **And the third row, a ligure, an agate, and an amethyst.** V.13. **And the fourth row, a beryl, an onyx, and a jasper; they were enclosed in ouches of gold in their inclosings,** in the settings by which they were fastened to the cloth. V.14. **And the stones were according to the names of the children of Israel, twelve, according to their names, like the engravings of a signet, everyone with his name, according to the twelve tribes.** V.15. **And** they made upon the breastplate chains at the ends, of wreathen work of pure gold, braided of gold wire. V.16. And they made two ouches of gold, the settings continued in the form of clasps, or buckles, and two gold rings; and put the two rings in the two ends of the breastplate. V.17. And they put the two wreathen chains of gold in the two rings on the ends of the breastplate. V.18. And the two ends of the two wreathen chains they fastened in the two ouches, in the clasps connected with the two onyx stones on the shoulders, and put them on the shoulderpieces of the ephod, before it. V.19. And they made two rings of gold, and put them on the two ends of the breastplate, upon the border of it, which was on the side of the ephod inward, on the lower end inside, facing the ephod. V.20. And they made two other golden rings, and put them on the two sides of the ephod underneath, on the ephod, in front, beneath the breastplate, toward the forepart of it, over against the other coupling thereof, where it was held together, above the curious girdle of the ephod. V.21. And they did bind the breastplate by his rings unto the rings of the ephod with a lace of blue, with threads made of the hyacinth-colored material, that it might be above the curious girdle of the ephod, and that the breastplate might not be loosed from the ephod, as the Lord commanded Moses. Cp. chap. 28, 15–29.

The other articles of wear. — V.22. And he made the robe of the ephod, over which the ephod was worn, of woven work, all of blue, a hyacinth-colored garment reaching to the knees. V.23. And there was an hole in the midst of the robe, for the head to pass through, as the hole of an habergeon, a strong linen shirt worn by soldiers, with

a band, a strong hem, or selvage, **round about the hole, that it should not rend.** v.24. **And they made upon the hems of the robe pomegranates of blue, and purple, and scarlet, and twined linen;** these were on the skirt of the garment, at the knees. V.25. **And they made bells of pure gold, and put the bells between the pomegranates upon the hem of the robe, round about between the pomegranates;** v.26. **a bell and a pomegranate, a bell and a pomegranate, round about the hem of the robe to minister in, as the Lord commanded Moses.** Cp. chap. 28, 31–34. V.27. **And they made coats of fine linen,** of shining byssus, **of woven work for Aaron and for his sons,** v.28. **and a miter of fine linen,** the high, turbanlike headdress, **and goodly bonnets,** ornamented caps, **of fine linen,** for the ordinary priests, **and linen breeches of fine twined linen,** v.29. **and a girdle of fine twined linen, and blue, and purple, and scarlet, of needlework,** of a damasklike fabric prepared from the various costly materials, **as the Lord commanded Moses.** The girdle of Aaron only is mentioned, since the girdles of the ordinary priests were patterned after his. V.30. **And they made the plate of the holy crown of pure gold,** a crown, or diadem, of holiness, **and wrote upon it a writing, like to the engravings of a signet, HOLINESS TO THE LORD.** V.31. **And they tied unto it a lace of blue,** a hyacinth-colored, ornamental string, **to fasten it on high upon the miter, as the Lord commanded Moses.** Cp. chap. 28, 39–42.

Moses approves the work. — V.32. **Thus was all the work of the Tabernacle of the Tent of the Congregation finished; and the children of Israel did according to all that the Lord commanded Moses, so did they.** V.33. **And**

they brought the Tabernacle unto Moses, both the inner
and the outer covering, the fine damask being intended
for the inner wall, and the curtains woven of goat-hair for
the outside, **the tent, and all his furniture, his taches,
his boards, his bars, and his pillars, and his sockets,**
v.34. **and the covering of rams' skins dyed red, and the
covering of badgers' skins,** the tough and pliant seacow
leather, which served to shelter the tent, something on the
order of a fly-top in our days, **and the veil of the covering,**
the curtain for the door of the Most Holy Place, v.35. **the
Ark of the Testimony, and the staves thereof, and the
mercy-seat,** v.36. **the table, and all the vessels thereof,
and the showbread,** v.37. **the pure candlestick, with the
lamps thereof, even with the lamps to be set in order,**
the burners as they were regularly to be renewed by trimming
and filling the lamps, **and all the vessels thereof, and the
oil for light,** v.38. **and the golden altar** of incense, **and
the anointing oil, and the sweet incense,** literally, the
incense of sweet odor, **and the hanging for the Tabernacle
door,** v.39. **the brazen altar and his grate of brass, his
staves and all his vessels, the laver and his foot,** v.40.
**the hangings of the court, his pillars, and his sockets,
and the hanging for the court gate, his cords, and his
pins, and all the vessels of the service of the Tabernacle
for the Tent of the Congregation,** the various articles
being enumerated in the order of their importance, v.41.
**the cloths of service to do service in the Holy Place,
and the holy garments for Aaron, the priest, and his
sons' garments, to minister in the priest's office.** V.42.
**According to all that the Lord commanded Moses, so
the children of Israel made all the work,** the majority

of them by donating the materials, and the artisans by producing the articles. V.43. **And Moses did look upon all the work, and, behold; they had done it as the Lord had commanded, even so had they done it;** a careful inspection showed that the instructions of the Lord had been carried out in every detail. **And Moses blessed them.** "The readiness with which the people had brought in abundance the requisite gifts for this work, and the zeal with which they had accomplished the work in half a year or less, were delightful signs of Israel's willingness to serve the Lord; and for this the blessing of God could not fail to be given." (Keil.)

41

Exodus 40

The Erection and the Dedication of the Tabernacle.

T he Tabernacle set up. — V.1. **And the Lord spake unto Moses, saying, v.2. On the first day of the first month shalt thou set up the Tabernacle of the Tent of the Congregation.** This was on the first of Nisan, or Abib, at the beginning of the second year after the children of Israel had left Egypt. The Tabernacle was to be in readiness for the first anniversary of the Passover Festival. V.3. **And thou shalt put therein the Ark of the Testimony,** where the Decalog, the testimony of the Lord to the people, was deposited, **and cover the ark with the veil,** hide it from the eyes of the people by the heavy curtain which screened the Most Holy Place. V.4. **And thou shalt bring in the table** of showbread, **and set in order the things,** literally, arrange the order, **that are to be set in order upon it; and thou shalt bring in the candlestick, and light the lamps thereof.** V.5. **And thou shalt set the altar of gold**

for the incense before the Ark of the Testimony, that is, to the east of it, before the veil of the Sanctuary, **and put the hanging of the door to the Tabernacle,** the door-curtain before the Holy Place. V.6. **And thou shalt set the altar of the burnt offering before the door of the Tabernacle of the Tent of the Congregation,** out in the open court. V.7. **And thou shalt set the laver between the Tent of the Congregation and the altar, and shalt. put water therein,** since it was to serve for the ablutions of the priests, both before entering the Sanctuary and before going up to the altar of burnt offering. V.8. **And thou shalt set up the court round about,** both the posts and the curtains, **and hang up the hanging at the court gate,** the splendid variegated entrance curtain. V.9. **And thou shalt take the anointing oil, and anoint the Tabernacle, and all that is therein, and shalt hallow it and all the vessels thereof; and it shall be holy,** set aside for the worship of Jehovah. V.10. **And thou shalt anoint the altar of the burnt offering and all his vessels, and sanctify the altar** for the service of the Lord; **and it shall be an altar most holy,** literally, holiness of holiness, everybody and everything that touched it being thereby consecrated to the Lord. V.11. **And thou shalt anoint the laver and his foot and sanctify it,** set it apart for the sacred use for which it was intended. V.12. **And thou shalt bring Aaron and his sons unto the door of the Tabernacle of the Congregation, and wash them with water,** chap. 29, 4. V.13. **And thou shalt put upon Aaron the holy garments, and anoint him, and sanctify him, that he may minister unto Me in the priest's office.** V.14. **And thou shalt bring his sons, and clothe them with coats,**

the white byssus garments which were the distinctive dress of the ordinary priests; v.15. **and thou shalt anoint them, as thou didst anoint their father, that they may minister unto Me in the priest's office; for their anointing shall surely be an everlasting priesthood throughout their generations.** The priesthood was hereditary among the sons of Aaron, but their consecration did not take place until the special ordinances of the sacrifices had been given. Cp. Lev. 8. V.16. **Thus did Moses; according to all that the Lord commanded him, so did he.**

The various appointments in place. — V.17. **And it came to pass in the first month in the second year, on the first day of the month, that the Tabernacle was reared up,** the great tent of worship was solemnly erected. V.18. **And Moses reared up the Tabernacle, and fastened his sockets,** the bases of the large planks, **and set up the boards thereof, and put in the bars thereof, and reared up his pillars,** those from which the two curtains were suspended. V.19. **And he spread abroad the tent over the Tabernacle,** first the splendid variegated curtain, and then the curtain of goats' hair, **and put the covering of the tent above upon it,** the protective covering of rams' skins and seacow leather, **as the Lord commanded Moses.** V.20. **And he took and put the testimony into the ark,** the stone tables with the Decalog, **and set the staves on the ark, and put the mercy-seat above upon the ark.** V.21. **And he brought the ark into the Tabernacle,** into the Most Holy Place, **and set up the veil of the covering, and covered the Ark of the Testimony,** shut it off from the gaze of all but the high priest on the great Day of Atonement, **as the Lord commanded Moses.** V.22. **And he put the table** of showbread **in** the Tent of the Congregation, in the Holy Place, **upon the side of the Tabernacle northward, without the veil,** on the right, or north, side of the altar of incense. V.23. **And he set the bread in order upon it before the Lord,** he arranged the showbread in the two heaps according to orders, **as the Lord had commanded Moses.** V.24. **And he put the candlestick in the Tent of the Congregation over against the table,** on the side opposite the table of showbread, **on the side of the Tabernacle southward,** to the left of the altar of incense. V.25. **And he lighted the lamps before the Lord, as the Lord commanded Moses.** V.26. **And he put the golden altar** of incense **in the Tent of the Congregation,** the Holy Place, **before the veil; v.27. and he burned sweet incense thereon, as the Lord commanded Moses.** V.28. **And he set up the hanging at the door of the Tabernacle,** suspending it from the pillars at the eastern entrance. V.29. **And he put the altar of burnt offering by the door of the Tabernacle of the Tent of the Congregation, and offered upon it the burnt offering and the meat-offering, as the Lord commanded Moses.** Both the burning of incense and the bringing of sacrifices at this time were extraordinary acts of Moses, and did not belong to the ordinary worship of the people, as it was done after the consecration of the Sanctuary. V.30. **And he set the laver between the Tent of the Congregation and the altar, and put water there to wash withal.** V.31. **And Moses and Aaron and his sons washed their hands and their feet thereat; v.32. when they went into the Tent of the Congregation, and when they came near unto the altar, they washed, as the Lord commanded Moses.** This signified that the Lord wanted not only clean hands, but clean hearts as well, in all those that were and are engaged in His worship. V.33. **And he reared up the court round about the Tabernacle and the altar, and set up the hanging of the court gate. So Moses finished the work.**

The cloud of God's glory. — V.34. **Then a cloud covered the Tent of the Congregation, and the glory of the Lord filled the Tabernacle,** shut off from the gaze of sinful men by the screen of cloud. So Jehovah Himself consecrated the Sanctuary by this manifestation of His glory in the sacred cloud, even before it was consecrated by the priesthood. V.35. **And Moses was not able to enter into the Tent of the Congregation,** not even he, the friend of Jehovah, **because the cloud abode thereon, and the glory of the Lord filled the Tabernacle.** This shows that the people had now again received the full pardon of the Lord, since He once more dwelt in their midst with His gracious presence. V.36. **And when the cloud was taken up from over the Tabernacle, the children of Israel went onward in all their journeys; v.37. but if the cloud were not taken up, then they journeyed not till the day that it was taken up.** The people broke camp and moved onward only with the moving of the cloud. V.38. **For the cloud of the Lord was upon the Tabernacle by day, and fire was on it by night, in the sight,** before the eyes, **of all the house of Israel, throughout all their journeys.** Thus did the presence of the covenant God accompany them in all their journeyings, and the Tabernacle served to hold before the congregation the object of its calling and the certain fulfillment of the promises to the patriarchs.

II

The Book of Leviticus

The Third of the Five Books of Moses

42

Introduction

The Third book of Moses received the name which me now apply to it because its precepts are concerned chiefly with the duties of the Levites and priests. It contains detailed ordinances describing the Levitic worship as it was to be observed in the Tabernacle and afterward in the Temple. The laws in Leviticus, mainly of a ceremonial character, constitute a handbook for the use of the priests in the performance of the various duties entrusted to them. A few supplementary rules to this Levitic law were added in the Book of Numbers.

Although this book contains no direct Messianic promise whatever, it is, by the intention of God, in reality one continuous sermon on the salvation of Jesus Christ; for, as the New Testament shows conclusively, the entire magnificent system of sacrifices was nothing less than a typical representation of the vicarious sacrifice of Jesus Christ, which was foreshadowed by every bloody offering on the sacred altars. And as far as the children of Israel were concerned, the laws of sacrifices taught them that God is holy,

and that man is sinful; that all are guilty before His Law; that
the man who transgresses His Law is worthy of His wrath
and displeasure, temporal death, and eternal damnation; that
without the shedding of blood there is no remission of sin;
that the holy God desire.: to enter into fellowship with sinful
man, and approaches him, and appoints this way of sacrifice
as an atonement for sin, and through His mercy accepts
the sacrifice of the victim instead of the death of the sinner.
Incidentally, it must be kept in mind throughout the book
that the whole system of sacrifices was merely temporary
and typical. "For it is not possible that the blood of bulls and
of goats should take away sins," Heb. 10, 4. No animal, no
mere man, no angel, could atone for sin. God alone could
do that, and therefore He became man that He might be able
to suffer and die for sin as man's substitute. "God was in
Christ, reconciling the world unto Himself," 2 Cor. 5, 19. All
sacrifices looked forward, therefore, to Christ, the Lamb of
God, which taketh away the sin of the world, and on which
God laid the iniquity of us all. The usages of the Jewish cult
were a shadow of things to come, but the body is of Christ,
Col. 2, 17.

"The Book of Genesis shows man's ruin and fall. Exodus
pictures the great redemption and salvation which God has
provided. Leviticus follows naturally, and is mainly occupied
with the way of access to God in worship and communion.
It is a book for a redeemed people. Its teaching in the light of
the New Testament is for those who have realized their lost
condition, and have accepted the redemption that is in Christ
Jesus, and are seeking to draw near into the presence of God.
It shows the holiness of God and the utter impossibility of
access except on the ground of atonement. Such is the main

lesson of Leviticus, and it is impressed upon us over and over again in a variety of ways. We come face to face with the great question of sacrifice for sin. The stress laid upon sacrifice is, no doubt, intended to give man a shock with regard to sin. The book stands out for all time as God's estimate of sin. To understand the seriousness of sin we must fathom three oceans-the ocean of human suffering, the ocean of the sufferings of the Lord Jesus Christ, the ocean of future suffering which awaits the impenitent sinners. What we have in type in Leviticus we have in reality in the cross of Christ. The cross was indeed an exhibition of God's love, the love of God the father, and of God the Son, who through the eternal Spirit offered Himself. But it was more than this-it was God's estimate of sin. The cross of Christ stands as God's estimate of what sin really is, something so deep and dreadful that it cost that. It was more even than this, it was the atoning sacrifice by which sin could forever be put away."[2]

The Book of Leviticus may be divided into three parts: the precepts concerning the sacrifices and the priesthood; the consecration of Israel for the service of Jehovah by the cleansing of the bodily life; the holiness of Israel as the people of God in life and worship.[3]

---

[2] *Concordia Bible Class,* Feb., 1919, 21-23.

[3] Fuerbringer, *Einleitung in das Alte Testament,* 25.

43

Leviticus 1

The Burnt offerings.

O F THE HERD. – V.1. **And the Lord called unto Moses, and spake unto him out of the Tabernacle of the Congregation,** out of the midst of the cloud which enveloped his glory, Ex. 40, 35, **saying, v.2. Speak unto the children of Israel, and say unto them, if any man of you bring an offering unto the Lord, ye shall bring your offering of the cattle, even of the herd and of the flock.** The sacrifices brought by individuals are described first, voluntary offerings, through which the worshiper intended to draw near to the Lord. The Hebrew word indicates the fact that sinful man, as such, does not dare to draw near to Jehovah. The sacrifice, therefore, is a symbol of his desire to enter into fellowship with Jehovah, and its value consisted in its foreshadowing the greater Sacrifice, through whom we have peace and access to the Father. The voluntary offering was regarded as a gift of the worshiper, no matter whether it was an actual sacrifice or a dedicatory offering. When the individual Israelite had determined to bring such a gift, the Lord's instructions as to the selection of the animal and as to the manner of offering were inclusive and exact. V.3. **If his offering be a burnt sacrifice of the herd, let him offer a male without blemish,** a strong, healthy animal, with all its limbs and members intact; **he shall offer it of his own voluntary will at the door of the Tabernacle of the Congregation before the Lord.** The formal dedication of the sacrifice to the Lord took place at the great entrance of the court, or perhaps inside the court itself, where the altar of burnt offering stood. At a later period such a perfect system of offering sacrifices was put into operation that both the slaughtering of the animals and their dissecting was performed with the greatest possible speed, a row of pillars holding heavy beams with hooks being used to suspend the animals after their blood had been caught by the officiating priests. V.4. **And he shall put his hand upon the head of the burnt offering**, in token of the transfer of his sin to the animal as his substitute, as the victim destined to die in the worshiper's stead; **and it shall be accepted for him to make atonement for him,** that his sins might be covered over before the face of the Lord. Note that here, as always, the acceptance of a substitute is in itself an act of grace and mercy on the part of the Lord. V.5. **And he shall kill the bullock before the Lord,** each worshiper, in a case of this kind, performing the function of a priest of the Lord, as a member of the kingdom of priests, Ex. 19, 6. **And the priests, Aaron's sons, shall bring the blood,** as it was caught up in basins after the slaughter of the animal, **and sprinkle the blood round about upon the altar,** against its four sides, **that is by the door of the Tabernacle of the Congregation.** The last was an exclusive priestly function, and even the catching of the blood was performed by the Levites only in cases of emergency. V.6. **And he shall flay the burnt offering,** this part of the work being done either by the offerer or by a Levite, **and cut it into his pieces,** dissect it according to the rule concerning the disposition of the various parts. V.7. **And the sons of Aaron, the priest, shall put fire upon the altar of burnt offering, and lay the wood in order upon the fire,** which was always kept burning; v.8. **and the priests, Aaron's sons, shall lay the parts, the head and the fat,** chiefly the loose fat of the abdominal and thoracic cavities, **in order upon the wood that is on the fire which is upon the altar;** v.9. **but his inwards and his legs,** the intestines, as the lower viscera, and the lower parts of the legs, especially beneath the knees, **shall he wash in water,** to remove any outward impurities that might be clinging to them; **and the priests shall burn all on the altar, to be a burnt sacrifice, an offering made by fire, of a sweet savor unto the Lord.** The animal, with its flesh and bones, was burned entire, for the offering signified that the worshiper dedicated himself to the Lord with all his heart and mind, with all the powers of his body and soul, and the rising of the smoke, as the animal was consumed, caused its essence to ascend as a pleasant, acceptable odor to the Lord. In other words, the Lord graciously accepted the worshiper and his service as a member of His Church on earth. God was well pleased with such sacrifices, if they were offered in faith.

OF THE FLOCK. - V.10. **And if his offering be of the**

flocks, namely, of the sheep or of the goats, for a burnt sacrifice, the worshiper being too poor to afford a bullock, **he shall bring it a male without blemish,** a perfect animal in every respect. V.11. **And he shall kill it on the side of the altar northward,** the usual place for slaughtering sacrifices, **before the Lord.** The various parts of the court were soon used for special purposes, its eastern end being used for the ashes of the altar, and the place south and southwest of the great altar being devoted to the priests. On the south side of the altar was also the incline for the officiating priests. **And the priests, Aaron's sons, shall sprinkle his blood round about upon the altar,** in the act symbolizing the atonement of sins. V.12. **And he shall cut it into his pieces,** as the disposition of the parts required, **with his head and his fat,** these parts being severed from the carcass; **and the priest shall lay them in order on the wood that is on the fire which is upon the altar.** V.13. **But he shall wash the inwards and the legs with water,** as in the case of the bullock. **And the priest shall bring it all and burn it upon the altar; it is a burnt sacrifice, an offering made by fire, of a sweet savor unto the Lord.**

OF FOWLS. - V.14. **And if the burnt sacrifice for his offering to the Lord be of fowls,** in the case of very poor people, **then he shall bring his offering of turtle-doves or of young pigeons,** either the mild or the tame species being acceptable for a gift-offering. V.15. **And the priest shall bring it unto the altar, and wring off his head,** separate his head from his body by pinching, **and burn it on the altar,** toss the head into the fire; **and the blood thereof shall be wrung out at the side of the altar,** since there was hardly enough to be sprinkled or poured. V.16. **And**

he shall pluck away his crop with his feathers, either the crop with the entire intestinal tract and its filth, or the entire intestinal tract while the dove was unplucked, **and cast it beside the altar on the east part, by the place of the ashes,** where all the refuse was heaped up. V.17. **And he shall cleave it with the wings thereof,** split it open lengthwise, or make an incision at its wings, **but shall not divide it asunder; and the priest shall burn it upon the altar, up on the wood that is upon the fire; it is a burnt sacrifice, an offering made by fire, of a sweet savor unto the Lord.** The sacrifice of the poor was just as acceptable to the Lord as the more costly sacrifice of the rich. The sacrificial worship was a shadow of things to come, in the person of the Messiah. In anticipation of the perfect sacrifice of Christ God accepted these figurative offerings as atonements for sin. But Christ is the only true Sacrifice, who bore the sins of all men in His body on the tree, burning under the wrath of the just God and dying as the Substitute for all men. In view of this sacrifice, whose blessings are ours through faith, we Christians are bound to offer ourselves to the Lord in daily obedience and service. Such sacrifice is a sweet savor to the Lord, a living sacrifice, holy, acceptable unto God, Rom. 12, 1. 2.

44

Leviticus 2

The Meat-Offerings.

THE VARIOUS KINDS OF MEAT-OFFERINGS. - V.1. **And when any will offer a meat-offering unto the Lord, his offering shall be of fine flour.** This also was an oblation, or gift, brought near to the Lord with the purpose of establishing true fellowship, and could be made by any member of the congregation, no matter whether man or woman. Only the finest wheat flour was to be used in these oblations. **And he shall pour oil upon it, and put frankincense thereon.** The incense was not mixed with the flour and the olive-oil, but added in such a manner as to permit its entire removal from the vessel in which it was offered. V.2. **And he shall bring it to Aaron's sons, the priests; and he** (the officiating priest) **shall take thereout his handful of the flour thereof and of the oil thereof with all the frankincense thereof,** as much as the hand would hold of flour and oil; **and the priest shall burn the memorial of it upon the altar,** to cause Jehovah to remember the worshiper in His mercy, **to be**

an offering made by fire, of a sweet savor unto the Lord, well-pleasing and acceptable to the Lord, as the burnt offering had been, chap. 1, 9. 13. 17. V.3. **And the remnant of the meat-offering shall be Aaron's and his sons;** all of it was offered to the Lord, who, in turn, bestowed the bulk of it upon the priests as a part of the emoluments due them; **it is a thing moat holy of the offerings of the Lord made by fire.** This is said of all sacrificial gifts which were wholly devoted to God, but of which portions were hallowed to Him by being given to the priests. These gifts the priests used for food in a place in the court of the Tabernacle of the Congregation, near the altar of burnt offering, chap. 6, 26; 10, 12. V.4. **And if thou bring an oblation of a meat-offering baken in the oven,** a small portable earthen oven in the form of a pot or jar, **it shall be unleavened cakes of fine flour, mingled with oil, or unleavened wafers, anointed with oil.** The unleavened dough used in making these cakes was mixed with olive-oil, and the thick, biscuitlike cakes were pierced with holes. V.5. **And if thy oblation be a meat-offering baken in a pan, it shall be of fine flour unleavened, mingled with oil,** the only difference between this sacrifice and the preceding one being this, that it was fried in an open pan. V.6. **Thou shalt part it in pieces and pour oil thereon; it is a meat-offering.** The finished cakes were to be broken into small fragments and then saturated with olive-oil. V.7. **And if thy oblation be a meat-offering baken in the frying-pan,** boiled in a pot, **it shall be made of fine flour with oil,** apparently cooked in the oil. The olive-oil, which figures so prominently in these sacrifices, is a symbol of the Holy Ghost. The good works of the believers are done in the power of the Holy Ghost. If these sacrifices are accompanied with the incense of prayer, they will be wellpleasing in the sight of the Lord. V.8. **And thou shalt bring the meat-offering that is made of these things unto the Lord; and when it is presented unto the priest,** as the representative of God, **he shall bring it unto the altar.** V.9. **And the priest shall take from the meat-offering a memorial thereof,** to bring the worshiper in remembrance before God, **and shall burn it upon the altar; it is an offering made by fire, of a sweet savor unto the Lord.** V.10. **And that which is left of the meat-offering shall be Aaron's and his sons'; it is a thing most holy of the offerings of the Lord made by fire.** The men that served in the Sanctuary were to receive their sustenance from these gifts, just as to-day they that preach the Gospel should live of the Gospel. V.11. **No meat-offering which ye shall bring unto the Lord shall be made with leaven,** leaven being considered an impure addition in this case on account of its fermenting property; **for ye shall burn no leaven nor any honey,** against which the same objection was made as against the leaven, **in any offering of the Lord made by fire.** There were certain offerings in which leavened bread was included, chap. 7, 13. 14; 23, 17. 20, and also honey, 2 Chron. 31, 5; but in the meat-offering they were strictly forbidden. Thus the believers will avoid all impurity and hypocrisy in word and deed.

THE MEAT-OFFERING OF THE FIRST-FRUITS. - V.12. **As for the oblation of the first-fruits, ye shall offer them unto the Lord,** bring them as gifts in order to establish or to confirm the fellowship with the Lord; **but they shall not be burned on the altar for a sweet savor.** In such offerings, therefore, even leaven and honey might be included. V.13. **And every oblation of thy meat-offering shalt thou season with salt,** this being both a purifier and a preservative; **neither shalt thou suffer the salt of the covenant of thy God to be lacking from thy meat-offering; with all thine offerings thou shalt offer salt.** Cp. Mark 9, 49; Col. 4, 6. This rule applied not only to meat-offerings, but to all offerings commanded by God. V.14. **And if thou offer a meat-offering of thy first-fruits unto the Lord,** of the first grain that was ready to harvested in the early summer, **thou shalt offer for the meat-offering of thy first-fruits green ears of corn dried by the fire, even corn beaten out of full ears.** The stalks of the grain were cut with the maturing ears, and the grain roasted at the fire while in the ear, such dried or roasted kernels, in the form of groats, being a favorite dish in the Orient to this day. V.15. **And thou shalt put oil upon it, and lay fankincense thereon,** as in the case of the fine flour; **it is a meat-offering.** V.16. **And the priest shall burn the memorial of it, part of the beaten corn thereof and part of the oil thereof, with all the frankincense thereof; it is an offering made by fire unto the Lord.** It is undoubtedly well-pleasing to the Lord if we, in addition to the regular sacrifices in good works, are found willing to offer to Him in extraordinary quantities, if He has blessed us in unusual measure.

45

Leviticus 3

The Peace-offerings.

OF THE HERD. – V.1. **And if his oblation be a sacrifice of peace-offering, if he offer it of the herd, whether it be a male or female, he shall offer it without blemish before the Lord.** The designation "peace-offering" seems to have been the more general term, for these sacrifices included also the thank-offerings and the salvation-offerings. Another division is that into thanksgiving-, vow-, and free-will offerings, chap. 7, 11-18. Some peace-offerings were made in times of distress, the idea associated with them being that of supplication for divine help, Judg. 20, 26; 21, 4; 1 Sam. 13, 9; 2 Sam. 14, 25. V.2. **And he shall lay his hand upon the head of his offering,** in the act which declared the animal to be the substitute for the worshiper in the sacrifice, **and kill it at the door of the Tabernacle of the Congregation; and Aaron's sons, the priests, shall sprinkle the blood upon**

the altar round about, for the purpose of atonement. V.3. **And he shall offer of the sacrifice of the peace-offering an offering made by fire unto the Lord,** certain parts of the animal offered for the purpose of establishing a closer fellowship with God were to be burned on the altar of burnt offering; **the fat that covereth the inwards,** the large net of adipose membrane in the abdominal cavity, **and all the fat that is upon the inwards,** that which is only loosely attached to the intestines and may be peeled off without difficulty, v.4. **and the two kidneys, and the fat that is on them, which is by the flanks,** attached to the muscles in the upper pelvic cavity, **and the caul above the liver,** the small net of adipose membrane extending from the liver to the kidneys, **with the kidneys,** that is, together with, or upon, the kidneys, as they lay in position, it shall he take away from the rest of the animal. V.5. **And Aaron's sons shall burn it,** these fatty parts with the kidneys, **on the altar upon the burnt sacrifice, which is upon the wood that is on the fire; it is an offering made by fire, of a sweet savor unto the Lord,** well-pleasing to Him if made in the right manner, if brought in true faith. These offerings were brought upon, that is, after the burnt offerings of the day.

OF THE FLOCK. – V.6. **And if his offering for a sacrifice of peace-offering unto the Lord be of the flock, male or female, he shall offer it without blemish.** The sex was immaterial, but the animal had to be perfect, as before. V.7. **If he offer a lamb for his offering, then shall he offer it before the Lord,** for the purpose of securing the good pleasure of the Lord. V.8. **And he** (the worshiper) **shall lay his hand upon the head of his offering, and kill it before the Tabernacle of the Congregation,** out in the open court; **and Aaron's sons shall sprinkle the blood thereof round about upon the altar,** the act having the same significance as before. V.9. **And he shall offer of the sacrifice of the peace-offering an offering made by fire unto the Lord,** that portion of the sacrificial victim burned upon the altar being known as the food of Jehovah and signifying the communion between Him and the worshiper brought about by the sacrifice; **the fat thereof and the whole rump,** the heavy fat-tail which is characteristic of a certain variety of sheep in Arabia and Palestine, **it shall he take off hard by the backbone; and the fat that covereth the inwards,** and all the fat that is upon the inwards, as in the case of the larger animal. v.3, v.10. **and the two kidneys, and the fat that is upon them, which is by the flanks, and the caul above the liver, with the kidneys,** that is, upon the kidneys, **it shall he take away.** Cp. v.4. V.11. **And the priest shall burn it upon the altar; it is the food of the offering made by fire unto the Lord,** a food offered by the believing Israelite by fire and rising up to the Lord in an odor well-pleasing to Him. In this manner the Lord partook of the sacrifice and entered in to fellowship with His people.

OF GOATS. - V.12. **And if his offering be a goat, then he shall offer it before the Lord.** V.13. **And he shall lay his hand upon the head of it, and kill it before the Tabernacle of the Congregation; and the sons of Aaron shall sprinkle the blood thereof,** as it was caught when the animal was slaughtered, upon the altar round about. V.14. **And he shall offer thereof his offering, even an offering made by fire unto the Lord;** the fat that covereth the inwards, and all the fat that is upon the inwards, v.15. **and**

the two kidneys, and the fat that is upon them, which is by the flanks, and the caul above the liver, with the kidneys, it shall he take away. V.16. **And the priest shall burn them upon the altar; it is the food of the offering made by fire for a sweet savor; all the fat is the Lord's,** that is, all the loose fatty parts that were enumerated in these three cases were to be the Lord's portion. V.17. **It shall be a perpetual statute for your generations throughout all your dwellings that ye eat neither fat nor blood.** As long as the children of Israel were in the wilderness, all the animals slaughtered for food had to be brought to the Sanctuary, chap. 17, 3-7; in the land of Canaan, they were permitted to slaughter such animals in their own cities. Deut. 12, 15, but all the sacrifices had to be made at the place of the Sanctuary. The prohibition, however, concerning the loose fat mentioned in this chapter and that regarding blood remained in force for the Jewish people. In the case of all peace-offerings the wave-breast and the heave-shoulder belonged to the priests, chap. 7, 30 ff., and the rest of the meat was to be eaten by the worshiper and his family in the court of the Tabernacle. This joyous sacrificial meal was to express the happiness which the believers felt because of their covenant with the God of their salvation, just as we Christians enjoy the blessings of God's covenant in the Sacrament of the Altar.

46

Leviticus 4

The Sin-offerings.

FOR A PRIEST. - V.1. **And the Lord spake unto Moses, saying,** v.2. **Speak unto the children of Israel, saying, if a soul shall sin through ignorance**, in an unintentional offense, **against any of the commandments of the Lord concerning things which ought not to be done, and shall do against any of them;** (the sacrifices enumerated till now were free-will offerings and could be brought even when there was no specific occasion, whenever the heart of the individual prompted him to seek the Lord's fellowship in sacrifice, prayer, and sacrificial meal; but there were times and occasions when certain sacrifices had to be made, as when an unintentional trespass had occurred. This included all sins of weakness, not only such as had been committed in ignorance, haste, and negligence, but also such in which the weakness of the flesh had overcome the good intention of the believer); v.3. **if the**

priest that is anointed do sin according to the sin of the people, the reference here very probably being to the high priest, who was in a special sense the anointed of the Lord among the priests; if this high priest in his official capacity, as the representative of the people, should become guilty of such an unintentional sin, **then let him bring for his sin which he hath sinned a young bullock without blemish unto the Lord for a sin-offering,** the most conspicuous sacrificial animal because of the priest's high position. V.4. **And he shall bring the bullock unto the door of the Tabernacle of the Congregation,** where all the sacrificial animals were officially delivered, **before the Lord, and shall lay his hand up on the bullock's head,** in the gesture signifying the transmission of his own guilt upon the substitute victim, **and kill the bullock before the Lord,** the animal taking the place of the guilty man. V.5. **And the priest that is anointed,** the high priest, **shall take of the bullock's blood, and bring it to the Tabernacle of the Congregation,** into the Holy Place; v.6. **and the priest shall dip his finger in the blood, and sprinkle of the blood seven times before the Lord, before the veil of the Sanctuary,** the heavy curtain that screened the ark in the Most Holy Place. V.7. **And the priest shall put some of the blood up on the horns of the altar of sweet incense before the Lord, which is in the Tabernacle of the Congregation,** the horns of the golden altar being used only in this case and when the entire nation was concerned, since the offense was considered especially grave; **and shall pour all the blood of the bullock,** the great bulk of it, but little haying been used for the ceremonies of the Holy Place, **at the bottom of the altar of the burnt offering, which**

is at the door of the Tabernacle of the Congregation, out in the open court. The sacrificial blood, which was to expiate the sin, was thus placed very prominently before the eyes of the Lord, in order to plead for His forgiveness. V.8. **And he shall take off from it all the fat of the bullock for the sin-offering; the fat that covereth the inwards,** the large net of adipose membrane in the abdominal cavity, **and all the fat that is up on the inwards,** the loose fat along the intestines, v.9. **and the two kidneys, and the fat that is up on them, which is by the flanks,** attached to the muscles of the upper pelvic region, **and the caul above the liver,** the small net of adipose membrane which extends from the liver to the kidneys, **with the kidneys, it shall he take away,** v.10. **as it was taken off from the bullock of the sacrifice of peace-offerings,** chap. 3, 3. 4; **and the priest shall burn them upon the altar of the burnt offering.** V.11. **And the skin of the bullock, and all his flesh, with his head, and with his legs, and his inwards, and his dung,** v.12. **even the whole bullock shall he carry forth without the camp unto a clean place, where the ashes are poured out** when they were carried out from time to time out of the court of the Tabernacle, **and burn him on the wood with fire; where the ashes are poured out shall he be burned.** This complete removal of the sacrifice of sin-offering signified that the sin for which it was brought was now put away entirely, and the whole ceremony was intended to express the fact that the fellowship with God, which had been disturbed or severed by the sinful act, was now once more restored to its original integrity.

FOR THE WHOLE CONGREGATION. - V.13. **And if the whole congregation of Israel sin through ignorance,** that is, through inadvertence due either to unconsciousness of the act's sinfulness or to lack of information on certain points of the Law, **and the thing be hid from the eyes of the assembly, and they have done somewhat** (something) **against any of the commandments of the Lord concerning things which should not be done, and are guilty,** although, for the time being, still in ignorance of that fact; v.14. **when the sin, which they have sinned against it, is known, then the congregation,** as a body, **shall offer a young bullock For the sin, and bring him before the Tabernacle of the Congregation.** V.15. **And the elders of the congregation,** as the representatives of the entire people, **shall lay their hands up on the head of the bullock before the Lord,** both in confessing the sin and expressing the transfer of the sin to the sacrificial animal; **and the bullock shall be killed before the Lord.** V.16. **And the priest that is anointed, the high priest, shall bring of the bullock's blood,** which was caught up as usual, **to the Tabernacle of the Congregation**, to the Holy Place; v.17. **and the priest shall dip his finger in some of the blood, and sprinkle it seven times before the Lord, even before the veil,** behind which was the throne of the Lord, the mercy-seat of the ark. V.18. **And he shall put some of the blood up on the horns of the altar which is before the Lord, that is in the Tabernacle of the Congregation,** the golden altar of incense, **and shall pour out all the blood at the bottom of the altar of the burnt offering, which is at the door of the Tabernacle of the Congregation.** V.19. **And he shall take all his fat from him, and burn it up on the altar.** V.20. **And he shall do with the bullock as he did with the bullock for a sin-**

offering, that offered by the high priest, **so shall he do with this; and the priest shall make an atonement For them, and it shall be forgiven them.** V.21. **And he shall carry forth the bullock without the camp and burn him as he burned the first bullock, it is a sin-offering for the congregation,** The high priest here acted as the mediator of the people, and the meaning of the entire ceremony was this, that the sin was covered, put out of sight, not, of course, as if the wrong could be undone, but that God had so hidden it as to have the sinner stand in His presence without fault. The sin-offering, in this case especially, was a symbol of the perfect sacrifice of Jesus Christ, as He gave Himself for the sins of the whole world, and of the atonement which He gained by it. At the same time we Christians must riot lose sight of the fact that, if we sin willfully after we have received the knowledge of the truth, there remaineth no more sacrifice for sins, Heb. 10, 26.

FOR A RULER. - V.22. **When a ruler,** one of the princes of the people, **hath sinned, and done somewhat through ignorance against any of the commandments of the Lord, his God, concerning things which should not be done, and is guilty;** v.23. **or if his sin wherein he hath sinned come to his knowledge,** if someone point out to him his deviation from the exact line of God's will, **he shall bring his offering, a kid of the goats, a Male without blemish,** a sacrifice which later, Num. 15, 24, is enumerated with that of the whole congregation; v.24. **and he shall lay his hand up on the head of the goat,** as the substitute victim, **and kill it in the place where they kill the burnt offering before the Lord; it is a sin-offering.** V.25. **And the priest shall take of the blood of the sin-offering**

with his finger, and put it up on the horns of the altar of burnt offering, and shall pour out his blood at the bottom of the altar of burnt offering. In this case the ceremonies of sprinkling before the veil of the Most Holy Place and of smearing the blood on the horns of the golden altar of incense were omitted. V.26. **And he shall burn all his fat upon the altar, as the fat of the sacrifice of peace-offerings,** chap. 3, 5; **and the priest shall make an atonement for him as concerning his sin, and it shall be forgiven him.** The ordinance concerning the disposition of the flesh is given chap. 6, 26-29.

FOR THE COMMON PEOPLE. - V.27. **And if any one of the common people,** any person, man or woman, native Jew or sojourning foreigner, Num. 15, **sin through ignorance,** in the same inadvertent manner as in the cases considered till now, **while he doeth somewhat against any of the commandments of the Lord concerning things which ought not to be done, and be guilty;** v.28. **or if his sin which he hath sinned come to his knowledge,** if some one informs him of the wrong which he has committed, **then he shall bring his offering, a kid of the goats,** the shaggy variety being specified here, as above, **a female without blemish, for his sin which he hath sinned,** to make atonement for him. V.29. **And he shall lay his hand upon the head of the sin-offering, and slay the sin-offering in the place of the burnt offering,** on the north side of the large altar in the court. V.30. **And the priest shall take of the blood thereof with his finger, and put it upon the horns of the altar of burnt offering, and shall pour out all the blood thereof at the bottom of the altar.** V.31. **And he shall take away all the fat** thereof, **as the fat is taken away from off the sacrifice of peace-offerings,** the same loose pieces of fat from the various parts of the abdominal cavity; **and the priest shall burn it upon the altar for a sweet savor unto the Lord; and the priest shall make an atonement for him, and it shall be forgiven him,** the Lord accepting the sacrifice in mercy, as an offering of propitiation. V.32. **And if he bring a lamb for a sin-offering, he shall bring it a female without blemish;** this was the alternative for a sacrificial animal. V.33. **And he (the worshiper) shall lay his hand upon the head of the sin-offering, and slay it for a sin-offering in the place where they kill the burnt offering.** V.34. **And the priest shall take of the blood of the sin-offering with his finger, and put it upon the horns of the altar of burnt offering, and shall pour out all the blood thereof at the bottom of the altar;** v.35. **and he shall take away all the fat thereof, as the fat of the lamb is taken away from the sacrifice of the peace-offerings,** chap. 3, 9. 10; **and the priest shall burn them upon the altar, of burnt offering, according to the offerings made by fire unto the Lord; and the priest shall make an atonement for his sin that he hath committed, and it shall be forgiven him.** Thus the Lord in mercy provided a way for the believers of the Old Testament by which, although in a symbolical manner, they received the assurance of the forgiveness of their sins, the blood of their sacrifices foreshadowing the greater, the perfect sacrifice of Jesus Christ, who has found an eternal redemption for us.

47

Leviticus 5

Of Sin- and Trespass-offerings.

SPECIAL CASES OF SIN-OFFERINGS. - V.1. **And if a soul sin, and hear the voice of swearing, and is a witness, whether he hath seen or known of it; if he do not utter it, then he shall bear his iniquity.** This is the first of several special cases in which a sin-offering was commanded. In the Jewish forms of trial the judge adjured those present, those summoned for that purpose, to tell the whole truth concerning the case, as they knew it, whether their knowledge was that of eye-witnesses or had been derived from other reliable sources. To feign ignorance at such a time and not to perform one's duty as required of witnesses made a person guilty before God, and unless this guilt was removed, the person in question had to suffer the consequences. Among these are mentioned sickness, childlessness, and even total extirpation of the family. V.2. **Or if a soul touch any unclean thing, whether it be a**

carcass of an unclean beast, of some wild animal, **or a carcass of unclean cattle,** of domestic animals, **or the carcass of unclean creeping things,** of reptiles, **and if it be hidden from him,** if he is not aware of it at the time, **he also shall be unclean and guilty.** V.3. **Or if he touch the uncleanness of man,** anything which caused a man to be ceremonially unclean, **whatsoever uncleanness it be that a man shall be defiled withal, and it be hid from him; when he knoweth of it,** that is, when he finds out about the defilement and yet omits the simple forms of purification which were provided in such cases, chap. 11, 24-40; 15, 5. 8. 21; Num. 19, 22, **then he shall be guilty,** atonement should be made for the sin which he committed, for the guilt which he heaped upon himself. V.4. **Or if a soul swear, pronouncing with his lips to do evil, or to do good, whatsoever it be that a man shall pronounce with an oath, and it be hid from him;** this is said of oaths as they are often made in trivial, foolish, unimportant matters, in heedlessness, recklessness, or passion, the person afterward forgetting or neglecting to keep the solemn promises and lightly disregarding the fact that such playing with sacred matters is sinful; **when he knoweth of it,** when it is brought to his attention and he does nothing to remove the sin, **then he shall be guilty in one of these,** in one of the three cases here enumerated. V.5. **And it shall be, when he shall be guilty in one of these things, that he shall confess that he hath sinned in that thing,** acknowledge the particular fault concerned before presenting the sacrificial animal. V.6. **And he shall bring his trespass-offering** (or guilt-offering) **unto the Lord for his sin which he hath sinned,** for the expiation of the guilt which he has loaded upon himself, **a female from the flock, a lamb or a kid of the goats, for a sin-offering; and the priest shall make an atonement for him concerning his sin,** cause his sin to be covered over before the face of the just and righteous God by virtue of the sacrifice which pointed forward to the perfect sacrifice of Jesus Christ. V.7. **And if he be not able to bring a lamb,** if, on account of poverty, he cannot afford the more expensive animal, **then he shall bring for his trespass which he hath committed two turtle-doves or two young pigeons unto the Lord, one for a sin-offering and the other for a burnt offering,** the two together forming a full sin-offering, and being given different names only on account of the different treatment which they received. V.8. **And he shall bring them unto the priest, who shall offer that which is for the sin-offering first, and wring off his head from his neck,** kill the bird by pinching off his neck immediately behind his head, **but shall not divide it asunder,** not sever it entirely; v.9. **and he shall sprinkle of the blood of the sin-offering upon the side of the altar,** none of it, in this case, being smeared on the horns, probably because the amount was so small; **and the rest of the blood shall be wrung out at the bottom of the altar; it is a sin-offering.** V.10. **And he shall offer the second for a burnt offering, according to the manner,** as the ordinance of the Lord prescribed: **and the priest shall make an atonement for him for his sin which he hath sinned, and it shall be forgiven him.** The ritual in this case was the same as when birds were offered for a burnt offering, chap. 1, 15-17. Through the symbolic rite of the atonement by blood the forgiveness of sins was secured for the believer. V.11. **But if**

he be not able to bring two turtle-doves or two young pigeons, if the condition of poverty be very extreme, **then he that sinned shall bring for his offering the tenth part of an ephah of fine flour** (about two and one half quarts) **for a sin-offering. He shall put no oil upon it, neither shall he put any frankincense thereon, as in the case of the meat-offerings;** for it is a sin-offering and, although offered without blood, was permitted in exceptional instances, since it was supplemented by the annual sacrifice on the Day of Atonement. V.12. **Then shall he bring it to the priest, and the priest shall take his handful of it, even a memorial thereof, and burn it on the altar,** the intention being to bring the worshiper into remembrance before God, **according to the offerings made by fire unto the Lord; it is a sin-offering,** and such an offering must not be mingled with the symbols of the Spirit and of the praise of God. V.13. **And the priest shall make an atonement for him as touching his sin that he hath sinned in one of these,** in the instances named above, **and it shall be forgiven him; and the remnant shall be the priest's, as a meat-offering.** This part was consecrated or set apart to be food for the priests in the holy place of the Sanctuary.

TRESPASS-OFFERINGS IN CASE OF IGNORANCE. V.14. **And the Lord spake unto Moses, saying,** v.15. **if a soul commit a trespass,** break the faith, neglect to discharge a debt due to God or man, the former sins only being considered here, **and sin through ignorance in the holy things of the Lord, then he shall bring for his trespass unto the Lord a ram without blemish out of the flocks, with thy estimation by shekels of silver, after**

the shekel of the Sanctuary, for a trespass-offering. The sin consisted here in withholding from the Lord the things that were consecrated to Him, first-fruits, tithes, or any gifts connected with the service of the Sanctuary. In the wilderness it was Moses, and afterward it was the officiating priest, who estimated the sacrificial animal, for its value had to be at least two shekels. V.16. **And he shall make amends for the harm that he hath done in the holy thing,** in neglecting to perform the services which were due to the Lord, **and shall add the fifth part thereto, and give it unto the priest,** as a penalty or forfeit for neglecting so important a duty toward the Lord; **and the priest shall make an atonement for him with the ram of the trespass-offering, and it shall be forgiven him,** the ceremony being performed as described in chap. 7. 1-6. V.17. **And if a soul sin and commit any of these things which are forbidden to be done by the commandments of the Lord;** the previous case was one of omission, the present case one of commission; **though he wist it not,** was not aware or did not realize the sinfulness of the act as it was being done, **yet is he guilty, and shall bear his iniquity.** By breaking a commandment of the Lord he had infringed upon some of the Lord's sovereign rights, and the guilt would rest upon him until such a time as atonement would be made, V.18. **And he shall bring a ram without blemish out of the flock, with thy estimation, for a trespass-offering, unto the priest; and the priest shall make an atonement for him concerning his ignorance wherein he erred and wist it not,** the transgressions of inadvertence, and it shall be forgiven him. V.19. **It is a trespass-offering; he hath certainly trespassed against**

the Lord. The sacrifice served for satisfaction, to make good the injury which had been inflicted. So far as the believers of the New Testament are concerned, they will take occasion regularly to examine their lives, and if they have become guilty of any transgression in word or deed, they will confess their sin to the Lord, asking forgiveness for the sake of Jesus.

48

Leviticus 6

A Summary Concerning offerings.

OF TRESPASS-OFFERINGS. - V.1. **And the Lord spake unto Moses, saying,** v.2. **if a soul sin and commit a trespass against the Lord,** break faith over against the Lord in some sin against his neighbor, - for the one included the other, - **and lie unto his neighbor in that which was delivered him to keep,** if he denies altogether having received anything of his neighbor in trust, **or in fellowship,** if he disclaims the receipt of some security, **or in a thing taken away by violence,** if he falsely states that he did not come into possession of his neighbor's property by sinful methods, **or hath deceived his neighbor,** in taking something from him by extortion or by a refusal to pay a just claim, if he invents excuses for the purpose of defrauding his neighbor, because he refuses to restore such property which he wrongfully holds; v.3. **or have found that which was lost, and lieth concerning it, and**

sweareth falsely, if he adds perjury to the sins which he has already committed against the Seventh Commandment; **in any of all these that a man doeth, sinning therein,** v.4. **then it shall be, because he hath sinned and is guilty, that he shall restore that which he took violently away, or the thing which he hath deceitfully gotten, or that which was delivered him to keep, or the lost thing which he found,** whether the sin was done secretly or openly, whether extortion or fraud was committed, with or without a show of right, v.5. **or all that about which he hath sworn falsely; he shall even restore it in the principal, and shall add the fifth part more thereto, as a penalty or forfeit, and give it unto him to whom it appertaineth, in the day of his trespass-offering.** The unlawfully gotten gain having been restored to his neighbor, the Lord also had to he reconciled, because the transgression was also directed against Him, Ps. 51, 4. So man could seek the divine forgiveness without having done all in his power to make amends for the wrong committed. V.6. **And he shall bring his trespass-offering unto the Lord, a ram without blemish out of the flock, with thy estimation, for a trespass-offering unto the priest;** v.7. **and the priest shall make an atonement for him before the Lord; and it shall be forgiven him for anything of all that he hath done in trespassing therein,** as in the trespass-offering which was concerned exclusively with the Lord, chap. 5, 14-19; for these verses really belong to that paragraph and are so given in the Hebrew text. If Christians have been overcome by sin and are in any way guilty over against their neighbors, they should hasten to confess their sins and ask God for forgiveness in Christ Jesus, At the same time it is self-evident that they will make amends as quickly as possible, and as far as in their power lies.

OF BURNT OFFERINGS. - V.8. **And the Lord spake unto Moses, saying,** v.9. **Command Aaron and his sons, saying, This is the law of the burnt offering: It is the burnt offering, because of the burning upon the altar all night unto the morning, and the fire of the altar shall be burning in it.** All the paragraphs following contain special instructions for the priests with regard to the various offerings. The first paragraph relates to the daily burnt offering of a lamb at evening and in the morning, which was made at the cost of the entire congregation. Cp. Ex. 29, 38; Num. 28, 3. "The slow fire of the evening sacrifice was to be so arranged as to last until the morning; that of the morning sacrifice was ordinarily added to by other offerings, or if not, could easily be made to last through the much shorter interval until the evening. The evening sacrifice is naturally mentioned first because, in the Hebrew division of time, this was the beginning of the day." V.10. **And the priest shall put on his linen garment,** Ex. 28, 40, **and his linen breeches shall be put upon his flesh, and take up the ashes which the fire hath consumed with the burnt offering on the altar;** the sacrifices having been turned to ashes in the burning, the officiating priest was to remove all these ashes; **and he shall put them beside the altar,** a special place being provided for that purpose on the east side of the court. V.11. **And he shall put off his garments, and put on other garments, and carry forth the ashes without the camp unto a clean place.** This duty was afterward performed by such members of the priestly family as were excluded from officiating at the altar by some bodily defect, chap. 21, 16-23. During the wilderness journey some clean place outside of the camp could be used for the ashes from the altar of burnt offering; when the sanctuary of the Lord was in the Temple at Jerusalem, a place outside of the city was chosen. V.12. **And the fire upon the altar shall be burning in it; it shall not be put out,** even when there were no sacrifices to be burned; **and the priest shall burn wood on it every morning,** build up a great, glowing fire from the embers that had kept the fire going during the night, **and lay the burnt offering in order upon it; and he shall burn there on the fat of the peace-offerings,** chap. 3. V.13. **The fire shall ever be burning upon the altar; it shall never go out.** It signified the continual, uninterrupted fellowship of the children of Israel with the covenant God. In the heart of the Christians the flame of love toward God should burn at all times with unabated vigor, until the worshiper passes from believing to seeing.

OF MEAT-OFFERINGS. - V.14. **And this is the law of the meat-offering,** as far as the priests were concerned: **The sons of Aaron shall offer it before the Lord, before the altar.** Cp. chap. 2, 2. 8. V.15. **And he,** the officiating priest, **shall take of it his handful, of the flour of the meat-offering,** as much as his hand would hold, **and of the oil thereof, and all the frankincense which is upon the meat-offering, and shall burn it upon the altar,** of burnt offering, **for a sweet savor, even the memorial of it, unto the Lord.** V.16. **And the remainder thereof shall Aaron and his sons eat,** this ordinance being an addition to the directions which had been given before; **with unleavened bread,** or as unleavened bread, **shall it be eaten in the Holy Place,** no leaven or yeast being permitted in the preparation of this bread; **in the court of the Tabernacle of the Congregation they shall eat it,** where they were stationed when on duty. V.17. **It shall not be baken with leaven. I have given it unto them for their portion of My offerings made by fire; it is most holy, as is the sin-offering and as the trespass-offering.** The entire offering was consecrated to the Lord, and He chose to give the greater portion of it to the priests for their maintenance. V.18. **All the males among the children of Aaron shall eat of it,** even such as were too young or too old to be actively engaged in the priestly functions. **It shall be a statute forever in your generations concerning the offerings of the Lord made by fire; every one that toucheth them shall be holy.** Only those that were set apart for the service of the Lord were permitted to partake of them, and any layman that touched them henceforth had the duty to keep himself from all uncleanness, just like the priests themselves. All Christians are priests of the most holy God and will therefore guard against defilement of every kind.

THE OFFERING OF CONSECRATION. - V.19. **And the Lord spake unto Moses, saying,** v.20. **This is the offering of Aaron and of his sons which they shall offer unto the Lord in the day when he is anointed,** when he was ordained and inducted into office, it being his daily sacrifice: **the tenth part of an ephah of fine flour for a meat-offering perpetual, half of it in the morning and half thereof at night;** it was the high priest's daily oblation, in order to maintain his fellowship with God. V.21. **In a pan it shall be made with oil; and when it is baken, thou shalt bring it in,** roasted or fried; **and the baken pieces of the meat-offering shalt thou offer for a sweet**

306

savor unto the Lord, the sacrifice in its finished form being broken in pieces in the act of offering. V.22. **And the priest of his sons that is anointed in his stead shall offer it,** this solemn ceremony being one of the first acts of every new high priest; **it is a statute forever unto the Lord; it shall be wholly burned,** for it was considered a part of a burnt offering, and in those the worshiper had no part. V.23. **For every meat-offering for the priest shall be wholly burned; it shall not be eaten.** The priest himself being the worshiper, the entire oblation went to the Lord.

OF SIN-OFFERINGS. - V.24. **And the Lord spake unto Moses, saying,** v.25. **Speak unto Aaron and to his sons, saying, This is the law of the sin-offering: in the place where the burnt offering is killed,** on the north side of the altar, in the court of the Tabernacle, **shall the sin-offering be killed before the Lord; it is most holy,** set apart for the Lord. V.26. **The priest that offereth it for sin shall eat it,** that is, all but the fat of the abdominal cavity and the kidneys, unless it was specifically ordered that the entire animal had to he burned outside the camp; **in the Holy Place shall it be eaten, in the court of the Tabernacle of the Congregation.** V.27. **Whatsoever shall touch the flesh thereof shall be holy** (cp. v.18); **and when there is sprinkled of the blood thereof upon any garment, thou shalt wash that whereon it was sprinkled in the Holy Place.** So strict was the Law in this case that the priest had to have the dress of the worshiper washed before he left the court of the Sanctuary, in case any of the blood of the sacrificial animal was spattered on it. The entire animal with its blood belonged to the Lord, and not even a drop of the latter could he carried out of the Sanctuary on the garment of the worshiper. V.28. **But the earthen vessel wherein it is sodden shall be broken,** since the blood and the juices of the flesh would he absorbed by the unglazed material; **and if it be sodden in a brazen pot, it shall be both scoured and rinsed in water,** so that no particle of the sacrifice would cling to it. V.29. **All the males among the priests shall eat thereof; it is most holy.** V.30. **And no sin-offering whereof any of the blood is brought in to the Tabernacle of the Congregation to reconcile withal in the Holy Place,** as in the sin-offering for the priest and for the entire congregation, also on the Day of Atonement, chap. 4; 16, 27, **shall be eaten; it shall be burnt in the fire.** Also in this respect the sin-offering for the whole congregation was a type of Christ, who suffered for our sins without the gate, Heb. 13, 11. 12.

49

Leviticus 7

Various Ordinances Concerning Sacrifices.

O F TRESPASS-OFFERINGS. - V.1. **Likewise this is the law of the trespass-offering: It is most holy.** The difference between the sin-offering and the trespass-offering may in general be said to consist in this, that the latter was required in the case of more serious offenses, V.2. **In the place where they kill the burnt offering shall they kill the trespass-offering,** that is, north of the altar in the court; **and the blood thereof shall he sprinkle round about upon the altar,** upon its four walls. V.3. **And he shall offer of it all the fat thereof; the rump, and the fat that covereth the inwards,** the large net of adipose membrane, v.4. **and the two kidneys, and the fat that is on them, which is by the flanks,** attached to the muscles in the upper part of the pelvic region, **and the caul,** the smaller net of adipose tissue, **that is above the liver, with the kidneys,** upon the kidneys, **it shall he** take away; v.5. **and the priest shall burn them upon the altar for an offering made by fire unto the Lord; it is a trespass-offering.** V.6. **Every male among the priests shall eat thereof,** as in the case of the sin-offering, chap. 6, 26; **it shall be eaten in the Holy Place; it is most holy.** V.7. **As the sin-offering is, so is the trespass-offering; there is one law for them,** for every act that brings guilt upon a person, whether it is a sin of ignorance or a more serious transgression, is in need of atonement; **the priest that maketh atonement therewith shall have it;** not the priests on duty in a body, but the individual officiating priest received the flesh of the sacrificial animal. V.8. **And the priest that offereth any man's burnt offering, even the priest, shall have to himself the skin of the burnt offering which he hath offered.** The Hebrew text brings out with great emphasis the fact that the skin of the slain animal was to belong to the officiating priest. It was a part of the payment for his services. V.9. **And all the meat-offering that is baken in the oven, and all that is dressed in the frying-pan,** cooked in the kettle, and in the pan, **shall be the priest's that offereth it,** with the exception, of course, of the handful which was burned as a memorial to the Lord. V.10. **And every meat-offering, mingled with oil, and dry, shall all the sons of Aaron have, one as much as another.** Thus was the distinction observed between the dry, or uncooked, meat-offering and that prepared on or in the oven. Incidentally, the people were always reminded of the fact that the laborer was worthy of his reward.

OF PEACE-OFFERINGS. - V.11. **And this is the law of sacrifice of peace-offerings which he shall offer unto the Lord.** The peace-offerings were made for the purpose of establishing and maintaining the fellowship with the covenant God, and may be divided into offerings of thanksgiving and into vow or voluntary offerings. V.12. **If he offer it for a thanksgiving,** in grateful acknowledgment of some special favor shown him by the Lord, **then he shall offer with the sacrifice of thanksgiving unleavened cakes mingled with oil, and unleavened wafers anointed with oil, and cakes mingled with oil, of fine flour, fried.** Cp. chap. 2, 4. 5. V.13. **Besides the cakes,** which were unleavened, **he shall offer for his offering leavened bread with the sacrifice of thanksgiving of his peace-offerings.** V.14. **And of it,** of the entire gift as presented to the Lord, **he shall offer one out of the whole oblation for an heave-offering unto the Lord,** one of each kind of cakes, **and it shall be the priest's that sprinkleth the blood of the peace-offerings,** the rest being returned to the worshiper for the sacrificial meal. The heave-offering was taken into the hands and waved up and down before the altar, but not placed upon it. V.15. **And the flesh of the sacrifice of his peace-offerings for thanksgiving shall be eaten the same day that it is offered; he shall not leave any of it until the morning.** This provision applied specifically to this form of the peace-offering: the sacrificial meal was to be held the same day. V.16. **But if the sacrifice of his offering be a vow or a voluntary offering,** brought whenever a believer felt the need of cementing the fellowship between himself and the Lord, **it shall be eaten the same day that he offereth his sacrifice; and on the morrow also the remainder of it shall be eaten,** two days being allowed in this case for consuming the flesh of the sacrificial animal; v.17. **but the remainder of the flesh of the sacrifice**

on the third day shall be burned with fire, and thus be destroyed completely. V.18. **And if any of the flesh of the sacrifice of his peace-offerings be eaten at all on the third day,** in violation of God's will, **it shall not be accepted,** the entire sacrifice would be made in vain, **neither shall it be imputed unto him that offereth it,** that is, as a sacrifice which is well-pleasing to the Lord; **it shall be an abomination,** hateful and nauseating to God, **and the soul that eateth of it shall bear his iniquity,** not only the worshiper immediately concerned, but also the members of his family and his friends who might partake of the meal. V.19. **And the flesh that toucheth any unclean thing shall not be eaten,** in such event it must be discarded at once; **it shall be burned with fire; and as for the flesh, all that be clean shall eat thereof,** that is, of the clean flesh of the sacrifice. V.20. **But the soul that eateth of the flesh of the sacrifice of peace-offerings that pertain unto the Lord,** that have been consecrated to Him by the offering, **having his uncleanness upon him,** any form of Levitical defilement, **even that soul shall be cut off from his people.** V.21. **Moreover, the soul that shall touch any unclean thing, as the uncleanness of man, or any unclean beast, or any abominable unclean thing,** cp. chaps. 12-15, **and eat of the flesh of the sacrifice of peace-offerings which pertain unto the Lord, even that soul shall be cut off from his people.** The abomination spoken of here included all the unclean fishes, birds, and smaller mammals, and the defilement of unclean animals was confined to their carcasses, carrion being considered especially filthy. The Lord indicates here that He wants pure hands and pure hearts in His service. But to this day true sacrifices of thanksgiving and the paying of vows are acts well-pleasing to the Lord, if they are done in true faith and love toward Him, Ps. 50, 14.

THE EATING OF FAT AND BLOOD FORBIDDEN. - **V.22. And the Lord spake unto Moses, saying,** v.23. **Speak unto the children of Israel, saying, Ye shall eat no manner of fat, of ox, or of sheep, or of goat.** This seems to apply to the fat of the abdominal cavity in sacrificial animals only, chap. 3, 17. V.24. **And the fat of the beast that dieth of itself,** its blood therefore not having a chance to drain out, **and the fat of that which is torn with beasts, may be used in any other use,** for purposes of every-day life; **but ye shall in no wise eat of it,** for animals that found their death in this manner were unclean and defiled those that ate of their flesh or of their fat. V.25. **For whosoever eateth the fat of the beast, of which men offer an offering made by fire unto the Lord,** the loose fat of the abdominal cavity, **even the soul that eateth it shall be cut off from his people.** V.26. **Moreover, ye shall eat no manner of blood,** a prohibition which had been given as early as the time of Noah, Gen. 9, 4; cp. chap. 3, 17; 17, 10-14, **whether it be of fowl or of beast, in any of your dwellings.** V.27. **Whatsoever soul it be that eateth any manner of blood, even that soul shall be cut off from his people.** The blood was regarded as the bearer of the soul of the animal, and the latter had been set apart for the atonement of men; hence its great value and the strictness of the prohibition. As a holy people, the children of Israel were to avoid every form of defilement.

THE PORTION OF JEHOVAH. - **V.28. And the Lord spake unto Moses, saying,** v.29. **Speak unto the children** of Israel, saying, **he that offereth the sacrifice of his peace-offerings unto the Lord shall bring his oblation unto the Lord of the sacrifice of his peace-offerings,** that special gift which belonged to the Lord and was intended to establish the fellowship between Him and the worshiper. V.30. **His own hands shall bring the offerings of the Lord made by fire,** the parts consecrated to Jehovah, **the fat with the breast, it shall he bring,** in person, not by the hands of a servant or messenger, **that the breast may be waved for a wave-offering before the Lord.** This part of the animal is now known as the brisket, and it was offered to the Lord by moving the hands back and forth in a motion of weaving. V.31. **And the priest shall burn the fat upon the altar; but the breast shall be Aaron's and his sons',** the common property of the priestly order. V.32. **And the right shoulder shall ye give unto the priest,** the officiating priest alone, **for an heave-offering of the sacrifices of your peace-offerings.** The ceremony of offering here consisted in a simple lifting up of the gift on high. V.33. **He among the sons of Aaron that offereth the blood of the peace-offerings and the fat shall have the right shoulder for his part.** V.34. **For the wave-breast and the heave-shoulder have I taken of the children of Israel from off the sacrifices of their peace-offerings, and have given them unto Aaron, the priest, and unto his sons by a statute forever from among the children of Israel.** As long as the Aaronic priesthood was to endure, so long were the Israelites to make their payment of fees to the priests as here set forth. V.35. **This is the portion of the anointing of Aaron and of the anointing of his sons,** these are the parts of the animals which were set aside for their emoluments, **out of the offerings of the Lord made by fire, in the day when he presented them to minister unto the Lord in the priest's office,** these were their fees beginning with the day that Moses inducted them into office; v.36. **which the Lord commanded to be given them of the children of Israel in the day that he** (Moses) **anointed them, by a statute forever throughout their generations.** V.37. **This is the law of the burnt offering, of the meat-offering, and of the sin-offering, and of the trespass-offering, and of the consecrations,** of the fillings of the hands which characterized the priest's work, Ex. 29, 19-28; Lev. 6, 20, **and of the sacrifice of the peace-offerings,** the whole law of sacrifice having been given in the preceding chapters; v.38. **which the Lord commanded Moses in Mount Sinai, in the day that He commanded the children of Israel to offer their oblations,** both their voluntary gifts and their stated sacrifices, **unto the Lord, in the Wilderness of Sinai.** All the sacrificial meals of the Old Testament were but weak types of the intimate fellowship with God which we, as the members of the household of God, enjoy in the Gospel, Luke 14, 15; 22, 30.

50

Leviticus 8

The Consecration of Aaron and His Sons.

PUTTING ON THE GARMENTS. - V.1. **And the
Lord spake unto Moses, saying, v.2. take Aaron
and his sons with him, and the garments, and
the anointing oil, and a bullock for the sin-offering,
and two rams, and a basket of unleavened bread; v.3.
and gather thou all the congregation together unto
the door of the Tabernacle of the Congregation.** The
detailed instructions of the Lord regarding the consecration
of the priests, Ex. 28, 29, and 40, were now to be carried out.
"This is the ordinance: first the persons; then the garments,
as symbols of the office: the anointing oil, the symbol of
the Spirit; the bullock for the sin-offering, the symbol of
the priest favored with the entrusted atonement, and yet
needing favor; the ram for the burnt offering, the symbol
of the sacrificial employment; the ram for the sacrifice of
consecration, the symbol of the priestly emoluments in true

316

sacrifices of consecration; and the basket of unleavened bread, the symbol of life's enjoyment of the priests, sanctified in every form by the oil of the Spirit." (Lange.) V.4. **And Moses did as the Lord commanded him; and the assembly was gathered together unto the door of the Tabernacle of the Congregation.** V.5. **And Moses said unto the congregation, This is the thing which the Lord commanded to be done.** Very likely Moses repeated the entire ordinance referring to the consecration of the priests before the act of consecration was begun, as he had recorded the Lord's words. V.6. **And Moses brought Aaron and his sons, and washed them with water,** very likely the whole body, a screen obviating the apparent impropriety, as on the Day of Atonement. This washing was symbolical of the purity of soul required in all those that draw near to God, and applies to all believers of the New Testament, as kings and priests before God and the Father. V.7. **And he put upon him the coat,** the long garment of shining byssus, **and girded him with the girdle, and clothed him with the robe,** the hyacinth-colored, close-fitting tunic, **and put the ephod upon him, and he girded him with the curious** (skillfully made) **girdle of the ephod,** of variegated material, **and bound it unto him there with.** V.8. **And he put the breastplate upon him,** fastening it to the front of the ephod; **also he put in the breastplate,** in the pocket formed by the doubling of the material, **the Urim and the Thummim.** Cp. Ex. 28, 30. V.9. **And he put the miter upon his head; also upon the miter, even upon his forefront, did he put the golden plate, the holy crown,** the diadem of holiness, with the inscription, "Holiness unto the Lord," **as the Lord commanded Moses.** V.10. **And Moses took the**

anointing oil, and anointed the Tabernacle, the curtains or hangings of the tent, **and all that was there in,** the Ark of the Covenant, the altar of incense, the table of showbread, the candlestick, and all their instruments, **and sanctified them.** V.11. **And he sprinkled thereof upon the altar,** namely, of burnt offering, **seven times**, **and anointed the altar and all his vessels, both the laver and his foot, to sanctify them,** Ex. 40, 6-10. V.12. **And he poured of the anointing oil upon Aaron's head, and anointed him, to sanctify him.** According to Jewish tradition, the anointing of the ordinary priests, which is not mentioned here, although referred to repeatedly, as in Num. 3, 3, differed from that of the high priest inasmuch as the oil was applied to their foreheads only. V.13. **And Moses brought Aaron's sons, and put coats upon them, and girded them with girdles, and put bonnets,** bound caps, **upon them, as the Lord commanded Moses.** The minuteness of the description shows how thoroughly the believers of the Old Testament were in bondage under externals, Gal. 4, 3, from whose dominion we have been freed by the work of Christ.

THE SACRIFICES. - V.14. **And he brought the bullock for the sin-offering,** Moses here, as the mediator of the covenant, performing the functions of the Lord's priest, **And Aaron and his sons laid their hands upon the head of the bullock for the sin-offering,** in token of the transfer of their guilt to the sacrificial animal. V.15. **And he slew it; and Moses took the blood, and put it upon the horns of the altar round about with his finger, and purified the altar, and poured the blood at the bottom of the altar, and sanctified it to make reconciliation upon it.** The altar of burnt offering, although consecrated to the Lord, was yet in need of the purifying blood, in order to sanctify it for the service of the priests, to cover the sins with which they, as sinful men, would defile it while performing the work of their ministry. V.16. **And he took all the fat that was upon the inwards, and the caul above the liver, and the two kidneys, and their fat, and Moses burned it upon the altar.** V.17. **But the bullock, and his hide, his flesh, and his dung he burned with fire without the camp,** as in the case of all sin-offerings, chap. 4, 8-12; **as the Lord commanded Moses,** Ex. 29, 12-14. V.18. **And he brought the ram for the burnt offering,** the second of the three great sacrifices; **and Aaron and his sons laid their hands upon the head of the ram,** which thereby was designated as their substitute in the sacrifice. V.19. **And he killed it; and Moses sprinkled the blood upon the altar round about.** V.20. **And he cut the ram in to pieces; and Moses burned the head and the pieces and the fat.** V.21. **And he washed the inwards, the intestines, and the legs in water; and Moses burned the whole ram upon the altar. It was a burnt sacrifice for a sweet savor, and an offering made by fire unto the Lord,** according to the ordinance, chap. 1, 3-9; **as the Lord commanded Moses,** Ex. 29, 15-18. V.22. **And he brought the other ram, the ram of consecration,** literally, the ram of fillings, that with which the hands of Aaron and his sons were to be filled for the wave-offering, as they were about to make it. The ceremony signified that the priests were now set apart for the service of bringing sacrifices in the name of the children of Israel. **And Aaron and his sons laid their hands upon the head of the ram.** V.23. **And he slew it; and Moses took of the blood of it, and put it upon the tip of Aaron's right ear, and upon**

319

**the thumb of his right hand, and upon the great toe
of his right foot,** to signify that he was to hear the Word
of the Lord, perform His will, and walk in the way of His
commandments. V.24. **And he brought Aaron's sons, and
Moses put of the blood upon the tip of their right ear,
and upon the thumbs of their right hands, and upon
the great toes of their right feet. And Moses sprinkled
the blood upon the altar round about.** Cp. Ex. 29, 19.
20. V.25. **And he took the fat, and the rump,** the fatty
tail which is found to this day in the Khirgiz variety of the
Asiatic sheep, **and all the fat that was upon the inwards,
and the caul above the liver, and the two kidneys, and
their fat,** all the fatty membranes and the loose fat of
the abdominal cavity, **and the right shoulder,** commonly
known as the heave shoulder; v.26. **and out of the basket
of unleavened bread that was before the Lord he took
one unleavened cake, and a cake of oiled bread, and
one wafer,** one piece of each variety of meat-offering, **and
put them on the fat and upon the right shoulder;** v.27.
**and he put all upon Aaron's hands and upon his sons'
hands, and waved them for a wave-offering before the
Lord.** He stretched out his hands beneath those of Aaron
and his sons, and then they all together moved their hands
back and forth in a weaving motion, an act which always
signified dedication to the Lord. V.28. **And Moses took
them from off their hands, and burned them on the
altar upon the burnt offering; they were consecrations
for a sweet savor,** sacrifices by which they were really
installed in their office. **It is an offering made by fire
unto the Lord.** Cp. Ex. 29, 22-25. V.29. **And Moses
took the breast and waved it for a wave-offering before**

the Lord; for of the ram of consecration it was Moses' part; as the Lord commanded Moses, Ex. 29, 27. V.30. And Moses took of the anointing oil, and of the blood which was upon the altar, and sprinkled it upon Aaron, and upon his garments, and upon his sons, and upon his sons' garments with him; and sanctified Aaron, and his garments, and his sons, and his sons' garments with him. This ceremony completed the consecration service on this and on each succeeding day. Cp. Ex. 29, 21. The priests were to perform the work of their service in the power of the Spirit of God.

FINAL INSTRUCTIONS. - V.31. And Moses said unto Aaron and to his sons, Boil the flesh at the door of the Tabernacle of the Congregation, in a holy place in the court, Ex. 29, 31; and there eat it with the bread that is in the basket of consecrations, as I commanded, saying, Aaron and his sons shall eat it. No lay person was permitted to partake of this sacrificial meal, for the food was holy, having served for the expiation and consecration of the priests. V.32. And that which remaineth of the flesh and of the bread shall ye burn with fire. Cp. chap. 7, 17. V.33. And ye shall not go out of the door of the Tabernacle of the Congregation, out of the great entrance which led to the Sanctuary, in seven days, until the days of your consecration be at an end; for seven days shall he consecrate you. V.34. As he hath done this day, so the Lord hath commanded to do, to make an atonement for you. On each one of the seven days the same rite was performed, at least so far as the sacrifices were concerned. V.35. Therefore shall ye abide at the door of the Tabernacle of the Congregation day and night

seven days, and keep the charge of the Lord, observe His precept, **that ye die not; for so I am commanded.** V.36. **So Aaron and his sons did all things which the Lord commanded by the hand of Moses.** Seven days they passed in holy seclusion in the court, seven days they brought the appointed sacrifices and lived on the sacrifice of consecration; what remained of it they did not devote to common or profane use, but they took care to burn it. For seven days they kept holy match, the watch of Jehovah, in the court of the Tabernacle, under the penalty of death. Moses made particularly prominent the symbolic force of this divine watch: it was Jehovah's express commandment.

51

Leviticus 9

Aaron enters upon His Office.

THE PREPARATIONS FOR THE SACRIFICES. - V.1. **And it came to pass on the eighth day,** after the seven days of consecration, **that Moses called Aaron and his sons and the elders of Israel,** for it was necessary that the priesthood be in active exercise of its duties at once. V.2. **And he said unto Aaron, take thee a young calf,** a bull calf, or very young bullock, **for a sin-offering, and a ram for a burnt offering, without blemish, and offer them before the Lord.** These first offerings of Aaron were made altogether under the directions of Moses as the mouthpiece of God, for he was just entering upon his office. The fact that Baron, in spite of the consecration with all its sacrifices, still began the work of his ministry with a sin-offering and a burnt offering, shows plainly that the sacrifices of the Old Testament cultus cannot make those perfect that offer them, Heb. 10, 1.

The temporary, the typical and symbolical character of the ancient sacrifices appears throughout. V.3. **And unto the children of Israel thou shalt speak, saying,** instructing them in the capacity of high priest, **take ye a kid of the goats for a sin-offering,** which was otherwise the offering for a prince. chap. 4, 23; **and a calf,** a young bullock, chap. 1, 5, **and a lamb, both of the first year, without blemish, for a burnt offering;** v.4. **also a bullock and a ram for peace-offerings, to sacrifice before the Lord; and a meat-offering mingled with oil,** representative sacrifices from every group; **for to-day the Lord will appear unto you,** that solemn manifestation was to be the climax of the day's events. V.5. **And they brought that which Moses commanded before the Tabernacle of the Congregation; and all the congregation drew near and stood before the Lord,** in the court of the Tabernacle and in its immediate neighborhood. V.6. **And Moses said, This is the thing which the Lord commanded that ye should do;** they should now witness the formal beginning of the worship by sacrifices, the explanation of Moses serving to make them attentive and intelligent witnesses; **and the glory of the Lord shall appear unto you.** This announcement was made in order to keep the people both interested and devout during the offering of the sacrifices. V.7. **And Moses said unto Aaron, Go unto the altar and offer thy sin-offering and thy burnt offering, and make an atonement for thyself and for the people, and offer the offering of the people, and make an atonement for them, as the Lord commanded.** That was the nucleus of the idea of the sacrifices, that was the purpose of the offerings at all times, to cover the sins in the sight of God, that He might forgive them. And all this was accomplished for the believing Israelites in view of the perfect atonement of Jesus Christ, of which the blood atonement made by their priests was but a dim picture.

THE FIRST OFFERINGS. - V.8. **Aaron, therefore, went unto the altar, and slew the calf of the sin-offering, which was for himself.** V.9. **And the sons of Aaron brought the blood unto him,** thus performing the work which was afterward assigned to the Levites in catching the blood of the slaughtered animal and keeping it from coagulating; **and he dipped his finger in the blood, and put it upon the horns of the altar, and poured out the blood at the bottom of the altar.** He brought no blood into the Holy Place, for the object at this time was the removal of the sin which might make his service in the name of the congregation displeasing to the Lord. The sin-offering served to remove the estrangement which existed between God and the people on account of the trespasses made by Israel, individually and collectively. V.10. **But the fat and the kidneys and the caul above the liver of the sin-offering he burned upon the altar, as the Lord commanded Moses,** chap. 4, 8. V.11. **And the flesh and the hide he burned with fire without the camp,** chap. 4, 11. V.12. **And he slew the burnt offering,** according to the ordinance, chap. 1, 3-9; 8, 18-21; **and Aaron's sons presented unto him the blood,** passed it to him as before, **which he sprinkled round about upon the altar.** V.13. **And they presented the burnt offering unto him with the pieces thereof and the head;** they passed the single pieces to him as he had dissected the animal; **and he burned them upon the altar.** This sacrifice expressed the complete and devout surrender of the worshipers to the Lord. V.14. **And he did wash the inwards and the legs, and burned them upon the burnt offering on the altar.** No mention is made of an oblation of meat-offering with this sacrifice, either because the special law referring to this rite was not yet given, Num. 15, 2 ff., or because it had already been made in connection with the morning sacrifice. V.15. **And he brought the people's offering,** which consisted of all three varieties of sacrifices, made in the usual order, **and took the goat, which was the sin-offering for the people, and slew it, and offered it for sin, as the first.** In this case also the blood was not brought into the Holy Place, for the purpose at this time was merely to make the proper beginning of the sacrificial worship. V.16. **And he brought the burnt offering,** the young bullock and the lamb, **and offered it according to the manner,** as the ordinance required it. V.17. **And he brought the meat-offering,** which accompanied the burnt offering, **and took an handful thereof, and burned it upon the altar beside,** that is, in addition to, **the burnt sacrifice of the morning;** for the usual offerings had been made on this morning, as always. V.18. **He slew also the bullock and the ram for a sacrifice of peace-offerings, which was for the people,** an act of thanksgiving for the grace received till now and a prayer for the maintenance of the merciful fellowship on the part of Jehovah. **And Aaron's sons presented unto him the blood, which he sprinkled upon the altar round about.** V.19. **And the fat of the bullock and of the ram, the rump,** that is, the heavy, fatty tail, **and that which covereth the inwards and the kidneys and the caul above the liver,** all the loose fat of the abdominal cavities; v.20. **and they put the fat upon the breasts,** upon the wave-breasts of the two animals, and passed it to Aaron in this manner; **and he burned the fat upon the altar;** v.21. **and the breasts and the right shoulder,** the wave-breasts and the heave-shoulders, **Aaron waved for a wave-offering before the Lord,** chap. 7, 30-34; **as Moses commanded.** V.22. **And Aaron,** standing upon the elevated slope which led to the altar of burnt offering, **lifted up his hand toward the people,** in a gesture transmitting the grace of the Lord, **and blessed them, and came down from offering of the sin-offering and the burnt offering and peace-offerings.** The various animals had been dissected and laid on the fire according to the ordinance of God, and the service was concluded with the blessing. Cp. Num. 6, 22-24. V.23. **And Moses and Aaron went into the Tabernacle of the Congregation;** for the latter had to be introduced to his future place of activity, as a part of the ceremony of installation; **and came out and blessed the people. And the glory of the Lord appeared unto all the people;** there was some glorious manifestation in the cloud which covered the Tabernacle, the presence of the Lord thus being demonstrated with great effectiveness. V.24. **And there came a fire out from before the Lord, and consumed upon the altar the burnt offering and the fat.** Either the entire cloud shone with a supernatural light, or there was a sudden flash of fire from the cloud, like a bolt of lightning, which in a moment completely devoured the sacrifices smoldering upon the altar. Similar manifestations of God's glory are related also at later times, especially at the dedication of the Temple of Solomon. **Which when all the people saw, they shouted,** they called out in glad wonder, thanksgiving, and praise, **and fell on their faces,** in the gesture expressing joyful and reverential awe, The awe which we Christians feel at the manifestation of Him in whom is life, and the life is the light of men, John 1, 4, will continue through time into eternity.

52

Leviticus 10

The Death of Nadab and Abihu and Its Lessons.

THE SIN OF NADAB AND ABIHU AND ITS PUNISHMENT. - V.1. **And Nadab and Abihu, the sons of Aaron, took either of them his censer, and put fire therein, and put incense thereon, and offered strange fire before the Lord, which he commanded them not.** Nadab and Abihu were probably the oldest sons of Aaron, and were distinguished by Moses in being selected to accompany him to the feast before the Lord, Ex. 24, 1. 9. The chances are that they were unduly exalted over their initiation into the priesthood and believed themselves competent to select their own methods of worshiping the Lord. They took two of the small vessels pertaining to the golden altar, put some fire in them which was not taken from the altar of burnt offering, and proceeded to offer incense to the Lord in these censers of their own selecting, whereas incense was to be offered only on the

329

golden altar by the officiating priest twice daily, Ex. 30, 7. 8. V.2. **And there went out fire from the Lord,** this time in consuming wrath, as it had shortly before flashed forth in an expression of mercy, **and devoured them; and they died before the Lord.** It was like a bolt of lightning which struck them dead without consuming their bodies or even their clothes. The punishment struck them while they were yet in the Sanctuary or in the court. Our God, in His jealousy, is a consuming fire, and will occasionally even now strike down such as blasphemously presume upon rights before Him which they do not possess. V.3. **Then Moses said unto Aaron, This is it that the Lord spake, saying, I will be sanctified in them that come nigh Me, and before all the people I will be glorified.** That was the explanation of this severe judgment. Since the two young men had omitted the proper preparation and had acted contrary to the commandment of the Lord, therefore He had sanctified Himself upon them by this punishment, which was to redound to His glory as the Holy One, who will not be mocked by disobedience. **And Aaron held his peace;** he was unable to gainsay the righteousness of the act of God, as set forth by Moses V.4. **And Moses called Mishael and Elzaphan, the sons of Uzziel, the uncle of Aaron,** Ex. 6, 18, and his own cousins, **and said unto them, Come near, carry your brethren from before the Sanctuary out of the camp.** The two dead men were the brethren, the relatives, of the men who were to perform the last rites over them: and they were buried in their linen coats, for these priestly garments had been defiled with the dead bodies. V.5. **So they went near and carried them in their coats out of the camp, as Moses had said,** the people meanwhile looking on in a kind of stupefied awe. V.6. **And Moses said unto Aaron and unto Eleazar and unto Ithamar, his sons, Uncover not your heads, neither rend your clothes,** the usual manner of showing a high degree of mourning being to let the hair of the head grow without trimming and cutting and to tear open the garments over the breast, **lest ye die, and lest wrath come up on all the people.** A transgression of the high priest, as the mediator between God and the people, involved the latter in the punishment of God. To mourn in this case would have been equivalent to expressing dissatisfaction with the judgments of the Lord and would have brought His punishment upon the offenders and upon all whom they represented. **But let your brethren, the whole house of Israel, bewail the burning which the Lord hath kindled,** the terrible expression of God's wrath in destroying the priests, the sad calamity that had befallen them. V.7. **And ye shall not go out from the door of the Tabernacle of the Congregation,** in order to join the funeral procession or in any way to permit an intermission to take place in the priestly functions, **lest ye die; for the anointing oil of the Lord is upon you. And they did according to the word of Moses.** The anointing oil was the symbol of the Spirit of the living God, who has nothing in common with death, but rather conquers death, and sin which causes death. Cp. chap. 21, 12.

INSTRUCTIONS TO THE PRIESTS. - V.8. **And the Lord spake unto Aaron, saying,** He now addressed Himself directly to the high priest to let him know His will, v.9. **Do not drink wine nor strong drink,** the latter being a very strongly intoxicating beverage made from barley, dates, and honey, **thou, nor thy sons with thee, when ye go in to the Tabernacle of the Congregation,** when engaged in the duties of the priesthood, **lest ye die; it shall be a statute forever through out your generations;** it was practically equivalent to absolute prohibition in the case of Aaron and his sons, for they must have been on duty continually, especially in the early days: later the priests were on duty in the Sanctuary only a short time during the year; v.10. **and that ye may put difference between holy and unholy, and between unclean and clean;** their minds had to be clear for the many cases which required careful distinguishing; v.11. **and that ye may teach the children of Israel all the statutes which the Lord hath spoken unto them by the hand of Moses.** The priests were at the same time the teachers of the people, and their minds did not dare to be befuddled with the fumes of intoxicating liquors while they mere engaged in the discharge of their duties. V.12. **And Moses spake unto Aaron, and unto Eleazar and unto Ithamar, his sons that were left, take the meat-offering that remaineth of the offerings of the Lord made by fire,** only a handful having been offered, chap. 9, 17, **and eat it without leaven beside the altar; for it is most holy.** It was used as food for the priests in a place provided for that purpose in the court. V.13. **And ye shall eat it in the Holy Place, because it is thy due;** it was a fee which was intended for the sustenance of the priests while they were on duty in the Sanctuary, **and thy sons' due, of the sacrifices of the Lord made by fire; for so I am commanded.** V.14. **And the wave-breast and heave-shoulder shall ye eat in a clean place; thou and thy sons and thy daughters with thee; for they be thy due and**

thy sons' due, which are given out of the sacrifices of peace-offerings of the children of Israel. This was the portion set aside for the priests and their families, fees or emoluments, a part of the salary, and this holy meal could be eaten outside of the court, in some clean place. V.15. **The heave-shoulder and the wave-breast shall they bring with the offerings made by fire of the fat, to wave it for a wave-offering before the Lord; and it shall be thine, and thy sons' with thee, by a statute forever, as the Lord hath commanded,** chap. 7, 31-34. V.16. **And Moses diligently sought the go at of the sin-offering,** for since its blood had been poured out at the altar of burnt offering, its flesh, being a sin-offering, should have been eaten by the priests in the Holy Place, **and, behold, it was burned; and he was angry with Eleazar and Ithamar, the sons of Aaron, which were left alive, saying,** V.17. **Wherefore have ye not eaten the sin-offering in the Holy Place, seeing it is most holy, and God hath given it you to bear the iniquity of the congregation, to make an atonement for them before the Lord?** The priests, being mediators of the people in offering the sacrifices, were bound to follow the ritual in all its details, and the eating of the flesh was an essential part of this service. V.18. **Behold, the blood of it was not brought in within the Holy Place,** to the altar of incense, as it was described chap. 4, 1-21; **ye should indeed have eaten it in the Holy Place, as I commanded.** Having undertaken the atonement for the people, the responsibility for the sins and that of carrying out every single precept of the sacrifice rested upon them. V.19. **And Aaron said unto Moses, Behold, this day have they offered their sin-offering and their burnt offering before the Lord,**

the priests had made these offerings for themselves; **and such things have befallen me,** in being bereft of two of his sons; **and if I had eaten the sin-offering to-day, should it have been accepted in the sight of the Lord?** The fearful accident which had happened had made Aaron and his remaining sons incapable of and unfit for eating. Cp. Hos. 9, 4. V.20. **And when Moses heard that, he was content,** literally, "it was good in his eyes," he was satisfied that no disregard of the Lord's precepts was intended, that the circumstances warranted Aaron and his sons in acting as they did. The law of love is the highest law and supersedes all others. It was so in the Old Testament, as it is in the New, that God desired mercy rather than sacrifice.

53

Leviticus 11

Ordinances Regarding Clean and Unclean Animals.

OF MAMMALS. - V.1. **And the Lord spake unto Moses and to Aaron, saying unto them,** Aaron bring included as the high priest consecrated for the purpose of making an atonement for the sins of the people, v.2. **Speak unto the children of Israel, saying, These are the beasts which ye shall eat among all the beasts that are on the earth.** From the animals in general the Lord distinguishes the domestic animals and those commonly used for food by the inhabitants of the countries round about. V.3. **Whatsoever parteth the hoof and is cloven-footed,** so that the hoof is not only partially, but completely divided into two parts, **and cheweth the cud, among the beasts,** as a member of the true ruminants, **that shall ye eat.** V.4. **Nevertheless these shall ye not eat of them that chew the cud, or of them that divide the hoof; as, the camel, because he cheweth the cud, but**

divideth not the hoof, there being only a partial division of the hoof; **he is unclean unto you**. V.5. **And the coney,** a marmot-like animal of the size of a hare living in caves and clefts of the rocks, **because he cheweth the cud,** making the characteristic mouth-movements of the ruminants, **but divideth not the hoof; he is unclean unto you.** V.6. **And the hare, because he cheweth the cud, but divideth not the hoof; he is unclean unto you.** Though the two last-named animals have not the three or four stomachs of the real ruminants, the motion which they make with their mouths as they sit before their burrows is that of chewing the cud. V.7. **And the swine, though he divide the hoof, and be cloven-footed, yet he cheweth not the cud; he is unclean to you.** Since pigs were nothing but scavengers in Oriental lands, and since the eating of pork in those circumstances often resulted in diseases of the skin, many of the ancient peoples considered them unclean. V.8. **Of their flesh shall ye not eat,** to slaughter these animals for food was strictly forbidden, **and their carcass shall ye not touch; they are unclean to you.**

OF ANIMALS LIVING IN WATER. - V.9. **These shall ye eat of all that are in the waters: whatsoever hath fins and scales in the waters, in the seas, and in the rivers, them shall ye eat,** all the animals that are fishes according to the common use of the word. V.10. **And all that have not fins and scales in the seas and in the rivers, of all that move in the waters,** all the smaller animals that throng the ocean, including also lobsters, crabs, oysters, and every other kind of marine animal, **and of any living thing which is in the waters, they shall be an abomination unto you;** v.11. **they shall be even an abomination unto you; ye shall**

not eat of their flesh, but ye shall have their carcasses in
abomination. V.12. **Whatsoever hath no fins nor scales
in the waters, that shall be an abomination unto you,**
was utterly to be abhorred.

OF ANIMALS OF THE AIR. - V.13. **And these are they
which ye shall have in abomination among the fowls;
they shall not be eaten, they are an abomination: the
eagle, and the ossifrage, and the osprey,** three varieties of
eagles, the latter two being more exactly identified as the sea
eagle and the black eagle, respectively, v.14. **and the vulture,**
a ravenous bird which may have been similar to a hawk
or falcon, **and the kite after his kind,** the class of hawks
which includes the chicken-hawk, v.15. **every raven after
his kind,** all the birds that belong to this family, including
crows and blackbirds of every description, v.16. **and the
owl,** literally, "the daughter of the desert," the ostrich, **and
the night-hawk,** very likely the desert owl, **and the cuckoo,**
either the desert hawk or the seagull, **and the hawk after
his kind,** the entire family of falcons, v.17. **and the little
owl,** often found in ruins, **and the cormorant,** or a kind of
pelican found in Syria, **and the great owl,** also a frequenter
of ruins in the desert, v.18. **and the swan,** probably an owl
with a dismal cry, **and the pelican, and the gier-eagle,** or
carrion vulture, v.19. **and the stork, the heron after her
kind,** the entire tribe of swamp birds, **and the lapwing,
and the bat,** which was at that time commonly enumerated
with the birds. V.20. **All fowls that creep, going upon
all four, shall be an abomination unto you.** As those
that had been mentioned until now were chiefly such as
lived on filth and carrion, they were unclean. They are
here classed with the vermin of the earth, with the smaller

337

animals equipped with wings for flight. V.21. **Yet these may ye eat of every flying, creeping thing that goeth upon all four, which have legs above their feet, to leap withal upon the earth,** whose strong hind legs are built for jumping; v.22. **even these of them ye may eat: the locust after his kind,** the migratory variety, **and the bald locust after his kind,** an exceptionally voracious variety, **and the beetle after his kind,** a very large, hopping variety of grasshopper, **and the grasshopper after his kind,** a variety with only rudimentary wings. The insects here named were very commonly used as food by the poorer classes of the Orient, either roasted or broiled in butter and eaten with spices and vinegar. Locusts are mentioned as the food of John the Baptist, Matt. 3, 4. V.23. **But all other flying, creeping things which have four feet,** that walk, not in an upright, but in a horizontal position, "on all fours," **shall be an abomination unto you. V.24. And For these ye shall be unclean; whosoever toucheth the carcass of them shall be unclean until the even;** contact with their dead bodies should be avoided under penalty of being declared unclean for the day. V.25. **And whosoever Beareth aught of the carcass of them,** even in removing it from his land, **shall wash his clothes and be unclean until the even. V.26. The carcasses of every beast which divideth the hoof, and is not cloven-footed nor cheweth the cud, are unclean unto you; every one that toucheth them shall be unclean. V.27. And whatsoever goeth upon his paws,** or, the bare soles of whose feet touch the ground, as in most beasts of prey, **among all manner of beasts that go on all four, those are unclean unto you; whoso toucheth their carcass shall be unclean until the even.** V.28. **And he** that bearest the carcass of them shall wash his clothes and be unclean until the even, being contaminated in even a higher degree than the one that merely touched the carcass; they are unclean unto you.

OF THE SMALLER ANIMALS. GENERAL PRECEPTS. - V.29. These also shall be unclean unto you among the creeping things that creep upon the earth: the weasel, which often entered houses and defiled foods, and the mouse, that is, the field-mouse, and the tortoise after his kind, the great lizard of the Orient, v.30. and the ferret, or rather a lizard with a sharp cry, and the chameleon, a salamander-like lizard living in old walls, and the lizard, and the snail, either the true lizard or one similar to the blind-worm of Europe, and the mole, the word here used seeming to point definitely to the chameleon. Note that the equivalent of the Hebrew names can be given only approximately in the English language, since we have no means of knowing to which of the species now occurring in the Orient the various words apply, or whether perhaps certain species are not extinct. V.31. These are unclean to you among all that creep; whosoever doth touch them when they be dead shall be unclean until the even. The ordinance concerning them was so strict, not because these animals in themselves were unusually filthy, but because there was greater likelihood of their coming in contact with clothes and with vessels in the houses. V.32. And upon whatsoever any of them, when they are dead, doth fall, it shall be unclean, for it might easily happen that one of them would fall out of a wall or from the open ceiling; whether it be any vessel of wood, or raiment, garments of every kind, or skin, used

339

for churning, for holding wine and other liquids, and for a variety of purposes, **or sack, whatsoever vessel it be, wherein any work is done,** that is, put to any use in the household or shop, **it must be put in to water, and it shall be unclean until the even; so it shall be cleansed.** V.33 **And every earthen vessel whereinto any of them falleth, whatsoever is in it shall be unclean; and ye shall break it,** since the porous nature of it would cause it to absorb some of the filthiness. V.34. **Of all meat which may be eaten, that on which such water cometh,** which has been in contact with the carcass of such a creature, **shall be unclean; and all drink that may be drunk in every such vessel shall be unclean,** it was defiled by the touch of the dead animal. V.35. **And everything whereupon any part of their carcass falleth shall be unclean, whether it be oven,** the larger bake-oven, **or ranges for pots,** small, portable ovens of earthenware, **they shall be broken down; for they are unclean and shall be unclean unto you.** V.36. **Nevertheless a fountain or pit, wherein there is plenty of water,** a spring or cistern with an abundance of fresh water or with the only water supply for an entire neighborhood, **shall be clean; but that,** or rather, he, **which toucheth their carcass,** in order to carry it away, **shall be unclean.** V.37. **And if any part of their carcass fall upon any sowing seed which is to be sown, it shall be clean,** the external filthiness on the dry grains being absorbed by the earth. V.38. **But if any water be put upon the seed, and any part of their carcass fall thereon, it shall be unclean unto you,** for in this case the uncleanness would be absorbed by the moisture in the kernels. V.39. **And if any beast of which ye may eat, die,** if an animal belonging to the category of clean animals die a natural death or be torn by wild beasts, **he that toucheth the carcass thereof shall be unclean until the even.** V.40. **And he that eateth of the carcass of it shall wash his clothes and be unclean until the even; he also that beareth the carcass of it shall wash his clothes and be unclean until the even.** In either case contact of the clothes with the dead animal was practically unavoidable. V.41. **And every creeping thing that creepeth upon the earth,** all crawling and four-footed vermin, **shall be an abomination; it shall not be eaten.** V.42. **Whatsoever goeth upon the belly,** as serpents and worms, **and whatsoever goeth upon all four,** as mice, rats, weasels, moles, **or whatsoever hath more feet among all creeping things that creep upon the earth,** as centipedes, spiders, and other arthropods, **them ye shall not eat; for they are an abomination.** V.43. **Ye shall not make yourselves abominable,** literally, "ye shall not make your souls an abomination," **with any creeping thing that creepeth, neither shall ye make yourselves unclean with them, that ye should be defiled thereby.** The children of Israel, as the people of the Lord, must keep away from every form of defilement.

A STRONG CONCLUDING ARGUMENT. - V.44. **For I am the Lord, your God; ye shall therefore sanctify yourselves, and ye shall be holy,** consecrated, holy persons, set aside for the service of God; **for I am holy; neither shall ye defile yourselves with any manner of creeping thing that creepeth up on the earth,** either by using such animals for food or by handling them needlessly. V.45. **For I am the Lord that bringeth you up out of the land of Egypt,** that was the mighty work in which He was then engaged, to be your God; ye shall therefore be holy, for I am holy. V.46. **This is the law of the beasts, and of the fowl, and of every living creature that moveth in the waters, and of every creature that creepeth up on the earth;** v.47. **to make a difference,** to observe the distinction, **between the unclean and the clean, and between the beast that may be eaten and the beast that may not be eaten.** Thus the regulating principle was laid down by which the children of Israel were to be governed in their selection of animals for food. We Christians of the New Testament are no longer bound by this Ceremonial Lair: for God has taught us not to regard anything as common and unclean. Acts 10, 15. In abstaining from using as food most of the animals mentioned in the list we are merely following the rules of hygiene, in the spirit of Christian liberty.

54

Leviticus 12

The Purification after Childbirth.

V.1. **And the Lord spake unto Moses, saying,** v.2. **Speak unto the children of Israel, saying, if a woman have conceived seed,** brought forth bodily issue, **and born a man child,** a boy, **then she shall be unclean seven days,** this being the time of her personal uncleanness, during which every person and thing touched by her itself became defiled; **according to the days of the separation for her infirmity shall she be unclean,** that is, during the average time of the flow following birth. V.3. **And in the eighth day the flesh of his foreskin shall be circumcised,** Gen. 17, this notice being here inserted lest this very necessary rite be neglected. V.4. **And she shall then,** counting from the eighth day, **continue in the blood of her purifying three and thirty days,** this making a total of forty days, during which she was to stay at home, although the restrictions of the first seven days were now made much lighter; **she shall touch no hallowed thing, nor come into the Sanctuary, until the days of her purifying be fulfilled.** Although free to perform the ordinary duties of the household, she could not take part in sacrificial meals, the Passover and other festivals, nor was she permitted to enter the court of the Sanctuary. The forty days were the symbolical time of purification, of exclusion from the world. V.5. **But if she bear a maid child, then she shall be unclean two weeks, as in her separation,** the extra seven days probably being an equivalent for the rite of circumcision in the case of the boy; **and she shall continue in the blood of her purifying,** for the average length of the entire flow, **threescore and six days,** this making a total of eighty days in the case of a girl. Natural sanitary reasons were probably the basis of the Levitical ordinance. V.6. **And when the days of her purification are fulfilled, for a son or for a daughter,** that is, depending upon the fact whether it was a boy or a girl that had been born, **she shall bring a lamb of the first year for a burnt offering, and a young pigeon or a turtledove for a sin-offering, unto the door of the Tabernacle of the Congregation, unto the priest,** v.7. **who shall offer it before the Lord, and make an atonement for her; and she shall be cleansed from the issue of her blood.** "The order of the offerings is a remarkable deviation from the general principle that, when the two offerings came together, the sin-offering always preceded. The reason of this exception appears to lie in the fact that at the birth of a child feelings of joy and gratitude are naturally uppermost; the thought of the child's heritage of sinfulness comes afterward." **This is the law for her that hath born a male or a female.** V.8. **And if she be not**

able to bring a lamb, if her poverty is such as to make it impossible for her to afford a lamb, **then she shall bring two turtles** (turtledoves) **or two young pigeons; the one for the burnt offering and the other for a sin-offering; and the priest shall make an atonement for her, and she shall be clean.** A significant light is thrown upon the external circumstances of Joseph's share in this world's goods by the fact that Mary was obliged to bring the sacrifice of the poor people at the time of her purification, Luke 2, 24. Note also: As the little Jewish baby was received into fellowship with the covenant God by the rite of circumcision, so Christian children, cleansed from the guilt of inherited sin by the mashing of Baptism, are placed in to the arms of their Savior for their soul's salvation.

55

Leviticus 13

Ordinances Concerning Leprosy.

V.1. **And the Lord spake unto Moses and Aaron, saying,** v.2. **When a man,** a person of either sex, **shall have in the skin of his flesh a rising,** a raised spot on the epidermis, or cuticle, of his skin, **a scab, or bright spot,** one of a whitish tinge, **and it be in the skin of his flesh like the plague of leprosy,** the characteristic spot or sore which indicated the presence of the dread disease, **then he shall be brought unto Aaron, the priest, or unto one of his sons, the priests;** v.3. **and the priest shall look on the plague,** on the spot or sore, **in the skin of the flesh; and when the hair in the plague,** on the suspicious spot, **is turned white,** this sign was all the more striking since the hair of the Jews was normally black, **and the plague in sight be deeper than the skin of his flesh,** when the spot appeared to have sunken into the skin, **it is a plague of leprosy; and the priest shall look**

on him and pronounce him unclean. The name leprosy is derived from a word meaning "to strike, to strike to the ground," the leper being a person who has been stricken or smitten by Cod. The sickness is contagious only, but was and is commonly treated as being infectious as well. Three forms of the disease were distinguished in olden times: the white leprosy, which was very prevalent among the Hebrews, the tubercular leprosy, or the Egyptian boil, and the black leprosy. 3) V.4. **If the bright spot be white in the skin of his flesh, and in sight be not deeper than the skin, and the hair thereof be not turned white, then the priest shall shut up him that hath the plague seven days,** keep him from intercourse with other people in order to see whether there would be decisive indications pointing to true leprosy. V.5. **And the priest shall look on him the seventh day; and, behold, if the plague in his sight be at a stay, and the plague spread not in the skin,** if the spot has not grown larger nor affected the surrounding parts, **then the priest shall shut him up seven days more.** V.6. **And the priest shall look on him again the seventh day; and, behold, if the plague be somewhat dark,** if the skin on the spot has regained its normal color, **and the plague spread not in the skin, the priest shall pronounce him clean; it is but a scab,** a harmless eruption of the skin; **and he shall wash his clothes and be clean,** for the mere suspicion has brought a taint upon that person, which would be removed by observing the precepts of cleanliness. V.7. **But if the scab spread much abroad in the skin, after he hath been seen of the priest for his cleansing, he shall be seen of the priest again;** this may refer either to the second examination or to a new process made necessary by a subsequent spread of the eruption; v.8. **and if the priest see that, behold, the scab spreadeth in the skin, then the priest shall pronounce him unclean; it is a leprosy.** V.9. **When the plague of leprosy is in a man,** when the preliminary stages have been ignored and the disease has reached the ulceration stage without an examination by a priest, **then he shall be brought unto the priest; v.10. and the priest shall see him; and, behold, if the rising be white in the skin, and it have turned the hair white, and there be quick raw flesh in the rising,** the sores having opened with the power of the disease, v.11. **it is an old leprosy,** an incurable form at this stage, **in the skin of his flesh, and the priest shall pronounce him unclean and shall not shut him up,** the case being so clear; **for he is unclean.** V.12. **And if a leprosy break out abroad in the skin, and the leprosy cover all the skin of him that hath the plague from his head even to his foot, wheresoever the priest looketh,** and as deeply as his eyes can penetrate, v.13. **then the priest shall consider; and, behold, if the leprosy have covered all his flesh, he shall pronounce him clean that hath the plague, the eruption; it is all turned white; he is clean.** It seems that the suspected person, in this instance, either had only a harmless skin disease, or the eruption of all the poisonous matter in the body at one time was the crisis and cleansed the blood and tissues from all impurities. V.14. **But when raw flesh appeareth in him, he shall be unclean.** V.15. **And the priest shall see the raw flesh, and pronounce him to be unclean; for the raw flesh is unclean,** the open sore indicated that the germs of the sickness were still present in the person; **it is a leprosy.** V.16. **Or if the raw flesh** turn again, and be changed unto white, he shall come unto the priest; v.17. and the priest shall see him; and, behold, if the plague be turned into white, the ulceration being due to some other cause and having healed with a white covering, or scab, then the priest shall pronounce him clean that hath the plague, the spot or sore: he is clean. V.18. The flesh also, in which, even in the skin thereof, was a boil, ulcer, or abscess, and is healed, v.19. and in the place of the boil there be a white rising, or a bright spot, white, and somewhat reddish, a whitish-red blotch, and it be showed to the priest; v.20. and if, when the priest seeth it, behold, it be in sight lower than the skin, and the hair thereof be turned white, the priest shall pronounce him unclean; it is a plague of leprosy broken out of the boil. These indications, if clear, settled the matter. V.21. But if the priest look on it, and, behold, there be no white hairs therein, and if it be not lower than the skin, but be somewhat dark, then the priest shall shut him up seven days; v.22. and if it spread much abroad in the skin, then the priest shall pronounce him unclean; it is a plague. V.23. But if the bright spot stay in his place and spread not, it is a burning boil, the scar of a burn or a wound; and the priest shall pronounce him clean. V.24. Or if there be any flesh, in the skin whereof there is a hot burning, a scar left from a burn, and the quick flesh that burneth have a white, bright spot, somewhat reddish, or white, becoming a swollen, shining spot, v.25. then the priest shall look upon it; and, behold, if the hair in the bright spot be turned white, and it be in sight deeper than the skin, it is a leprosy broken out of the burning; wherefore the priest shall pronounce him

unclean; it is the plague of leprosy. Such spots favored the development of leprosy, the infection could easily take hold in them. V.26. **But if the priest look on it, and, behold, there be no white hair in the bright spot, and it be no lower than the other skin, but be somewhat dark, then the priest shall shut him up seven days;** v.27. **and the priest shall look upon him the seventh day; and if it be spread much abroad in the skin, then the priest shall pronounce him unclean; it is the plague of leprosy.** V.28. **And if the bright spot stay in his place, and spread not in the skin, but it be somewhat dark, it is a rising of the burning,** a slight elevation due to the scar, **and the priest shall pronounce him clean; for it is an inflammation of the burning.** V.29. **If a man or woman have a plague,** a spot or sore, **upon the head or the beard,** v.30. **then the priest shall see the plague; and, behold, if it be in sight deeper than the skin, and there be in it a yellow thin hair,** the natural hair being replaced with thin hair of a golden sheen, **then the priest shall pronounce him unclean; it is a dry scall,** a malicious scurf, **even a leprosy upon the head or beard.** V.31. **And if the priest look on the plague of the scall, and, behold, it be not in sight deeper than the skin, and that there is no black hair in it,** this being an indication that it was a harmless skin eruption, **then the priest shall shut up him that hath the plague of the scall seven days;** v.32. **and in the seventh day the priest shall look on the plague; and, behold, if the scall spread not, and there be in it no yellow hair, and the scall be not in sight deeper than the skin,** v.33. **he shall be shaven, but the scall shall he not shave,** this being reserved for further observation; **and the**

priest shall shut up him that hath the scall seven days more; v.34. **and in the seventh day the priest shall look on the scall; and, behold, if the scall be not spread in the skin, nor be in sight deeper than the skin,** the sore being neither deep-seated nor virulent, **then the priest shall pronounce him clean; and he shall wash his clothes and be clean.** V.35. **But if the scall spread much in the skin after his cleansing,** if after the priest's examination the sore causes trouble, V.36. **then the priest shall look on him; and, behold, if the scall be spread in the skin, the priest shall not seek for yellow hair,** there being enough symptoms for a definite diagnosis; he is unclean. V.37. **But if the scall be in his sight,** so far as he can judge upon a careful examination, **at a stay, and that there is black hair grown up therein, the scall is healed, he is clean; and the priest shall pronounce him clean.** V.38. **If a man also or a woman have in the skin of their flesh bright spots, even white bright spots,** v.39. **then the priest shall look; and, behold, if the bright spots in the skin of their flesh be darkish white,** without the luster peculiar to an inner swelling and inflammation, **it is a freckled spot that groweth in the skin; he is clean.** "It is an eruption on the skin, appearing in somewhat elevated spots or rings of unequal sizes and a pale-white color, which do not change the hair; it causes no inconvenience, and lasts from two months to two years." (Keil.) V.40. **And the man whose hair is fallen off his head, he is bald; yet is he clean.** This is spoken of cases in which the hair begins to fall out at the crown. V.41. **And he that hath his hair fallen off from the part of his head toward his face,** in the front, beginning above the temples, **he is forehead-bald; yet is**

he clean. V.42. **And if there be in the bald head or bald forehead a white, reddish sore, it is a leprosy sprung up in his bald head or his bald forehead.** Baldness did not render unclean, but leprosy might develop on the bare skin of the head as well as on the body. V.43. **Then the priest shall look upon it; and, behold, if the rising of the sore be white reddish in his bald head or in his bald forehead, as the leprosy appeareth in the skin of the flesh,** v.44. **he is a leprous man, he is unclean; the priest shall pronounce him utterly unclean; his plague is in his head,** the ulcer of leprosy is developing on his head. V.45. **And the leper in whom the plague is,** every person that has been pronounced a leper by the priest, **his clothes shall be rent,** as a mark of great mourning and affliction, **and his head bare,** uncovered and unkempt, **and he shall put a covering upon his upper lip** to hide his usually hideous aspect, Ezek. 24, 17. 22, **and shall cry, Unclean, unclean!** as a warning to passers-by. V.46. **All the days wherein the plague shall be in him he shall be defiled,** the Law thus, with all its strictness, taking into consideration a possible recovery of the leper; **he is unclean; he shall dwell alone,** in order to avoid contact with healthy people; **without the camp shall his habitation be.** Cp. Num. 5, 2-4; 12, 14. 15; 2 Kings 15, 5; Luke 17, 12. In Palestine the lepers lived outside the city walls, but they were permitted to attend the synagogs in a place set apart for them, the Law demanding, however, that they come after the opening of services and leave in such a way as not to come in contact with healthy persons. V.47. **The garment also that the plague of leprosy is in,** probably such as were contaminated by contact with a leprous person, **whether** it be a woolen garment or a linen garment, these two being the common materials used for woven clothes; v.48. whether it be in the warp or woof, no matter which part of the cloth would first show the infection; of linen or of woolen; whether in a skin or in anything made of skin, in cloaks, mantles, or receptacles for liquids; v.49. and if the plague be greenish or reddish in the garment, whether the mold indicating the presence of the disease have the one color or the other, or in the skin, either in the warp or in the woof, even in unfinished garments and cloth, or in anything of skin, in any vessel made of leather, - it is a plague of leprosy and shall be showed unto the priest; v.50. and the priest shall look upon the plague, and shut up it that hath the plague seven days. V.51. And he shall look on the plague on the seventh day. If the plague, the infected spot, be spread in the garment, either in the warp, or in the woof, or in a skin, or in any work that is made of skin, the plague is a fretting leprosy, a corroding infection; it is unclean. V.52. He shall therefore burn that garment, whether warp or woof, in woolen or in linen, or anything of skin, wherein the plague is; for it is a fretting leprosy; it shall be burned in the fire, that being the most effective way of removing all danger of infection. V.53. And if the priest shall look, and, behold, the plague be not spread in the garment, either in the warp, or in the woof, or in anything of skin, v.54. then the priest shall command that they, the owners, wash the thing wherein the plague is, and he shall shut it up seven days more; v.55. and the priest shall look on the plague after that it is washed; and, behold, if the plague have not changed his color, and the plague be

not spread, it is unclean; thou shalt burn it in the fire; it is fret inward, whether it be bare within or without. The terms in the Hebrew are here used in the same way as those concerning baldness in human beings. Whether the right or the wrong side of the cloth still showed the mark or spot distinctly, the garment was to be condemned. V.56. **And if the priest look, and, behold, the plague be somewhat dark after the washing of it,** the spot less distinct than before the cloth was washed, **then he shall rend it out of the garment or out of the skin or out of the warp or out of the woof.** It was a matter of wise precaution to remove the suspected spot. V.57. **And if it appear still in the garment,** if the same kind of mold reappeared, **either in the warp or in the woof or in anything of skin, it is a spreading plague; thou shalt burn that wherein the plague is with fire.** V.58. **And the garment, either warp or woof, or whatsoever thing of skin it be, which thou shalt wash, if the plague be departed from them, then it shall be washed the second time and shall be clean.** V.59. **This is the law of the plague of leprosy in a garment of woolen or linen, either in the warp or woof or anything of skins, to pronounce it clean or to pronounce it unclean.** These were wise sanitary precautions which were here embodied in the Ceremonial Law. The Lord, in His theocratic government, did not ignore the needs of the body.

56

Leviticus 14

The Cleansing from Leprosy.

THE MANNER OBSERVED IN PURIFYING A LEPER. - V.1. **And the Lord spake unto Moses, saying, v.2. This shall be the law of the leper in the day of his cleansing,** when he is found cured of the terrible disease with which he had been suffering: **He shall be brought unto the priest; v.3. and the priest shall go forth out of the camp; and the priest shall look, and, behold, if the plague of leprosy be healed in the leper,** literally, healed away from, that is, healed and gone away from, a careful inspection showing that all symptoms and marks of the disease have disappeared; v.4. **then shall the priest command to take for him that is to be cleansed two birds alive and clean, and cedar-wood, and scar let, and hyssop.** The purpose was to make the person that had been sick Levitically clean. The living birds signified that the leper's dead flesh, the body that was all but dead, was restored to life and vigor; the cedar-wood denoted restoration from evil-smelling rotting of the tissues and the endurance of life: the scarlet (wool or thread or a bit of cloth), restoration of the color of health and freshness to the skin; the fragrant hyssop, the restoration from the exceedingly bad odor of the disease and the purity of life which was now to be expected of the patient. V.5. **And the priest shall command that one of the birds be killed in an earthen vessel,** which could afterward be destroyed, **over running water,** the vessel having been partly filled with water from a spring or brook. V.6. **As for the living bird,** which yet remained, **he shall take it, and the cedar-wood, and the scarlet, and the hyssop, and shall dip them and the living bird in the blood of the bird that was killed over the running water,** so that the mixture of water and blood would cling to the feathers of the bird and to the other objects; v.7. **and he** (the priest) **shall sprinkle upon him that is to be cleansed from the leprosy seven times,** as on similar occasions of peculiar solemnity, **and shall pronounce him clean, and shall let the living bird loose in to the open field.** This signified that the former leper was released from the fetters of his sickness and could once more return to the enjoyment of full social and religious fellowship with the other people of his nation. V.8. **And he that is to be cleansed shall wash his clothes, and shave off all his hair,** on his whole body, **and wash himself in water that he may be clean; and after that he shall come in to the camp, and shall tarry abroad out of his tent seven days.** "This remaining restriction seems designed still further to impress upon the mind the fearful character of the disease from which the leper had recovered; and still more, to postpone the full restoration of the leper to his family until he had first, by the prescribed sacrifices, been restored to fellowship with God." (Lange.) **V.9. But it shall be on the seventh day that he shall shave all his hair off his head and his beard and his eyebrows, even all his hair he shall shave off,** for a second thorough cleansing; **and he shall wash his clothes, also he shall wash his flesh in water, and he shall be clean,** restored to full Levitical purity. He was now in a condition to offer the prescribed sacrifices of the eighth day. **V.10. And on the eighth day he shall take two he-lambs without blemish, and one ewe lamb of the first year without blemish, and three-tenth deals of fine flour for a meat-offering,** one-tenth of an epha (about two and one half quarts) being figured for each sacrificial animal, **mingled with oil, and one log** (about seven-tenths of a pint) of oil. **V.11. And the priest that maketh him clean shall present the man that is to be made clean, and those things,** all the prescribed sacrifices, **before the Lord, at the door of the Tabernacle of the Congregation; v.12. and the priest shall take one he-lamb, and offer him for a trespass-offering, and the log of oil, and wave them for a wave-offering before the Lord,** this ceremony distinguishing the leper's sacrifice from others of the same kind and serving for the worshiper's consecration; **v.13. and he shall slay the lamb in the place where he shall kill the sin-offering and the burnt offering, in the Holy Place,** north of the altar of burnt offering: **for as the sin-offering is the priest's, so is the trespass-offering; it is most holy. V.14. And the priest shall take some of the blood of the trespass-offering, and the priest shall put it upon the tip,** or lobe, **of the right ear of him that is to be cleansed, and upon the**

thumb of his right hand, and upon the great toe of his right foot, to consecrate the organs of the hearing of the Word, of doing the will of the Lord, and of walking in the path of His commandments, as in the consecration of the priests. V.15 **And the priest shall take some of the log of oil, and pour it into the palm of his own left hand;** v.16. **and the priest shall dip his right finger in the oil that is in his left hand, and shall sprinkle of the oil with his finger seven times before the Lord,** before the altar in the court; V.17. **and of the rest of the oil that is in his hand shall the priest put upon the tip of the right ear of him that is to be cleansed, and upon the thumb of his right hand, and upon the great toe of his right foot, upon the blood of the trespass-offering** which he had just applied in the same manner; v.18. **and the remnant of the oil that is in the priest's hand he shall pour upon the head of him that is to be cleansed,** to restore him to the privilege of his priestly kingship, from which he had been excluded by his disease; **and the priest shall make an atonement for him before the Lord.** Thus was the propitiation made and the gulf which had existed between God and man bridged over and covered. V.19. **And the priest shall offer the sin-offering, and make an atonement for him that is to be cleansed from his uncleanness,** for the leprosy was only the outward expression of the inner impurity of sin; **and afterward he shall kill the burnt offering,** the ewe lamb which had been provided. V.20. **And the priest shall offer the burnt offering and the meat-offering up on the altar; and the priest shall make an atonement for him, and he shall be clean.** All this was but a shadow and figure of the sacrifices of good works in which the believers of the New Testament are diligent. V.21. **And if he be poor and can not get so much, then he shall take one lamb for a trespass-offering to be waved,** instead of the two animals which the more well-to-do were expected to bring, **to make an atonement for him, and one tenth deal of fine flour** (about two and one half quarts), **mingled with oil for a meat-offering, and a log of oil** (about seven-tenths of a pint); v.22. **and two turtle-doves, or two young pigeons, such as he is able to get,** as he can afford, according to his means; **and the one shall be as in-offering and the other a burnt offering. V.23. And he shall bring them on the eighth day,** after the first ceremony of washing or lustration, vv. 4-8, **for his cleansing unto the priest, unto the door of the Tabernacle of the Congregation, before the Lord. V.24. And the priest shall take the lamb of the trespass-offering and the log of oil, and the priest shall wave them for a wave-offering before the Lord,** to distinguish the leper's offering from the ordinary sacrifices of the same kind and to symbolize his renewed consecration to the Lord V.25. **And he shall kill the lamb of the trespass-offering; and the priest shall take some of the blood of the trespass-offering, and put it up on the tip of the right ear of him that is to be cleansed, and up on the thumb of his right hand, and up on the great toe of his right foot; v.26. and the priest shall pour of the oil in to the palm of his own left hand; v.27. and the priest shall sprinkle with his right finger some of the oil that is in his left hand seven times before the Lord; v.28. and the priest shall put of the oil that is in his hand up on the tip of the right ear of him that is to be cleansed, and up on the thumb of his right hand, and up on the great**

toe of his right foot, up on the place of the blood of
the trespass-offering; v.29. **and the rest of the oil that
is in the priest's hand he shall put up on the head of
him that is to be cleansed, to make an atonement for
him before the Lord,** as before, vv. 16-18, and with the
same significance. V.30. **And he shall offer the one of
the turtle-doves or of the young pigeons, such as he can
get,** v.31. **even such as he is able to get, the one for a
sin-offering and the other for a burnt offering, with the
meat-offering; and the priest shall make an atonement
for him that is to be cleansed before the Lord.** The
necessity of atonement, of propitiation, of bridging the gulf
between God and sinful man by means of the sacrifices that
prefigured the perfect offering of Christ, is brought out
again and again. V.32. **This is the law of him in whom is
the plague of leprosy, whose hand is not able to get that
which pertaineth to his cleansing,** who is actually not in
a position to afford the more expensive sacrifices. While
cleansing was absolutely necessary, the Lord did not intend
to place insuperable obstacles in the way of the person who
wished to be restored to full communion with God and full
fellowship with the covenant people.

LEPROSY IN A HOUSE. - V.33. **And the Lord spake
unto Moses and unto Aaron, saying,** v.34. **When ye be
come in to the land of Canaan, which I give to you for
a possession,** which is here definitely foreseen, **and I put
the plague of leprosy in a house of the land of your
possession,** if it should be found that the Lord had afflicted
a house in this way, as a reminder of the fact that not only
their bodies, but also their places of habitation should be
considered consecrated to the Lord, v.35. **and he that**

owneth the house shall come and tell the priest, saying, It seemeth to me there is as it were a plague in the house, v.36. **then the priest shall command that they empty the house,** clear the house by moving all the furniture and utensils out, **before the priest go in to it to see the plague, that all that is in the house be not made unclean,** for all the furniture mould be looked upon as unclean if it were still in the house when the sentence of condemnation would be passed upon the structure. **And afterward the priest shall go in to see the house;** v.37. **and he shall look on the plague,** on the spot or area which seems to be infected, **and behold, if the plague be in the walls of the house with hollow strakes, greenish or reddish, which in sight are lower than the wall,** the reference undoubtedly being to fungous growths which partake of the nature of diseases, are often poisonous, and eat into the stones, v.38. **then the priest shall go out of the house to the door of the house and shut up the house seven days.** V.39. **And the priest shall come again the seventh day,** according to the division of time usually observed in ceremonies of this kind, **and shall look; and, behold, if the plague be spread in the walls of the house,** v.40. **then the priest shall command that they take away the stones in which the plague is,** which were affected by the fungous disease, **and they shall cast them into an unclean place without the city.** V.41. **And he shall cause the house to be scraped within round about,** to remove all the loose and soft particles of lime or sand from the stones; **and they shall pour out the dust that they scrape off without the city into an unclean place;** v.42. **and they shall take other stones, and put them in the place of those stones;**

and he shall take other mortar, and shall plaster the house. V.43. **And if the plague come again, and break out in the house, after that he hath taken away the stones, and after he hath scraped the house, and after it is plastered,** the infection thus being not merely on the surface, but indicating a deep-seated trouble, v.44. **then the priest shall come and look, and, behold, if the plague be spread in the house, it is a fretting leprosy in the house,** an infection which eats away the substance of the stones; **it is unclean. V.45. And he shall break down the house,** that is, the priest shall cause this to be done, **the stones of it, and the timber thereof, and all the mortar of the house,** all the building materials used in its construction; **and he shall carry them forth out of the city into an unclean place. V.46. Moreover, he that goeth into the house all the while that it is shut up shall be unclean until the even. V.47. And he that lieth in the house,** reclining there for the purpose of eating or sleeping, **shall wash his clothes; and he that eateth in the house shall wash his clothes,** not so much on account of the danger of infection as to prevent the contraction of symbolical uncleanness. **V.48. And if the priest shall come in and look upon it, and, behold, the plague hath not spread in the house after the house was plastered,** after the removal of the infected stones, **then the priest shall pronounce the house clean, because the plague is healed. V.49. And he shall take to cleanse the house two birds, and cedar-wood, and scarlet, and hyssop;** v.50. **and he shall kill the one of the birds in an earthen vessel over running water;** v.51. **and he shall take the cedar-wood, and the hyssop, and the scarlet, and the living bird, and dip them in the blood of**

the slain bird and in the running water, the blood being mixed with the water in the earthen vessel, and sprinkle the house seven times. V.52. **And he shall cleanse the house with the blood of the bird, and with the running water, and with the living bird, and with the cedar-wood, and with the hyssop, and with the scarlet;** v.53. **but he shall let go the living bird out of the city into the open fields, and make an atonement for the house,** as a structure infected with the uncleanness of sin, as it appeared in the fungous growth on the walls; **and it shall be clean.** The rite thus was exactly the same as that used for the leper without the camp, vv. 4-7, and the house was restored from its taint to its proper relations and purposes. V.54. **This is the law for all manner of plague of leprosy, and scall**, scab or scurf, v.55. **and for the leprosy of a garment, and of a house,** v.56. **and for a rising, and for a scab, and for a bright spot,** v.57. **to teach when it is unclean, and when it is clean; this is the law of leprosy,** as it is contained in these two chapters.

57

Leviticus 15

Special Forms of Uncleanness and Their Cleansing.

IN THE CASE OF MEN. - V.1. **And the Lord spake unto Moses and to Aaron, saying,** v.2. **Speak unto the children of Israel, and say unto them, When any man hath a running issue out of his flesh,** either a catarrhal affection of the urethra or a latent flowing of semen with a continuous discharge, **because of his issue he is unclean,** Levitically impure. V.3. **And this shall be his uncleanness in his issue: whether his flesh run with his issue, or his flesh be stopped from his issue,** that is, whether the matter flows without stopping, or whether it is sometimes temporarily retained, **it is his uncleanness.** V.4. **Every bed whereon he lieth that hath the issue is unclean; and everything,** every piece of furniture, **whereon he sitteth shall be unclean. V.5. And whosoever toucheth his bed shall wash his clothes, and bathe himself in water, and be unclean until the even.**

V.6. **And he that sitteth on anything whereon he sat that hath the issue shall wash his clothes, and bathe himself in water, and be unclean until the even. V.7. And he that toucheth the flesh,** that is, the body, **of him that hath the issue shall wash his clothes, and bathe himself in water, and be unclean until the even. V.8. And if he that hath the issue spit upon him that is clean,** as might inadvertently happen, **then he** (the clean person) **shall wash his clothes, and bathe himself in water, and be unclean until the even. V.9. And what saddle soever,** wagon or seat of a wagon, **he rideth upon that hath the issue shall be unclean. V.10. And whosoever toucheth anything that was under him,** any garment, saddle, or vessel upon which the unclean person lay or sat, **shall be unclean until the even; and he that beareth any of those things shall wash his clothes, And bathe himself in water, and be unclean until the even. V.11. And whomsoever he toucheth that hath the issue, and hath not rinsed his hands in water, he shall wash his clothes, and bathe himself in water, and be unclean until the even.** The washing of the hands prevented the communication of the uncleanness on the part of the person suffering with the issue, for the uncleanness was of a symbolical character. V.12. **And the vessel of earth that he toucheth which hath the issue shall be broken; and every vessel of wood shall be rinsed in water.** V.13. **And when he that hath an issue is cleansed of his issue,** when the flow has stopped, **then he shall number to himself seven days for his cleansing,** to be sure that a recurrence of the trouble was excluded, **and wash his clothes, and bathe his flesh,** his body, **in running water, and shall be clean.** V.14.

And on the eighth day he shall take to him two turtle-doves or two young pigeons, offerings of the humblest kind indeed, but serving just the same for the purpose of upholding the relation between God and the sinner, **and come before the Lord unto the door of the Tabernacle of the Congregation, and give them unto the priest;** v.15. **and the priest shall offer them, the one for a sin-offering and the other for a burnt offering. And the priest shall make an atonement for him before the Lord for his issue.** On account of the uncleanness there had existed an estrangement between God and the afflicted person, and this was now removed by the sacrifice of faith. V.16. **And if any man's seed of copulation go out from him,** inadvertently, during sleep, **then he shall wash all his flesh in water, and be unclean until the even.** V.17. **And every garment and every skin whereon is the seed of copulation shall be washed with water, and be unclean until the even.** The law seems to refer to involuntary emissions only, but its provisions naturally would serve to check the terrible sin of self-pollution. V.18. **The woman also with whom man shall lie,** in the chief relation peculiar to the marital estate, **with seed of copulation, they shall both bathe themselves in water, and be unclean until the even.** This law must have acted as a very effective check upon mere sensual passions. Cp. Ex. 19, 15; 1 Sam. 21, 5. 6; 2 Sam. 11, 4. "This defilement is connected with the general sinful condition of man, and did not pertain to his original state."

IN THE CASE OF WOMEN. - V.19. **And if a woman have an issue, and her issue in her flesh be blood,** the regular menstrual flow, **she shall be put apart seven days;**

and whosoever toucheth her shall be unclean until the even; every form of contact, even if it was ever so slight, rendered unclean for the day. V.20. And everything that she lieth upon in her separation shall be unclean; everything also that she sitteth upon shall be unclean; beds and chairs and every other article of furniture upon which she rested were here included. V.21. And whosoever toucheth her bed shall wash his clothes, and bathe himself in water, and be unclean until the even, having become Levitically defiled by the mere outward contact. V.22. And whosoever toucheth anything that she sat upon shall wash his clothes, and bathe himself in water, and be unclean until the even. V.23. And if it, any of the menstrual discharge, be on her bed, or on anything whereon she sitteth, when he, any person, toucheth it, he shall be unclean until the even. V.24. And if any man lie with her at all, in the specific marital relation, and her flowers, some of the discharge, be upon him, he shall be unclean seven days; and all the bed whereon he lieth shall be unclean; he will enter into the condition of her Levitical uncleanness. V.25. And if a woman have an issue of her blood many days out of the time of her separation, beyond the normal limit of seven days, as in the case of the woman whom Jesus healed, Matt. 9, 20-22, or if it run beyond the time of her separation, all the days of the issue of her uncleanness shall be as the days of Her separation; she shall be unclean; during that whole period she was to be regarded as being in the uncleanness of menstruation. V.26. Every bed whereon she lieth all the days of her issue shall be unto her as the bed of her separation; and whatsoever she sitteth upon shall

be unclean, as the uncleanness of her separation. V.27. **And whosoever toucheth those things shall be unclean, and shall wash his clothes, and bathe himself in water, and be unclean until the even.** V.28. **But if she be cleansed of her issue, then she shall number to herself Seven days,** as in the case of the man, v.13. **and after that she shall be clean.** V.29. **And on the eighth day she shall take unto her two turtles,** the wild turtle-doves, **or two young pigeons, and bring them unto the priest, to the door of the Tabernacle of the Congregation.** V.30. **And the priest shall offer the one for a sin-offering and the other for a burnt offering; and the priest shall make an atonement for her before the Lord For the issue of her uncleanness.** While ordinary menstruation required no sacrifice, this abnormal flow, being an uncleanness which estranged from God, made an offering of atonement necessary, for the Lord wanted external, physical purity as a mark and expression of internal cleanness in all the members of His people. V.31. **Thus shall ye separate the children of Israel from their uncleanness,** set them apart as people consecrated to the Lord, **that they die not in their uncleanness when they defile my Tabernacle that is among them.** The measures here ordered were not merely sanitary, but they also regulated sexual life among the Israelites, besides being typical of the perfect purity which the Lord expects from all His children at all times. V.32. **This is the law of him that hath an issue, and of him whose seed goeth from him and is defiled therewith,** v.33. **and of her that is sick of her flowers,** with the menstrual flow, **and of him that hath an issue, of the man, and of the woman, and of him that lieth with her**

that is unclean. Christian spouses will keep in mind at all times that they know how to possess their organs and vessels in sanctification and honor, not in the loathsome lust of concupiscence, as the Gentiles that know not God, 1 Thess. 4, 4. 5.

58

Leviticus 16

The Sacrifices of the Great Day of Atonement.

ARON'S SACRIFICES FOE HIMSELF. - V.1. **And the Lord spake unto Moses after the death of the two sons of Aaron, when they offered before the Lord and died,** their unauthorized act bringing down upon them the destroying wrath of God, chap. 10, 1. 2. V.2. **And the Lord said unto Moses, Speak unto Aaron, thy brother, that he come not at all times,** at any time that he might choose, **into the Holy Place within the veil,** into the Most Holy Place, **before the mercy-seat, which is upon the ark,** the corer, or lid, of the chest which contained the tables of the covenant, **that he die not; for I will appear in the cloud upon the mercy-seat.** That was the place appointed for the peculiar manifestation of God in the glory of His mercy, Ex. 25, 22; for this cloud revealed the presence of God to the representatives of the people. To step into this place of highest consecration in an arbitrary way, without the special direction of God, would result in death to the offender. V.3. **Thus shall Aaron come into the Holy Place,** into the innermost section of the Tabernacle: **with a young bullock for a sin-offering and a ram for a burnt offering.** These were the sacrificial offerings for the faults of the high priest and for those of the entire priesthood. V.4. **He shall put on the holy linen coat, and he shall have the linen breeches upon his flesh, and shall be girded with a linen girdle, and with the linen miter,** the turbanlike head-dress, **shall he be attired; these are the holy garments; therefore shall he wash his flesh in water, and so put them on.** These white garments were reserved for the special ceremonies of this day, whereas upon other occasions the high priest appeared in his variegated dress, Ex. 28. The white color indicated that no unclean person, no sinner, should step into the presence of the holy God. V.5. **And he shall take of the congregation of the children of Israel,** as the joint offering of the entire people, and therefore supplied by them, **two kids of the goats for a sin-offering and one ram for a burnt offering.** Although the ritual dealt with the two young goats in an entirely different manner, yet they both together constituted a single sin-offering. Thus the sacrificial victims both for the priesthood and for the congregation were provided. V.6. **And Aaron shall offer his bullock of the sin-offering, which is for himself, and make an atonement for himself and for his house,** the term here apparently including not only the immediate family of the high priest, but the whole order of priests. Since all the priests were representatives and mediators of the people in their dealings with the Lord, it was necessary that their own sin, first of all, be covered and expiated in the sight of God. V.7. **And he shall take the two goats, and present them before the Lord at the door of the Tabernacle of the Congregation,** formally set them forth in their character as sacrificial animals, before the face of the Lord. According to Jewish tradition the two goats were of the same size and otherwise as identical as possible in their markings. V.8. **And Aaron shall cast lots upon the two goats,** the lots being drawn from an urn by some attendant; **one lot for the Lord and the other lot for the scapegoat,** or *Azazel*, as the Hebrew has it, for the "Remover of Sin." 4) Both he-goats bore the sins of the people, the one through the act of sacrifice, the other by complete removal into the wilderness. V.9. **And Aaron shall bring the goat upon which the Lord's lot fell, and offer him for a sin-offering,** in the manner prescribed for such sacrifices. V.10. **But the goat on which the lot fell to be the scapegoat,** to symbolize the complete removal of all transgression and iniquity, **shall be presented alive before the Lord, to make an atonement with him, and to let him go for a scapegoat into the wilderness.** So much for the preparation for the sacrifices. V.11. **And Aaron shall bring the bullock of the sin-offering, which is for himself, and shall make an atonement for himself and for his house,** for the entire priesthood, **and shall kill the bullock of the sin-offering which is for himself.** This was the first stage of the day's sacrifices. V.12. **And he shall take a censer,** a pan or vessel, **full of burning coals of fire from off the altar before the Lord,** from the altar of burnt offering, **and his hands full of sweet incense beaten small,** the form in which its perfume would be strongest, **and bring it within the veil,** into the Most Holy Place; v.13. **and he shall put the incense upon the fire before the Lord, that the cloud of the incense** arising from its burning in the censer **may cover the mercy-seat that is upon the testimony,** that covers the tables of the testimony, **that he die not.** The cloud of incense protected the high priest, a sinful human being as he was, from the angry glance of the holy God. V.14. **And he shall take of the blood of the bullock,** which had been caught up by some attendant and meanwhile kept from coagulating by constant stirring, **and sprinkle it with his finger upon the mercy-seat eastward,** on the side which faced the east; **and before the mercy-seat,** between the ark and the veil, **shall he sprinkle of the blood with his finger seven times.** This was the second stage of the special sacrifices of the day, whereby the atonement for the priesthood was completed. The atonement was made, not without blood, for without the shedding of blood there is no remission, and for the high priest and his house first, Heb. 5, 1-3; 9, 7.

THE OFFERINGS FOR THE PEOPLE. - V.15. **Then shall he kill the goat of the sin-offering that is for the people,** the slaying taking place, of course, outside in the court, **and bring his blood within the veil,** into the Most Holy Place, **and do with that blood as he did with the blood of the bullock, and sprinkle it upon the mercy-seat and before the mercy-seat;** v.16. **and he shall make an atonement for the Holy Place,** the Sanctuary itself being in need of cleansing, **because of the uncleanness of the children of Israel, and because of their transgressions in all their sins,** for it was exposed to defilement in the midst of a sinful people; **and so shall ha do for the Tabernacle of**

the Congregation, that remaineth among them in the
midst of their uncleanness. Thus both the sins of the
priests, with which they had contaminated the Sanctuary,
and the transgressions of the people, which also defiled the
habitation of God in their midst, had to be expiated on the
great Day of Atonement. V.17. And there shall be no man
in the Tabernacle of the Congregation when he goeth in
to make an atonement in the Holy Place, until he come
out, and have made an atonement for himself, and for
his household, for the entire priesthood, and for all the
congregation of Israel. Everything and every person that
was defiled had to be kept away from the Most Holy Place
during this most solemn part of the ceremony, and the entire
responsibility rested upon the high priest alone. While all the
members of the congregation were, on this day, to feel the
damnable nature of sin, the high priest was to be particularly
conscious of this fact, since he acted in the name of all the
children of Israel. V.18. And he shall go out unto the altar
that is before the Lord, to the altar of incense, and make
an atonement for it; and shall take of the blood of the
bullock, and of the blood of the goat, and put it upon
the horns of the altar round about. So the blood of both
kinds of sin-offering was mingled in the expiatory rite, the
faults of both the priests and the people being atoned for in
the sight of God by this third stage of the day's sacrificial
ceremonies. Note that even the altar, as an instrument
used for purposes of purification and atonement, had to
be cleansed of the defilement clinging to it by reason of the
worship of sinners. V.19. And he shall sprinkle of the
blood upon it with his finger seven times, and cleanse
it, and hallow it from the uncleanness of the children

of Israel. The ceremonies of the great Day of Atonement were largely Messianic types. Christ is the true High Priest, holy, blameless, undefiled, separate from sinners, and made higher than the heavens, Heb. 7, 26. By His own blood He entered in once into the Holy Place, having obtained eternal redemption for us, Heb. 9, 12. V.20. **And when he hath made an end of reconciling the Holy Place and the Tabernacle of the Congregation and the altar, he shall bring the live goat,** the second animal of the sin-offering. V.21. **And Aaron shall lay both his hands upon the head of the live goat,** not only one, as in the ordinary sacrifices, **and confess over him all the iniquities of the children of Israel,** individually and collectively, **and all their transgressions in all their sins,** all the misdeeds and trespasses which brought upon them the wrath of Jehovah, **putting them upon the head of the goat,** the "remover of sins," **and shall send him away by the hand of a fit man in to the wilderness,** one who stood ready to go upon the instant, without loss of time; v.22. **and the go at shall bear upon him all their iniquities unto a land not inhabited,** into a desert and desolate place, for complete removal; **and he shall let go the goat in the wilderness.** Thus the fourth part of the special ceremonies of the day was brought to a close. V.23. **And Aaron shall come in to the Tabernacle of the Congregation, and shall put off the linen garments which he put on when he went in to the Holy Place, and shall leave them there,** since they were used only in the rite of atonement on this one day in the year; v.24. **and he shall wash his flesh with water in the Holy Place,** where the ablutions of the priests were ordinarily performed, at the laver near the entrance of the Tabernacle, and **put on his garments,** the ordinary vestments of his office made of the fine variegated cloth, **and come forth, and offer his burnt offering and the burnt offering of the people,** in either case a ram, **and make an atonement for himself and for the people.** V.25. **And the fat of the sin-offering shall he burn upon the altar.** All this could be done only after the defilement of sin had been entirely removed. V.26. **And he that let go the goat for the scapegoat,** for the complete removal of the sin placed upon his head, **shall wash his clothes, and bathe his flesh in water, and afterward come into the camp,** thus also cleansing himself of the impurity of contact with the sin-offering. V.27. **And the bullock for the sin-offering, and the goat for the sin-offering, whose blood was brought in to make atonement in the Holy Place, shall one carry forth without the camp; and they shall burn in the fire their skins and their flesh and their dung.** V.28. **And he that burneth them shall wash his clothes, and bathe his flesh in water, and afterward he shall come into the camp.** He also had to be cleansed from the contamination which came to him by touching the sin-offering. The second goat is also a type of Christ, who is the true "Remover of Sin." The Lord laid on Him the iniquity of us all, Is. 53, 6, and He not only bore them, but He took them away, John 1, 29, removed them SO completely that their guilt no longer rests upon us. Thus Christ has earned an eternal redemption for us.

THE PURPOSE OF THE DAY. - V.29. **And this shall be a statute forever unto you: that in the seventh month, on the tenth day of the month, ye shall afflict your souls,** bowed down in penitence and humiliation, **and do**

no work at all, whether it be one of your own country, or a stranger **that sojourneth among you.** The tenth day of the first month of the civil year, known first as Ethanim, and afterwards as Tishri, although not included in the great festivals, was yet of such importance as to give it the name of being the most solemn day in the year, and it was often designated simply as "the day." V.30. **For on that day shall the priest make an atonement for you, to cleanse you, that ye may be clean from all your sins before the Lord.** V.31. **It shall be a Sabbath of rest unto you,** be regarded in every way as a true Sabbath, **and ye shall afflict your souls,** by fasting, as an expression of the deepest humiliation and shame, **by a statute forever.** V.32. **And the priest, whom he shall anoint, and whom he shall consecrate to minister in the priest's office in his father's stead,** the intimation being that the high-priestly office was hereditary, **shall make the atonement, and shall put on the linen clothes, even the holy garments,** those especially set aside for the service of this day; v.33. **and he shall make an atonement for the holy sanctuary,** the Most Holy Place, **and he shall make an atonement for the Tabernacle of the Congregation,** the Holy Place, **and for the altar,** the golden altar of incense, **and he shall make an atonement for the priests, and for all the people of the congregation.** V.34. **And this shall be an everlasting statute unto you, to make an atonement for the children of Israel for all their sins once a year. And he,** Aaron, **did as the Lord commanded Moses.** When the time came, this festival day was duly kept and all the ceremonies carried out in accordance with the will of the Lord. By reason of their symbolism and through the faith

377

of the true Israelites the rites of the great Day of Atonement had power and efficacy until Christ made His great sacrifice, with its eternal power.

59

Leviticus 17

Warning against Desecration of Sacrifices.

ANIMALS TO BE SLAIN BY PRIESTS. - V.1. **And the Lord spake unto Moses, saying,** v.2. **Speak unto Aaron and unto his sons and unto all the children of Israel, and say unto them: This is the thing which the Lord hath commanded, saying,** v.3. **What man soever there be of the house of Israel that killeth an ox, or lamb, or goat,** the most common sacrificial animals, **in the camp, or that killeth it out of the camp,** even if the underlying thought be merely that of slaughtering the animal for food, v.4. **and bringeth it not unto the door of the Tabernacle of the Congregation to offer an offering unto the Lord before the Tabernacle of the Lord,** in some form of peace-offering, **blood shall be imputed unto that man; he hath shed blood,** he would be considered guilty of slaughtering an animal without authorization; **and that man shall be cut off from among**

his people, expelled from the congregation of the Lord; v.5. **to the end that the children of Israel may bring their sacrifices,** all the clean animals slaughtered for food, **which they offer in the open field, even that they may bring them unto the Lord, unto the door of the Tabernacle of the Congregation, unto the priest, and offer them for peace-offerings unto the Lord.** As a voluntary sacrifice the flesh of these animals could then be eaten on the same day or on the nest, chap. 7, 1 6. 17. V.6. **And the priest shall sprinkle the blood upon the altar of the Lord at the door of the Tabernacle of the Congregation, and burn the fat for a sweet savor unto the Lord.** By this provision both the eating of blood and of the loose fat of the abdominal cavity, which was expressly forbidden, chap. 7, 23-26, was made practically impossible. V.7. **And they shall no more offer their sacrifices unto devils, after whom they have gone a-whoring.** The idols referred to are demons commonly pictured as he-goats, of which the Egyptians especially believed that they lived in the wilderness. By slaughtering animals in their honor superstitious people thought they could prevent evil influences. It seems that the Egyptian custom had found lodgment among the children of Israel, at least to some extent, and the Lord wanted this form of idolatry eradicated. **This shall be a statute forever unto them throughout their generations.** V.8. **And thou shalt say unto them, Whatsover man there be of the house of Israel, or of the strangers which sojourn among you, that offereth a burnt offering or sacrifice,** in the foolish or insolent presumption that he had the right to worship the Lord anywhere, v.9. **and bringeth it not unto the door of the Tabernacle of the Congregation to offer it unto the**

Lord, in line with the ordinances which he had set forth, **even that man shall be cut off from among his people.** This command was to quench all tendencies of the people to choose their own places of worship, as was later done so widely. Israel had its law of sacrifices, and the Lord wanted this law to be observed in all its details. It is true for all times that not only gross idolatry, but also all self-chosen Worship is an abomination unto the Lord and cuts off the willful transgressor from fellowship with the Lord.

EATING OF BLOOD FORBIDDEN. - V.10. **And whatsoever man there be of the house of Israel, or of the strangers that sojourn among you, that eateth any manner of blood, I will even set My face against that soul that eateth blood, and will cut him off from among his people.** Cp. 7, 27. The Lord Himself threatens to be the executor in this case, for the transgression of this law was inconsistent with membership among the holy people of God. V.11. **For the life of the flesh is in the blood,** is carried by the blood; **and I have given it to you upon the altar to make an atonement for your souls; for it is the blood that maketh an atonement for the soul.** Since the blood was the bearer of the soul of the sacrificial animal, therefore the Lord had ordered it to be used as the means of expiation for the souls of men and had forbidden its use for food. V.12. **Therefore I said unto the children of Israel, No soul of you shall eat blood, neither shall any stranger that sojourneth among you eat blood. V.13. And whatsoever man there be of the children of Israel, or of the strangers that sojourn among you, which hunteth and catcheth any beast or fowl that may be eaten,** those that had been declared unclean being, of course, excepted, chap. 11, **he shall even pour out the blood thereof, and cover it with dust,** to prevent any desecration of the blood as the means of the expiation and atonement for sins. V.14. **For it is the life of all flesh; the blood of it is the life thereof. Therefore I said unto the children of Israel, Ye shall eat the blood of no manner of flesh; for the life of all flesh is the blood thereof; whosoever eateth it shall be cut off.** He that ate blood or permitted dogs or other animals to eat blood which he had shed, desecrated that which the Lord had set apart as consecrated to Himself, and thus became guilty. V.15. **And every soul that eateth that which died of itself, or that which was torn with beasts, whether it be one of your own country or a stranger, he shall both wash his clothes, and bathe himself in water, and be unclean until the even; then shall he be clean.** Cp. chap. 22. 8; Ex. 22, 31. V.16. **But if he wash them not, nor bathe his flesh, then he shall bear his iniquity.** He that ate of such food was polluted, and he that touched it was defiled. The Lord's intention was to have the inner purity of the heart symbolized by a strict outward Levitical cleanness, just as He expects the Christians to give evidence of their regenerated hearts in the sanctity of their lives.

60

Leviticus 18

Purity in Sexual Life Demanded.

U NLAWFUL MARRIAGES. - V.1. **And the Lord spake unto Moses, saying, v.2. Speak unto the children of Israel and say unto them, I am the Lord, your God.** Because the Lawgiver was Jehovah God, the covenant God, therefore the observance of these laws was a matter of covenant obligation. V.3. **After the doings of the land of Egypt wherein ye blood shall ye not do, and after the doings of the land of Canaan whither I bring you shall ye not do; neither shall ye walk in their ordinances.** The children of Israel were absolutely to avoid all practices, whether they were of Egyptian or Canaanitish origin, which desecrated the marriage relation or showed immorality in any form. The propagation of the human race is to take place in lawful wedlock only, and unlawful marriages, illegal sexual intercourse, and degenerate lusts are an abomination to the Lord. V.4. **Ye shall do My judgments**

and keep Mine ordinances to walk there in; I am the Lord, your God. His authority, as the only true God, was absolute. V.5. **Ye shall therefore keep My statutes and My judgments,** both those precepts which concerned them only, as the people of the Lord in a peculiar sense, and the ordinances which were natural laws, and which all men should recognize as binding upon them, also the Egyptians and Canaanites; **which if a man do, he shall live in them,** for a perfect keeping of the Law will have the enjoyment of eternal life as its reward, Luke 10, 28; **I am the Lord.** V.6. **None of you shall approach to any that is near of kin to him, to uncover their nakedness; I am the Lord.** The literal translation is: "Any man at all, to any flesh of his flesh shall he not come near to uncover shame." That is the fundamental rule: Sexual intercourse, the peculiar relation which is characteristic of the married state and is absolutely prohibited outside of holy wedlock, should not take place within the second degree of relationship, whether by blood (consanguinity) or by marriage (affinity). 5) V.7. **The nakedness of thy father or the nakedness of thy mother shalt thou not uncover: she is thy mother; thou shalt not uncover her nakedness.** This refers to a man's own, natural mother. V.8. **The nakedness of thy father's wife,** the stepmother, **thou shalt not uncover; it is thy father's nakedness.** V.9. **The nakedness of thy sister, the daughter of thy father or daughter of thy mother,** that is, the half-sister, **whether she be born at home or born abroad,** that is, in a former marriage, **even their nakedness thou shalt not uncover.** V.10. **The nakedness of thy son's daughter or of thy daughter's daughter,** of the granddaughter, **even**

there with; neither shall any woman stan[d]
beast to lie down thereto, to permit carnal [i]
is confusion, a most abominable and revol[ting]
V.24. Defile not ye yourselves in any
in these bestial perversions of sexual
these the nations are defiled whic[h]
you; v.25. and the land is defiled; [t]
iniquity thereof upon it, and t'
out her inhabitants. The stor[y]
extent unnatural vices were
of Canaan, to a degree that
endure them. V.26. Ye sh[all]
and My judgments, an[d]
abominations, neith[er]
stranger that sojournet[h]
ancestors of Israel were not all[o]
iniquity of the Amorites not yet full[y]
become filled with a mass of festering m[...]
Its inhabitants were to be cast out and the h[...]
planted in their stead. It could not be allowed that
stranger' should again introduce the pollutions which were
now being so severely punished." Lange), v.27. (for all these
abominations have the men of the land done which
were before you, and the land is defiled,) v.28. that
the land spue not you out also when ye defile it, as it
spued out the nations that were before you. The land
is personified as a creature which is obliged to vomit forth
some form of indigestible food with every indication of re-
vulsion. V.29. For whosoever shall commit any of these
abominations, even the souls that commit them shall
be cut off from among their people. V.30. Therefore

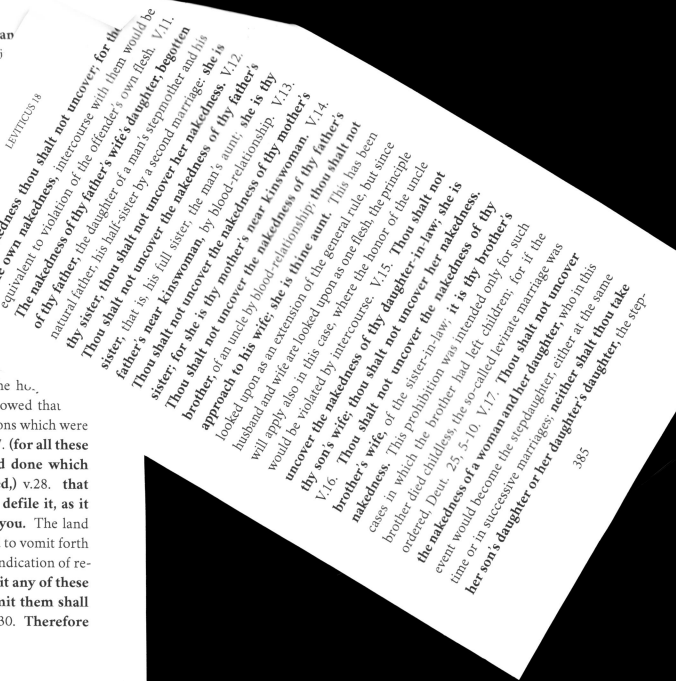

their nakedness thou shalt not uncover; for th[eir]
thine own nakedness, intercourse with them would be
equivalent to violation of the offender's own flesh. V.11.
The nakedness of thy father's wife's daughter, begotten
of thy father, the daughter of a man's stepmother and his
natural father, his half-sister by a second marriage: she is
thy sister, thou shalt not uncover her nakedness. V.12.
Thou shalt not uncover the nakedness of thy father's
sister, that is, his full sister, the man's aunt; she is thy
father's near kinswoman, by blood-relationship. V.13.
Thou shalt not uncover the nakedness of thy mother's
sister; for she is thy mother's near kinswoman. V.14.
Thou shalt not uncover the nakedness of thy father's
brother, of an uncle by blood-relationship; thou shalt not
approach to his wife; she is thine aunt. This has been
looked upon as an extension of the general rule, but since
husband and wife are looked upon as one flesh, the principle
will apply also in this case, where the honor of the uncle
would be violated by intercourse. V.15. Thou shalt not
uncover the nakedness of thy daughter-in-law; she is
thy son's wife; thou shalt not uncover the nakedness of thy
brother's wife, of the sister-in-law; it is thy brother's
nakedness. This prohibition was intended only for such
cases in which the brother had left children; for if the
brother died childless, the so-called levirate marriage was
ordered, Deut. 25, 5-10. V.17. Thou shalt not uncover
the nakedness of a woman and her daughter, who in this
event would become the stepdaughter, either at the same
time or in successive marriages; neither shalt thou take
her son's daughter or her daughter's daughter, the step-

shall ye keep Mine ordinance, the precept covering this matter based upon natural law, **that ye commit not any one of these abominable customs which were committed before you, and that ye defile not yourselves therein. I am the Lord, your God,** and the just and holy God cannot endure such customs of abomination, as in those days, so in our times. There is a hint in this chapter which has been sustained abundantly by history, namely, that any relaxation of sexual purity will usually be accompanied by the perversion or denial of some fundamental doctrine.

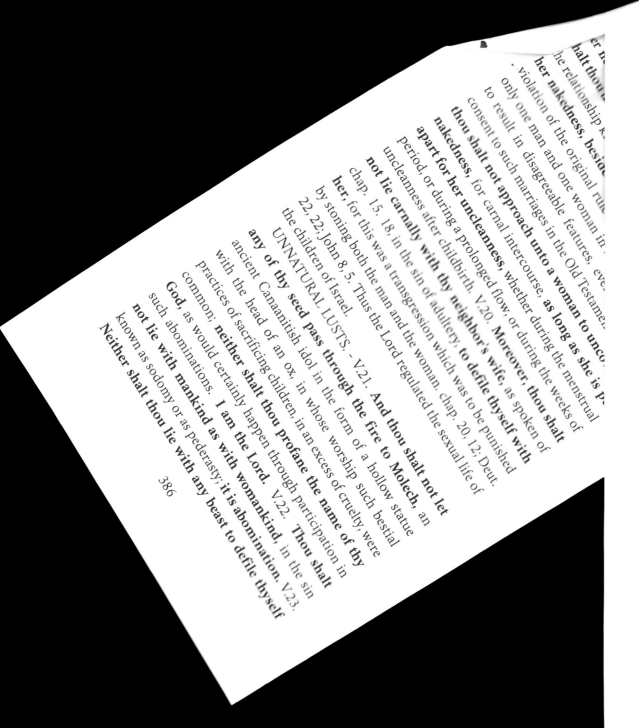

her **nakedness, beside** the relationship ... violation of the original rule ... only one man and one woman in ... to result in disagreeable features, even consent to such marriages in the Old Testament, **thou shalt not approach unto a woman** to uncover her **nakedness,** for carnal intercourse, whether during the weeks of **apart for her uncleanness,** as spoken of period, or during a prolonged flow, or during the menstrual uncleanness after childbirth. V20. **Moreover, thou shalt not lie carnally with thy neighbor's wife, to defile thyself with** chap. 15. 18, in the sin of adultery, which was to be punished her, for this was a transgression regulated the sexual life of by stoning both the man and the woman. chap. 20, 12; Deut. 22, 22; John 8, 5. Thus the Lord UNNATURAL LUSTS. – V.21. **And thou shalt not let the children of Israel. any of thy seed pass through the fire to Molech,** an ancient Canaanitish idol in the form of a hollow statue with the head of an ox, in whose worship such bestial practices of sacrificing children, in an excess of cruelty, were common; **neither shalt thou profane the name of thy God,** as would certainly happen through participation in such abominations. **I am the Lord.** V.22. **Thou shalt not lie with mankind as with womankind,** in the sin known as sodomy or as pederasty; **it is abomination.** V.23. **Neither shalt thou lie with any beast to defile thyself**

386

61

Leviticus 19

A Summary of Various Laws.

CHIEFLY OF THE FIRST TABLE. - V.1. **And the Lord spake unto Moses, saying,** v.2. **Speak unto all the congregation of the children of Israel and say unto them, ye shall be holy; for I, the Lord, your God, am holy.** They were not only to be pure and sinless, but their entire life was to present a definite and unvarying contrast to sin and transgression in any form. That is the fundamental thought of the chapter. V.3. **Ye shall fear every man his mother and his father.** The mother is here mentioned first, as the children are chiefly dependent upon her and associated with her, especially in the first years of their lives. Reverence to the mother of the home is essential for the proper social relationship, and the importance of this relation is seen from the fact that the family is the unit of civilization. **And keep My Sabbaths,** all the festival days sacred to the Lord. **I am the**

Lord, your God. This observance governed the entire social organization of the Jews. V.4. **Turn ye not unto idols, nor make to yourselves molten gods. I am the Lord, your God.** "If the heart of man becomes benumbed to the use of images of false gods of any kind, he sinks down to the level of the idols which are his ideals, and becomes as dumb and unspiritual as they are." (Lange.) It is significant that the word here used for idols really means "nothingnesses," thus describing the idols in their true character. Cp. Ps. 96, 5; 115, 8; 135, 18; Is. 40, 18; 44, 10. V.5. **And if ye offer a sacrifice of peace-offerings unto the Lord, ye shall offer it at your own will.** Unless the offerings were made in this spirit, with a right good will, from the heart, they would have no value in the sight of God. V.6. **It shall be eaten the same day ye offer it, and on the morrow,** for that was the rule with regard to voluntary sacrifices, chap. 7, 16; **and if aught remain until the third day, it shall be burned in the fire.** V.7. **And if it be eaten at all on the third day, it is abominable; it shall not be accepted,** the object of the sacrifice was not attained, its purpose was made void by the deliberate disregard of God's rule. V.8. **Therefore every one that eateth it shall bear his iniquity, because he hath profaned the hallowed thing of the Lord,** in eating of flesh which had been devoted to the Lord as a gift after it had become unclean; **and that soul shall be cut off from among his people.** This threat involved excommunication on the part of the congregation and the punishment of death on the part of God, who is a holy, jealous God.

CHIEFLY OF THE SECOND TABLE. - V.9. **And when ye reap the harvest of your land, thou shalt not wholly reap the corners of thy field,** to the very edge of the property line, **neither shalt thou gather the gleanings of thy harvest,** single stalks and ears that dropped when the sheaves were bound. V.10. **And thou shalt not glean thy vineyard** after the first picking, **neither shalt thou gather every grape of thy vineyard,** those that had fallen to the ground during the picking; **thou shalt leave them for the poor and stranger. I am the Lord, your God.** Love toward one's neighbor was emphasized again and again as a fundamental requirement of the Law. V.11. **Ye shall not steal, neither deal falsely,** hypocritically, **neither lie one to another,** said of deceit and perfidiousness. Note that falsehood and fraud are enumerated with theft, for the three go together. V.12. **And ye shall not swear by My name falsely;** true oaths are indeed permitted, those in the interest of one's neighbor, but not false oaths; **neither shalt thou profane the name of thy God,** desecrate it by taking it in vain. **I am the Lord.** V.13. **Thou shalt not defraud, oppress, thy neighbor, neither rob him,** in any manner whatever deprive him of something which is due him; **the wages of him that is hired shall not abide with thee all night until the morning.** The day-laborer was to receive his pay at the end of each day, Deut. 24. 14. 15. V.14. **Thou shalt not curse the deaf,** the poor man not being able to hear the maledictions and to defend himself, **nor put a stumbling-block before the blind,** to cause him to fall, a decidedly ill-conceived form of practical joke, **but shalt fear thy God,** who both hears and sees, and will avenge the wrong in due time. **I am the Lord.** V.15. **Ye shall do no unrighteousness in judgment,** not let personal interests influence you to disregard the demands of justice. **Thou shalt not respect the person of**

the poor, take his part from false sympathy, **nor honor the person of the mighty,** with the aim of gaining his favor; **but in righteousness shalt thou judge thy neighbor.** V.16. **Thou shalt not go up and down as a talebearer among thy people; neither shalt thou stand against the blood of thy neighbor,** as the false witness often does. **I am the Lord.** This involves, of course, "casting aside all inhumane conduct, all ill will, as manifested in malicious belittling, blackening, and slandering, and especially in attempts against the life of a neighbor, whether in court or in private life." (Lange.) V.17. **Thou shalt not hate thy brother in thine heart, not bear him any grudge. Thou shalt in any wise rebuke thy neighbor,** frankly and openly tell him his fault in the event of a transgression, as the Lord also bids us do, Matt. 18, 15-17, **and not suffer sin upon him,** that is, not bear a sin on his account by remaining silent, when a remonstrance in time might save one's neighbor from severe transgressions. So even the Israelites, according to this precept, would become partakers of other men's sins. V.18. **Thou shalt not avenge,** seek and take revenge for a wrong which has been inflicted, **nor bear any grudge against the children of thy people,** Rom. 12, 19, after a wrong has been committed, but thou shalt love thy neighbor as thyself. I am the Lord. Cp. Matt. 19, 19; 22, 39. Many of these cases, if not all, are applications of the law of love, and therefore require to be observed by Christians to this day.

VARIOUS STATUTES. - V.19. **Ye shall keep My statutes,** those special precepts which applied particularly to the conditions under which the Jews lived. **Thou shalt not let thy cattle gender with a diverse kind,** for the production of hybrids. **Thou shalt not sow thy field with mingled**

seed, for the same reason; neither shall a garment mingled of linen and woolen come upon thee. V.20. **And whosoever lieth carnally with a woman that is a bondmaid,** a slave, **betrothed to an husband,** probably after the manner spoken of Ex. 21, 7-11, **and not at all redeemed, nor freedom given her,** these being the two ways in which a slave could gain his liberty; **she shall be scourged,** or rather, there shall be a punishment of both guilty persons; **they shall not be put to death, because she was not free** and could not legally contract marriage. V.21. **And he,** the guilty man, **shall bring his trespass-offering unto the Lord, unto the door of the Tabernacle of the Congregation, even a ram for a trespass-offering.** V.22. **And the priest shall make an atonement for him with the ram of the trespass-offering before the Lord for his sin which he hath done,** in the manner prescribed by God, chap. 7, 1-7; **and the sin which he hath done shall be forgiven him.** V.23. **And when ye shall come in to the land, and shall have planted all manner of trees for food,** fruit-trees and nut-trees, **then ye shall count the fruit thereof as uncircumcised,** and therefore not to be used; **three years shall it be as uncircumcised unto you; it shall not be eaten of.** V.24. **But in the fourth year all the fruit thereof shall be holy to praise the Lord withal,** hallowed to Jehovah, and fit to be used as an offering of first-fruits. V.25. **And in the fifth year shall ye eat of the fruit thereof, that it may yield unto you the increase thereof** through the blessing of the Lord. **I am the Lord, your God.** This manner of treating the trees incidentally increased the yield of the orchard. V.26. **Ye shall not eat anything with the blood,** flesh from which the blood had not thoroughly drained, chap. 17. 10; **neither shall ye use enchantment,** any form of soothsaying, **nor observe times,** another form of witchcraft, that of using the evil eye. V.27. **Ye shall not round the corners of your heads,** cut or shave the hair in a circle from one temple to the other, **neither shalt thou mar the corners of thy beard,** crop or trim the ends. This seems to have reference to a custom followed by some heathen nations in honor of certain idols. V.28. **Ye shall not make any cuttings in your flesh for the dead,** such tattooing and such incisions as the Jews must have seen done among the Egyptians, **nor print any marks upon you,** in the form of pictures, letters, or figures. **I am the Lord.** V.29. **Do not prostitute thy daughter,** induce her to permit her body to he used for immoral purposes, **to cause her to be a whore,** a sin which profanes the body in the most specific and emphatic sense, **lest the land fall to whoredom, and the land become full of wickedness,** full of abominable deeds. The reference is probably to religious immorality, as it was joined with many idolatrous worships and is to this day, in which women voluntarily abandoned their chastity as priestesses of the idol. V.30. **Ye shall keep My Sabbaths,** all the prescribed festivals, **and reverence My Sanctuary. I am the Lord.** The entire social and domestic life of the Israelites was to be pervaded by the fear of God and characterized by chasteness and propriety. V.31. **Regard not them that have familiar spirits, neither seek after wizards to be defiled by them;** literally: "Do not turn to the spirits of the dead, and after the spirits of soothsaying do not follow." **I am the Lord, your God.** All intercourse with conjurors of the dead and with wizards was equivalent to desecration of the holy relation with God, "The chief means used by both these classes of persons was the consulting with the spirits of the departed. While this furnishes an incidental testimony all along to the belief of the Israelites in the life beyond the grave, it is self-evident that all such attempts to secure knowledge which God has not put in the power of living man to acquire are a resistance to His will, and a chafing against the barriers He has imposed. It is remarkable that such attempts should have been persisted in through all ages and in all lands." (Gardiner.) 6) V.32. **Thou shalt rise up before the hoary head, and honor the face of the old man, and fear thy God. I am the Lord.** The respect for old age, coming under the Fourth Commandment, is here associated with the fear of God, who demands this showing of respect. V.33. **And if a stranger sojourn with thee in your land, ye shall not vex,** that is, oppress, him, make him feel that he is an outcast. V.34. **But the stranger that dwelleth with you shall be unto you as one born among you,** be treated with all kind regard, just as though he were an inhabitant of the land, **and thou shalt love him as thyself; for ye were strangers in the land of Egypt,** and the remembrance of the oppression suffered there was to have a wholesome influence in teaching them mercy, **I am the Lord, your God.** V.35. **Ye shall do no unrighteousness in judgment,** in any matter that is to be decided in court, **in mete-yard,** in measurements of length, **in weight, or in measure,** both dry and liquid measure being included. V.36. **Just balances,** for measures of weight, **just weights,** stones used as standards of weight, **a just ephah,** as a standard for dry measure, **and a just hin,** as the standard for liquid measure, **shall ye have. I am the Lord,** your God, which brought you out of the land of

Egypt. It is clear that equity in the affairs of daily life is here made to rest upon the foundation of duty toward God. V.37. **Therefore shall ye observe all My statutes and all My judgments,** the precepts flowing out of the natural law inscribed in the hearts of all men as well as those given to the Jews in particular, **and do them. I am the Lord,** Love is still the fulfillment of the Law, the advantage which the Christians have consisting chiefly in this, that its application in the individual cases is left to the judgment of the believer, as a spur to his ingenuity.

62

Leviticus 20

Punishments for Various Sins.

FOR SINS AGAINST THE SIXTH, SECOND, AND FOURTH COMMANDMENTS. - V.1. **And the Lord spake unto Moses, saying,** v.2. **Again, thou shalt say to the children of Israel, Whosoever he be of the children of Israel, or of the strangers that sojourn in Israel, that giveth any of his seed unto Molech,** in the double sin of masturbation or onanism and idolatry, or, more likely, in immolating children, chap. 18, 21, **he shall surely be put to death; the people of the land shall stone him with stones.** The offender, after the forms of the law had been observed, Deut. 17, 6; 19, 15, was to suffer summary execution by being stoned and literally buried under the thrown stones. V.3. **And I will set My face against that man,** in case the people should neglect the punishment in due time, **and will cut him off from among his people,** pursue the offender and his followers with His judgment, until He has exterminated all that are associated in his guilt, **because he hath given of his seed unto Molech,** the abomination of the Canaanites, **to defile My Sanctuary, and to profane My holy name.** V.4. **And if the people of the land do anyways hide their eyes from the man when he giveth of his seed unto Molech,** consecrating it as an act of worship, **and kill him not,** v.5. **then I will set My face against that man and against his family, and will cut him off and all that go a-whoring after him,** in the double sense of committing an immoral act and of becoming guilty of idolatry, **to commit whoredom with Molech, from among their people.** As no sacrifice to false gods was permitted in the land, so this special worship of Molech was an abomination which could under no circumstances be tolerated. V.6. **And the soul that turneth after such as have familiar spirits, and after wizards,** after men and women that consult with the spirits of the dead and use other forms of soothsaying, chap. 19, 31, **to go a-whoring after them,** becoming unfaithful to the true God by such idolatrous practices. **I will even set My face against that soul, and I will cut him off from among his people.** Excommunication and death was to be his punishment for engaging in apostasy and for corrupting the people of the Lord. V.7. **Sanctify yourselves, therefore, and be ye holy; for I am the Lord, your God,** and Jehovah God, Himself the absolutely sinless and pure personality, wanted His people not only to abstain from sin, but also to abhor sin with an undying enmity. V.8. **And ye shall keep My statutes and do them. I am the Lord which sanctify you.** By training them to observe the ordinances of His holy will God was consecrating them to be a holy people in His service. V.9. **Fore very one that curseth his father or his mother shall be surely put to death; he hath cursed his father or his mother,** the representatives of God in the home, in the family; his blood shall be up on him. This shows the emphasis which the Lord at all times placed upon the honor of parents and the keeping of the Fourth Commandment.

FOR UNLAWFUL MARRIAGES. - V.10. **And the man that committeth adultery with another man's wife, even he that committeth adultery with his neighbor's wife,** who, according to chap. 18, 20, is restricted to her husband, so far as sexual relations are concerned, 1 Cor. 7, 4. 5, **the adulterer and the adulteress shall surely be put to death. V.11. And the man that lieth with his father's wife,** with his stepmother, **hath uncovered his father's nakedness. Both of them shall surely be put to death; their blood shall be up on them. V.12. And if a man lie with his daughter-in-law, both of them shall surely be put to death; they have wrought confusion,** become guilty of a revolting defilement; **their blood shall be up on them. V.13. If a man also lie with mankind as he lieth with a woman,** in the sin of pederasty, **both of them have committed an abomination,** a bestial crime, contrary to nature, a horror; **they shall surely be put to death; their blood shall be upon them. V.14. And if a man take a wife and her mother,** in revolting incest, **it is wickedness,** a most horrible act, an unheard-of deed of shame; **they shall be burned with fire, both he and they,** after they have been stoned, for thus the abnormality of their crime was emphasized; **that there be no wickedness among you.** In all these cases, both persons are alike guilty, because even the passive part consented to the act, permitted the seduction to take place. In the case of rape the Lord's judgment is different. Deut. 22, 26. 27. V.15. **And if a man lie with a beast, he shall surely be put to death; and ye shall slay the beast.** V.16. **And if a woman approach unto any beast and lie down thereto, thou shalt kill the woman and the beast; they shall surely be put to death; their blood shall be upon them.** "With the beastly human being the beast itself was also to be destroyed." (Lange.) V.17. **And if a man shall take his sister, his father's daughter or his mother's daughter,** his (older) half-sister, **and see her nakedness and she see his nakedness, it is a wicked thing,** a disgraceful act; **and they shall be cut off in the sight of their people; he hath uncovered his sister's nakedness; he shall bear his iniquity,** his misdeed. V.18. **And if a man lie with a woman having her sickness,** her menstrual period, **and shall uncover her nakedness,** knowingly and intentionally, **he hath discovered her fountain,** exposed her life-spring, **and she hath uncovered the fountain of her blood; and both of them shall be cut off from among their people.** For the penalty of the unintentional offense, see chap. 15, 24. V.19. **And thou shalt not uncover the nakedness of thy mother's sister nor of thy father's sister; for he uncovereth his near kin; they shall bear their iniquity.** This transgression was not punished with death by the government, but the Lord Himself would take their case in hand. V.20. **And if a man shall lie with his uncle's wife,** his aunt by marriage, **he hath uncovered his uncle's nakedness; they shall bear their sin; they shall die childless.** While the marriage was not annulled, the Lord's punishment was very severe, for childlessness was classed with bereavement in the estimation of the Jews. V.21. **And if a man shall take his brother's wife,** in any case but that of the levirate marriage, **it is an unclean thing,** calling forth God's curse of the first degree; **he hath uncovered his brother's nakedness; they shall be childless.** The aim of all these provisions was to purify sexual life among the Hebrews, since the entire nation was consecrated to the Lord as a royal priesthood, Ex. 19, 6. Christians will keep in mind at all times that marriage is honorable in all and the bed undefiled, Heb. 13, 4.

ADMONITION TO HOLINESS. - V.22. **Ye shall therefore keep all My statutes and all My judgments,** both general and special, **and do them, that the land whither I bring you to dwell therein spue you not out,** chap. 18, 25. 28. V.23. **And ye shall not walk in the manners of the nation which I cast out before you,** the nation of the Canaanites with all its branches; **for they committed all these things, and therefore I abhorred them.** This implies that the sins enumerated in the list above were offenses against the natural law, against the summary of God's will as it was implanted in the hearts of men at the beginning. They were unnatural sins and vices. V.24. **But I have said unto you, Ye shall inherit their land, and I will give it unto you to possess it, a land that floweth with milk and honey,** of unusual fruitfulness. **I am the Lord, your God, which have separated you from other people,** to be a peculiar people, and one distinguished in His service. V.25. **Ye shall therefore put difference between clean beasts and unclean, and between unclean fowls and clean,** observe the distinctions set forth in chapter 11; **and ye shall not make your souls abominable by**

beast or by fowl or by any manner of living thing that creepeth on the ground, which I have separated from, you as unclean. V.26. **And ye shall be holy unto Me; for I, the Lord, am holy, and have severed you from other people that ye should be Mine.** "The sacred observance of the laws of food was thus a constant reminder for Israel of its theocratic sanctity and dignity." (Lange.) V.27. **A man also or woman that hath a familiar spirit, or that is a wizard,** that consults with the spirits of the dead or practices necromancy, **shall surely be put to death; they shall stone them with stones; their blood shall be upon them.** In this way every defilement through idolatrous abominations was prevented, and Israel was kept consecrated for the service of the Lord.

63

Leviticus 21

The Holiness of the Priests.

T HEIR OUTWARD APPEARANCE AND RELA-
TIONS. V.1. **And the Lord said unto Moses,
Speak unto the priests, the sons of Aaron, and
say unto them, There shall none be defiled for the dead
among his people** (for a person became unclean not only
by touching a dead body, but also by being in the same
tent or room with a deceased person, Num 19, 11. 14)
v.2. **but for his kin that is near unto him, that is, for
his mother, and for his father, and for his son, and for
his daughter, and for his brother,** v.3. **and for his sister,
a virgin,** as long as she is unmarried, **that is nigh unto
him, which hath had no husband; for her may he be
defiled.** After her marriage she belonged to her husband's
family, and the intimate ties of relationship were naturally
severed. A daughter always retains her affection for her
parents, while a married sister is usually estranged from her

brother V.4. **But he shall not defile himself being a chief among his people, to profane himself;** that is, he was not permitted to become unclean on account of any person related to him by marriage, but only on account of blood-relatives. V.5. **They shall not make baldness upon their head,** by shaving off the hair, **neither shall they shave off the corner of their beard, crop or trim the edges, nor make any cuttings in their flesh,** all these being extreme marks of severe mourning and grief. Cp. chap. 19, 27. 28; Deut. 14, 1. V.6. **They shall be holy unto their God, and not profane the name of their God,** as they would do by expressions of passionate grief, which are often equivalent to rebellion against His dispensations; **for the offerings of the Lord made by fire, and the bread of their God, they do offer,** thus serving Jehovah, drawing near to the Lord who has revealed Himself to His people as the Holy One; **therefore they shall be holy.** V.7. **They shall not take a wife that is a whore,** a public prostitute, or profane, a fallen woman, or one of illegitimate birth; **neither shall they take a woman put away from her husband,** a divorced woman; **for he** (the priest) **is holy unto his God.** The wives of the priests had to be of unblemished and spotless character. V.8. **Thou shalt sanctify him therefore; for he offereth the bread of thy God,** in the various sacrifices; **he shall be holy unto thee; for I, the Lord, which sanctify you, am holy.** The entire life and surroundings of the priests were to be in harmony with their calling. V.9. **And the daughter of any priest, if she profane herself by playing the whore, she profaneth her father,** brings disgrace not only upon his person, but also upon his office; **she shall be burned with fire,** after having suffered the punishment of death.

V.10. **And he that is the high priest among his brethren,** selected for that position from among his brethren, the children of Levi, **upon whose head the anointing oil was poured, and that is consecrated to put on the garments, shall not uncover his head,** go about with unkempt hair, **nor rend his clothes,** another of the accustomed marks of mourning, a precept which was disregarded by Caiaphas during the trial of Christ, Matt. 26, 65; v.11. **neither shall he go into any dead body, nor defile himself for his father or for his mother,** contact with the dead body of even these nearest relatives being forbidden; v.12. **neither shall he go out of the Sanctuary,** namely, for the purpose of visiting the home of his relatives at such a time, **nor profane the Sanctuary of his God** by bringing uncleanness upon his person in this manner; **for the crown of the anointing oil of his God is upon him. I am the Lord.** As a high priest of the Lord, set apart for the work of the Sanctuary by the oil of consecration, he was strictly to avoid all contamination, since this would bring disgrace upon Jehovah.

WIVES OF PRIESTS; BLEMISHES. - V.13. **And he shall take a wife in her virginity,** a pure virgin. V.14. **A widow, or a divorced woman, or profane,** a fallen woman, **or an harlot, these shall he not take,** v.7. **but he shall take a virgin of his own people to wife, a daughter of Israel.** V.15. **Neither shall he profane his seed among his people** by being joined in wedlock in a way which would not harmonize with the sanctity of his position; **for I, the Lord, do sanctify him.** v.16. **And the Lord spake unto Moses, saying,** v.17. **Speak unto Aaron, saying, Whosoever he be of thy seed in their generations,** among all his

405

coming descendants, **that hath any blemish,** any bodily defect, **let him not approach to offer the bread of his God,** the sacrifices in general, for these culminated in the showbread. V.18. **For whatsoever man he be that hath a blemish, he shall not approach: a blind man, or a lame, or he that hath a flat nose,** misshapen or slit, **or anything superfluous,** abnormal members of the body, v.19. **or a man that is broken-footed,** that has broken-down arches, **or broken-handed,** v.20. **or crookbacked,** one that has a hump, **or a dwarf,** one that is abnormally slender, **or that hath a blemish in his eye,** that is, a white spot conspicuous enough to draw attention, **or be scurvy,** affected with a growth which resembled leprosy, **or scabbed,** with a disfiguring skin-disease, **or hath his stones broken,** affected with a disease of the sexual organs; v.21. **no man that hath a blemish of the seed of Aaron, the priest, shall come nigh to offer the offerings of the Lord made by fire; he hath a blemish; he shall not come nigh to offer the bread of his God,** he was excluded from the characteristic work of the priesthood. V.22. **He shall eat the bread of his God, both of the most holy,** chap. 2, 3, **and of the holy,** of the wave-breast and of the heave-shoulder, of first-fruits, tithes, and gifts. This compassionate provision compensated, in a way, for the exclusion of these men from active service in the Sanctuary. V.23. **Only he shall not go in unto the veil, nor come nigh unto the altar,** he shall not discharge the official functions of the high priest or of the priests, **because he hath a blemish; that he profane not My sanctuaries; for I, the Lord, do sanctify them.** V.24. **And Moses told it unto Aaron and to his sons and unto all the children of Israel;** for the entire congregation was interested in the observance of these ordinances. In the New Testament the congregation of the believers is even more interested in the keeping of God's ordinances, because the discrimination between a special priesthood and a laity no longer exists, and every member is responsible for matters of doctrine and of life.

64

Leviticus 22

Further instructions For the priests.

WARNING AGAINST PROFANATION OF HAL-
LOWED THINGS. - V.1. **And the Lord spake
unto Moses, saying,** v.2. **Speak unto Aaron
and to his sons that they separate themselves from
the holy things of the children of Israel, and that they
profane not My holy name in those things which they
hallow unto Me. I am the Lord.** The priests were not to
profane the holy gifts of the people by approaching them
at a time when they themselves were in a condition of
uncleanness, which made their priestly services unlawful.
In these gifts were also included those parts of the sacrifices
which the Lord had set aside for maintenance of the priests.
V.3. **Say unto them, Whosoever he be of all your seed
among your generations,** of any descendant of Aaron
entrusted with priestly functions, **that goeth unto the
holy things which the children of Israel hallow unto**

408

the Lord, **having his uncleanness upon him,** any form of Levitical defilement, such as were discussed in chaps. 13 to 15, **that soul shall be cut off from My presence,** deprived of his priestly office, and perhaps punished in a more severe manner. **I am the Lord. V.4. What man soever of the seed of Aaron is a leper, or hath a running issue,** chap. 15, 2, **he shall not eat of the holy things until he be clean. And whoso toucheth anything that is unclean by the dead,** because of contact with a dead body, **or a man whose seed goeth from him; v.5. or whosoever toucheth any creeping thing, whereby he may be made unclean,** any one of the lower forms of animal life whose contact defiled a man, **or a man of whom he may take uncleanness, whatsoever uncleanness he hath;** v.6. **the soul which hath touched any such shall be unclean until even,** according to the general rule, which thus applied to the priests also, **and shall not eat of the holy things, unless he wash his flesh with water. V.7. And when the sun is down,** at the end of the day and at the beginning of the new day, **he shall be clean, and shall afterward eat of the holy things, because it is his food;** he was dependent upon the priests' share of the offerings for his daily bread and should no longer be deprived of this, after having fasted all day. The divine legislation always shows this considerate character. **V.8. That which dieth of itself, or is torn with beasts, he shall not eat to defile himself therewith,** for that was forbidden to all the children of Israel, Ex. 22, 31. **I am the Lord. V.9. They shall therefore keep Mine ordinance, lest they bear sin for it and die there for, if they profane it. I, the Lord, do sanctify them.** Death was the general penalty of a priest's neglect to follow the precepts of the Lord with regard to purity of service in his Sanctuary. Having now stated in what condition a priest was not to eat of things sanctified, the Lord excludes from their share of the sacrifices all those that were not members of the priestly family. V.10. **There shall no stranger eat of the holy thing; a sojourner of the priest,** any visitor not belonging to his family, to the tribe of Levi, **or an hired servant, shall not eat of the holy thing.** V.11. **But if the priest buy any soul with his money, he shall eat of it, and he that is born in his house; they shall eat of his meat.** In either case the slave was a member of the priest's family and dependent upon the food which he received for his own maintenance. V.12. **If the priest's daughter also be married unto a stranger,** to a man not belonging to the priestly family, **she may not eat of an offering of the holy things.** V.13. **But if the priest's daughter be a widow or divorced,** spurned by her husband, **and have no child, and is returned unto her father's house, as in her youth, she shall eat of her father's meat,** of the food which her father was entitled to as a part of his emoluments as priest; **but there shall no stranger eat thereof.** If the priest's daughter should have children, she formed with her children a household of her own, even if she was widowed or divorced. V.14. **And if a man eat of the holy thing unwittingly,** without intention, without being aware of the fact at the time, **then he shall put the fifth part thereof unto it,** that is, the equivalent of the food which was profaned together with a penalty, **and shall give it unto the priest with the holy thing,** thereby making restitution for the fault. V.15. **And they shall not profane the holy things of the children of Israel which they offer unto the Lord,** v.16. **or suffer**

them to bear the iniquity of trespass, load themselves with the crime of the guilt in permitting such a profanation on the part of unauthorized people, **when they eat their holy things; for I, the Lord, do sanctify them.** So the priests were charged with the supervision of these matters, in order to keep the sanctified things from profanation, just as the pastors of the Christian Church should carry out the function of watchmen in warning the people entrusted to them by the Lord of the Church against all transgressions of God's holy Law.

SOME QUALIFICATIONS OF SACRIFICES. - V.17. **And the Lord spake unto Moses, saying,** v.18. **Speak unto Aaron and to his sons and unto all the children of Israel, and say unto them, whatsoever he be of the house of Israel or of the strangers in Israel that will offer his oblation for all his vows and for all his free-will offerings, two forms of peace-offerings, chap. 7, 16, which they will offer unto the Lord for a burnt offering,** v.19. **ye shall offer at your own will,** for the purpose of gaining the good pleasure of the Lord: **a male without blemish, of the beeves, of the sheep, or of the goats.** The point that the animal offered had to be physically perfect stands out with special emphasis. V.20. **But whatsoever hath a blemish, that shall ye not offer; for it shall not be acceptable for you.** V.21. **And whosoever offereth a sacrifice of peace-offerings unto the Lord to accomplish his vow,** in payment of some promise made to the Lord, **or a free-will offering in beeves or sheep,** any animal from the flocks, **it shall be perfect to be accepted; there shall be no blemish therein.** V.22. **Blind or broken,** that is, ruptured, **or**

maimed, with some deep incision or wound, **or having a wen,** a festering sore, **or scurvy,** an eruption like leprosy, **or scabbed,** with a putrid skin disease, **ye shall not offer these unto the Lord, nor make an offering by fire of them upon the altar unto the Lord. V.23. Either a bullock or a lamb that hath anything superfluous or lacking in his parts,** members too many or too few, or members and organs of an abnormal shape in either direction, so long as they were not diseased, **that mayest thou offer for a free-will offering,** for in this case an exception was permitted; **but for a vow it shall not be accepted.** V.24. **Ye shall not offer unto the Lord that which is bruised, or crushed, or broken, or cut,** for by these four ways was sterility produced in male animals; **neither shall ye make any offering thereof in your land;** the Israelites were not to make such mutilations a practice, for a perfect animal included its fitness for breeding. V.25. **Neither from a stranger's hand shall ye offer the bread of your God of any of these, because their corruption is in them, and blemishes be in them; they shall not be accepted for you.** We Christians should also keep in mind that it is not whatever remains after we have had our fill which we ought to give to the Lord, but that He expects perfect gifts at our hands. V.26. **And the Lord spake unto Moses, saying,** v.27. **When a bullock or a sheep or a go at is brought forth, then it shall be seven days under the dam,** to get its nourishment from its mother; **and from the eighth day and thenceforth it shall be accepted for an offering made by fire unto the Lord.** "The reason for this was that the young animal had not attained to a mature and self-sustained life during the first week of its existence." (Keil.)

Animals became admissible for sacrifices at the same age as that when a male child was received into the covenant relationship with God by the sacrament of circumcision. V.28. **And whether it be cow or ewe, a female from the flock, ye shall not kill it and her young both in one day.** Cp. Ex. 23, 19; Deut. 22, 6. 7. V.29. **And when ye will offer a sacrifice of thanksgiving unto the Lord, offer it at your own will;** it was essential that the gift be voluntary. V.30. **On the same day it shall be eaten up; ye shall leave none of it until the morrow. I am the Lord.** Cp. chap. 7, 15: 19, 5. 6. V.31. **Therefore shall ye keep My commandments and do them. I am the Lord.** V.32. **Neither shall ye profane My holy name** in any of the ways discussed in this chapter; **but I will be hallowed among the children of Israel,** given that obedience, honor, and reverence which pertains to Him as the one true God. **I am the Lord which hallow you,** v.33. **that brought you out of the land of Egypt to be your God: I am the Lord.** Just as the Lord at that time stressed the necessity of cheerful willingness on the part of the worshipers, so the truly good works of the Christians flow from the love of their hearts based upon their faith in their Savior.

Leviticus 23

The Feasts of the Lord.

THE SABBATH. - V.1. **And the Lord spake unto Moses, saying, v.2. Speak unto the children of Israel and say unto them, Concerning the feasts of the Lord which ye shall proclaim to be holy convocations, even these are My feasts.** The word originally means fixed or appointed times, which the Lord had marked out, separated, distinguished from the ordinary course of daily life, and therefore found its chief application in the case of the festivals. While the chapter contains a calendar of the festivals, its purpose is chiefly, as the restricting relative clause indicates, to mark those festivals upon which there should be solemn meetings for the purpose of worship. V.3. **Six days shall work be done,** the ordinary business of life should be done on the six days of the week, and the words are not merely a permission, but a command; **but the seventh day is the Sabbath of rest, an holy**

convocation; ye shall do no work therein. The Sabbath was to be distinguished not only by the fact that the Jews desisted from work, but chiefly because they assembled for the purposes of worship; **it is the Sabbath of the Lord in all your dwellings.** By the last expression the convocation of the Sabbath is distinguished from that of all the annual festivals, for the Sabbath was usually celebrated at home, in the country, in town, in village, in hamlet, throughout the land, and wherever the Jews lived, while the great festivals were celebrated chiefly, if not entirely, at the places where the Lord's Sanctuary was erected.

THE PASSOVER AND THE OFFERING WHICH FOLLOWED IT. - V.4. **These are the feasts of the Lord,** in the narrower sense, **even holy convocations, which ye shall proclaim in their seasons.** This instruction was carried out with strict literalness in after-years, the exact date of the new moon in each month being fixed by the elders of the Jews and announced with great solemnity. V.5. **In the fourteenth day of the first month,** of the month Abib, or Nisan, with which the church-year began, at even, **is the Lord's Passover.** Cp. Ex. 12, 6-20. V.6. **And on the fifteenth day of the same month is the Feast of Unleavened Bread unto the Lord; seven days ye must eat unleavened bread.** Although at a later period the two festivals were considered as one, for all practical purposes, and often identified, yet the distinction was observed, and careful writers did not neglect to refer to it, Mark 14, 1. V.7. **In the first day ye shall have an holy convocation,** a solemn assembly for purposes of worship; **ye shall do no servile work therein.** On this day all business and work was strictly suspended, as on a most solemn Sabbath.

415

V.8. **But ye shall offer an offering made by fire unto the Lord seven days,** although these days were not closed to the ordinary work in the house, in the shop, and on the farm. **In the seventh day is an holy convocation; ye shall do no servile work therein,** as on the first day. Of the annual festivals, the Passover, with the Feast of Unleavened Bread connected with it, came first in the cycle of the church-year, first in the great historic event it commemorated, first in its obligation, and first in its spiritual and typical significance. V.9. **And the Lord spake unto Moses, saying,** v.10. **Speak unto the children of Israel and say unto them, When ye come in to the land which I give unto you,** for it was only at that time that this special instruction was to come into force, **and shall reap the harvest thereof, then ye shall bring a sheaf of the first-fruits of your harvest unto the priest,** a sheaf of barley, which ripens in Palestine in April; v.11. **and he shall wave the sheaf before the Lord,** by which the gift was sanctified to Jehovah, who then designated it for the use of the priests, **to be accepted for you; on the morrow after the Sabbath,** after the first day of the holy convocation, on the sixteenth of Nisan, **the priest shall wave it.** V.12. **and ye shall offer that day when ye wave the sheaf an he-lamb without blemish of the first year for a burnt offering unto the Lord.** As Israel, by the offering of the sheaf of first-fruits, consecrated the entire new harvest and the daily bread depending upon this harvest to the Lord and confessed that its maintenance depended upon the divine goodness, so, by the burnt offering, the people declared their unworthiness of the Lord's goodness and their need of His mercy. V.13. **And the meat-offering thereof,** to accompany the burnt offering, **shall be two-tenth deals** (somewhat over five quarts) **of fine flour,** wheaten flour, **mingled with oil, an offering made by fire unto the Lord for a sweet savor; and the drink-offering thereof shall be of wine, the fourth part of an hin,** a trifle more than a quart. V.14. **And ye shall eat neither bread, nor parched corn,** roasted at the fire, **nor green ears,** of the new harvest, **until the selfsame day that ye have brought an offering unto your god; it shall be a statute forever throughout your generations in all your dwellings,** in the land of Canaan, as long as the Levitical priesthood endured. The use of the new grain for food in any form whatever before the ceremony of waving on the sixteenth of Nisan was absolutely forbidden. All our possessions, all the members of our bodies, should be consecrated to the Lord for diligence in good works.

THE FEAST OF WEEKS. - V.15. **And ye shall count unto you from the morrow after the Sabbath,** from the sixteenth of Nisan, **from the day that ye brought the sheaf of the wave-offering; seven Sabbaths,** or weeks, **shall be complete.** V.16. **Even unto the morrow after the seventh Sabbath shall ye number fifty days, and ye shall offer anew meat-offering unto the Lord,** one prepared from the grain of the new harvest. V.17. **Ye shall bring out of your habitations,** not from the Temple revenues, this being an extra offering, **two wave-loaves of two-tenth deals** (a little more than five quarts), bread like that used for daily food. **They shall be of fine flour,** of wheaten flour; **they shall be baken with leaven,** as the bread was always prepared in the homes; **they are the first-fruits unto the Lord.** V.18. **And ye shall offer with the breads even lambs without blemish of the first year and one**

417

young bullock and two rams; they shall be for a burnt offering unto the Lord, with their meat-offering and their drink-offerings, even an offering made by fire, of sweet savor unto the Lord. V.19. **Then ye shall sacrifice one kid of the goats for a sin-offering, and two lambs of the first year for a sacrifice of peace-offerings.** "The sin-offering was to excite the feeling and consciousness of sin on the part of the congregation of Israel, that, whilst eating their daily leavened bread, they might not serve the leaven of their old nature, but seek and implore from the Lord, their God, the forgiveness and cleansing away of their sin." (Keil.) V.20. **And the priest shall wave them with the bread of the first-fruits for a wave-offering before the Lord,** the name being derived from the movement of the body and of the arms which accompanied the presentation to the Lord, **with the two lambs; they shall be holy to the Lord for the priest.** Thus the character of the festival, as one of joyful gratitude for God's goodness and mercy, was emphasized. V.21. **And ye shall proclaim on the selfsame day that it may be an holy convocation unto you; ye shall do no servile work therein,** as on the first and the last day of the Feast of Unleavened Bread; **it shall be a statute forever in all your dwellings throughout your generations.** V.22. **And when ye reap the harvest of your land, thou shalt not make clean riddance of the corners of thy field when thou reapest,** in mowing to the very border of the land, **neither shalt thou gather any gleaning of thy harvest,** the stalks and ears that dropped out in harvesting; **thou shalt leave them unto the poor and to the stranger. I am the Lord, your God.** To celebrate a festival of thanksgiving to the Lord for the blessings of His goodness and at the same time to ignore the needs of the poor is a combination which will hardly meet with the approval of the Lord,

THE FEAST OF TRUMPETS. - V.23. **And the Lord spake unto Moses, saying,** v.24, **Speak unto the children of Israel, saying, In the seventh month, in the first day of the month, shall ye have a Sabbath, a memorial of blowing of trumpets, an holy convocation.** It was a feast Sabbath, distinguished from the ordinary new moons, and a Sabbath of memorial. The feature of the day was the sounding of the trumpets, horns, or trombones, which belonged to the equipment of the Sanctuary, Num. 10, 2. V.25. **Ye shall do no servile work there in; but ye shall offer an offering made by fire unto the Lord.** The day was afterward, if not at that time, celebrated as the Sew Year's Day of the civil year, and the solemn assembly marked its prominence, as the Jews said, because it commemorated the creation, when all the sons of God shouted for joy, Job 38, 7. The blowing of horns was afterward not confined to the Sanctuary, but was indulged in very generally throughout the land. The burnt offering of the day is specified exactly in Num. 29, 1-6.

THE DAY OF ATONEMENT. - V.26. **And the Lord spake unto Moses, saying,** v.27. **Also on the tenth day of this seventh month,** the seventh month of the church-year, known as Tishri, **there shall be a day of atonement; it shall be an holy convocation unto you; and ye shall afflict your souls,** show the grief and mourning which you feel on account of your sins by a complete fast, **and offer an offering made by fire unto the Lord.** Cp. chap. 16. The offerings are specified in detail Num. 29, 8-11.

419

V.28. **And ye shall do no work in that same day; for it is a day of atonement, to make an atonement for you before the Lord, your God,** the annual restoration of the relation between the covenant God and His people by the sprinkling of blood in the Most Holy Place. V.29. **For whatsoever soul it be that shall not be afflicted in that same day,** not join the rest of the people in the fasting which showed the intensity of their mourning, **he shall be cut off from among his people.** V.30. **And whatsoever soul it be that doeth any work in that same day, the same soul will I destroy from among his people,** for the strictest form of Sabbath rest was here demanded. V.31. **Ye shall do no manner of work; it shall be a statute forever throughout your generations in all your dwellings.** V.32. **It shall be unto you a Sabbath of rest, and ye shall afflict your souls. In the ninth day of the month at even, from even unto even, shall ye celebrate your Sabbath.** The exact length of the fast is specified, and the great rigor is to be noted with which the penalty of death was held forth for every transgression against the rest of the Sabbath and against the fast. The children of Israel mere to be made conscious, at least to some extent, of the heinousness and of the guilt of sin, that they might enter upon the celebration of the Day of Atonement with hearts full of genuine repentance.

THE FEAST OF TABERNACLES. - V.33. **And the Lord spake unto Moses, saying,** v.34. **Speak unto the children of Israel, saying, The fifteenth day of this seventh month,** of the month Tishri, corresponding to the latter part of our September and the first part of our October, **shall be the Feast of Tabernacles for seven days unto the Lord,** named the Feast of Booths on account of the temporary structures in which the children of Israel lived during that week, as described below. V.35. **On the first day shall be an holy convocation; ye shall do no servile work therein,** as on the other great festivals. V.36. **Seven days ye shall offer an offering made by fire unto the Lord,** in addition to the daily burnt offerings, as described Num. 29, 13-38. **On the eighth day shall be an holy convocation unto you; and ye shall offer an offering made by fire unto the Lord; it is a solemn assembly,** concluding the festivities of the week in a manner befitting their importance; **and ye shall do no servile work therein.** V.37. **These are the feasts of the Lord,** as enumerated in this chapter, **which ye shall proclaim to be holy convocations,** this being the feature which is stressed here, **to offer an offering made by fire unto the Lord, a burnt offering, and a meat-offering, a sacrifice, and drink-offerings,** the libations of wine, **every thing upon his day;** v.38. **beside the Sabbaths of the Lord, and beside your gifts, and beside all your vows, and beside all your free-will offerings which ye give unto the Lord.** V.39. **Also in the fifteenth day of the seventh month, when ye have gathered in the fruit of the land, ye shall keep a feast unto the Lord seven days,** for the Feast of Tabernacles was the festival of the completed harvest, not only of grain, but also of fruit. **On the first day shall be a Sabbath, and on the eighth day shall be a Sabbath,** as stated above. V.40. **And ye shall take you on the first day the boughs of goodly trees,** literally, "fruit of ornamental trees." whose long composite leaves would serve well for purposes of decoration, **branches of palm-trees, and the boughs of thick trees,** such with

421

POPULAR COMMENTARY ON EXODUS AND LEVITICUS

heavy foliage, **and willows of the brook,** all these being used in the construction of booths; **and ye shall rejoice before the Lord, your God, seven days.** Cp. Neh. 8, 15 ff. V.41. **And ye shall keep it a feast unto the Lord seven days in the year. It shall be a statute forever in your generations; ye shall celebrate it in the seventh month.** V.42. **Ye shall dwell in booths seven days; all that are Israelites born shall dwell in booths,** the strangers being excluded in the ordinance, since the second purpose of the festival was to remind the Israelites of their dwelling in tents in the wilderness, v.43. **that your generations may know that I made the children of Israel to dwell in booths when I brought them out of the land of Egypt. I am the Lord, your God.** The keynote of the festival, therefore, was joy to the point of exultation, since the contrast between the fullness of the blessings enjoyed in Palestine, as it appeared in every harvest, and the desolation of the wilderness was so marked. Cp. Deut. 8. V.44. **And Moses declared unto the children of Israel the feasts of the Lord.** The Feast of Tabernacles is probably symbolic of the everlasting festival of joy which we shall celebrate with all the elect in heaven, where our hosannas will rise to the throne of the Lamb in endless refrain.[4]

[4] For a full discussion of the Hebrew festivals, see *Syn.-Ber.,* Iowa Dist., 1919.

66

Leviticus 24

Additional Ordinances. Punishment of Blasphemy.

O F THE OIL AND THE SHOWBREAD. - V.1. **And the Lord spake unto Moses, saying,** v.2. **Command the children of Israel that they bring unto thee pure oil olive beaten for the light, to cause the lamps to burn continually.** Cp. Ex. 27, 20. 21. This oil was exceptionally pure, because all leaves, parts of branches and twigs, and all other foreign matter was removed; and the olives from which this oil was gained were not stamped or pressed in presses, but merely cut and beaten, a process which caused the oil to drain off without any other juices of the fruit. V.3. **Without the veil of the testimony,** the curtain which hid the Ark of the Covenant with the tables of the testimony from the eyes of all the children of Israel, **in the Tabernacle of the Congregation,** in the Holy Place, **shall Aaron order it from the evening unto the morning before the Lord continually,** that is, he was to place the lamps filled with the pure oil on the seven-armed candlestick and light them in the evening, and put them in order in the morning by cleaning them and trimming their wicks. **It shall be a statute forever in your generations.** V.4. **He shall order the lamps upon the pure candlestick before the Lord continually.** This was a function which was expressly delegated to the priests while the Levitical precepts were in force. V.5. **And thou shalt take fine flour, wheaten flour, and bake twelve cakes thereof; two-tenth deals** (a little more than five quarts) **shall be in one cake.** V.6. **And thou shalt set them in two rows,** or heaps, **six on a row, upon the pure table before the Lord,** upon the table of showbread made of pure gold, on the north side of the altar of incense, in the Holy Place, V.7. **And thou shalt put pure frankincense upon each row,** the pure natural gum, as a gift from the people, the twelve tribes of Israel being represented by the twelve cakes of the showbread. The frankincense, according to Jewish tradition, was placed beside each heap of showbread in golden censers, **that it may be on the bread for a memorial, even an offering made by fire unto the Lord,** its sweet odor serving to bring the people into remembrance before the Lord. v.8. **Every Sabbath he,** the priest on duty, **shall set it in order before the Lord continually, being taken from the children of Israel by an everlasting covenant.** In this unbloody sacrifice the congregation brought the fruit of its activity, of its life, and of its sanctification before the face of the Lord, and thus presented itself to Him as a people diligent in good works. V.9. **And it shall be Aaron's and his sons';** and they shall eat it in the holy place,** it belonged to the food which they consumed somewhere in the Sanctuary or in its court; **for it is most holy unto him of the offerings of the Lord made by fire by a perpetual statute.** It was a symbol and guarantee of the eternal covenant which existed between Jehovah and His people. We Christians have a more perfect table, at which our communion with God and the covenant of His mercy are renewed as often as we come in true faith, namely, the table of His Supper.

A BLASPHEMER STONED. - V.10. **And the son of an Israelitish woman, whose father was an Egyptian,** one of the mixed multitude that went up with the children of Israel out of Egypt, Ex. 12, 38, **went out among the children of Israel,** he left his tent and that part of the camp appointed for his people and mingled with the true Israelites; **and this son of the Israelitish woman and a man of Israel strove together in the camp,** engaged in a quarrel; v.11. **and the Israelitish woman's son blasphemed the name of the Lord and cursed;** he uttered "the Name" (of God) with irreverence and contempt, the climax being reached in his bold denunciation of Jehovah. Any blasphemy against the name of Jehovah, as against the name above all names, was not only blasphemy against the God of Israel, but also against the religion of His revelation, against the covenant with Jehovah, and thus against the holy source of all consecrations, as one commentator has it. **And they brought him unto Moses,** that is, those that were witnesses of the blasphemy; **(and his mother's name was Shelomith, the daughter of Dibri, of the tribe of Dan;)** v.12. **and they put him in ward,** they secured or imprisoned him, **that the mind of the Lord might be showed them,** for the measure of punishment and the form of death in such a case had not yet been expressly stated. V.13. **And the**

Lord spake unto Moses, saying, v.14. **Bring forth him that hath cursed without the camp; and let all that heard him lay their hands upon his head,** thereby ridding themselves of all complicity in the guilt which might have rested upon them on account of their being witnesses of the sin, **and let all the congregation stone him.** Under the form of government which was directly responsible to God capital punishment was imposed for transgressions of this nature. V.15. **And thou shalt speak unto the children of Israel, saying,** with reference to this execution, **Whosoever curseth his God shall bear his sin,** that is, the guilt and then also the punishment of sin as the Lord laid it upon the people under His direct government. V.16. **And he that blasphemeth the name of the Lord,** utters the name above all names in a spirit of levity and contempt, **he shall surely be put to death, and all the congregation shall certainly stone him,** the emphasis upon the execution being very strong; **as well the stranger as he that is born in the land,** Israelite or non-Israelite, all that were under the jurisdiction of the government, **when he blasphemeth the name of the Lord, shall be put to death.** And the Lord now expands this ordinance to include some other cases in which He demanded similar punishment. V.17. **And he that killeth any man,** strikes him down so that his life is taken, **shall surely be put to death.** V.18. **And he that killeth a beast shall make it good, beast for beast.** V.19. **And if a man cause a blemish in his neighbor,** any bodily harm or the loss of any organ; **as he hath done, so shall it be done to him:** v.20. **breach for breach, eye for eye, tooth for tooth; as he hath caused a blemish in a man, so shall it be done to him again,** for the law of restitution demanded reparation. V.21. **And he that killeth a beast, he shall restore it; and he that killeth a man, he shall be put to death. V.22. Ye shall have one manner of law, as well for the stranger as for one of your own country; for I am the Lord, your God.** The same laws that were given to the Israelites were to apply to the non-citizen that chose to live in their country. Cp. Ex. 21, 12 ff. V.23. **And Moses spake to the children of Israel that they should bring forth him that had cursed out of the camp, and stone him with stones. And the children of Israel did as the Lord commanded Moses,** thus putting away the evil out of their midst. A Christian congregation has no jurisdiction over life and death, but notorious and unrepentant sinners, such as blasphemers, should be excluded from their organization; and it is self-evident among Christians that the law of love demands restoration of all goods in which one's neighbor has been harmed.

67

Leviticus 25

The Sabbath Years.

THE SEVENTH YEAR. - V.1. **And the Lord spake unto Moses in Mount Sinai,** while the children of Israel were still encamped in its vicinity, saying, v.2. **Speak unto the children of Israel, and say unto them, When ye come in to the land which I give you,** the certainty of this event being set forth time and again, **then shall the land keep a Sabbath unto the Lord,** the soil should be given periods of rest, in which the land should lie fallow. V.3. **Six years thou shalt sow thy field, and six years thou shalt prune thy vineyard, and gather in the fruit thereof;** v.4. **but in the seventh year shall be a Sabbath of rest unto the land, a Sabbath for the Lord; thou shalt neither sow thy field, nor prune thy vineyard.** The earth was to be saved from the hand of man, lest its strength be exhausted for earthly purposes, and man was to be saved from the uninterrupted drudgery which

428

tended to chain his thoughts to the soil and to the bitter labor in the sweat of his brow which was connected therewith. V.5. **That which groweth of its own accord of thy harvest,** the volunteer grain from the kernels that had dropped out at the last harvest, **thou shalt not reap, neither gather the grapes of thy vine undressed,** the grapes which grew in the vineyard without the attention of the husbandman; **for it is a year of rest unto the land.** V.6. **And the Sabbath of the land shall be meat for you; for thee and for thy servant and for thy maid,** both male and female slaves being named, **and for thy hired servant, and for thy stranger that sojourneth with thee.** So all the volunteer grain and the volunteer fruit was not to be harvested, but was to be eaten out of the field, as the need for food arose, this rule applying not only to men, but also to animals, both domestic and wild; v.7. **and for thy cattle, and for the beast that are in thy land shall all the increase thereof be meat,** be used as food. The Sabbatical Pear was a civil year, which began after the harvest, in the late fall, for in the next fall, at the beginning of the eighth year, the cultivation of the land was resumed. God wanted to signify to the people of His covenant that He was well able to keep them, even without the labor of their hands, if they would strive to keep His covenant and he satisfied with His mercy.

THE YEAR OF JUBILEE. - V.8. **And thou shalt number seven Sabbaths of years unto thee, seven times seven years; and the space of the seven Sabbaths of years shall be unto thee forty and nine years.** V.9. **Then shalt thou cause the trumpet of the jubilee to sound on the tenth day of the seventh month,** which formally opened this special Sabbatical Year; **in the Day of Atonement**

shall ye make the trumpet sound throughout all your land. After the solemn quiet of the day on which all the people afflicted their souls, and after the great rites of the annual propitiation had been completed, probably at the end of the evening sacrifices, the glad sounding of the trumpets proclaimed the Year of Jubilee. V.10. **And ye shall hallow the fiftieth year, and proclaim liberty throughout all the land unto all the inhabitants thereof.** This proclamation of freedom from the toil and drudgery which came into the world as a consequence of sin was most fitting just after the great reconciliation of the people with the covenant God had been completed. Twice in every century two fallow years followed upon each other, and the land had an opportunity to recover its strength. **It shall be a jubilee unto you; and ye shall return every man unto his possession, and ye shall return every man unto his family,** as the further ordinances prescribed. V.11. **A jubilee shall that fiftieth year be unto you; ye shall not sow, neither reap that which groweth of itself in it, nor gather the grapes in it of thy vine undressed,** as in the Sabbatical Year, v.4. V.12. **For it is the jubilee; it shall be holy unto you; ye shall eat the increase thereof out of the field,** directly from the stalks, from the vine, from the trees, without harvesting or storing in granaries. V.13. **In the year of this jubilee ye shall return every man unto his possession,** to the land which had been in the possession of his family from the beginning. V.14. **And if thou sell aught unto thy neighbor, or buyest aught of thy neighbor's hand, ye shall not oppress one another,** not overreach or practice fraud; v.15. **according to the number of years after the jubilee thou shalt buy of thy**

neighbor, and according unto the number of years of the fruits he shall sell unto thee; v.16. according to the multitude of years thou shalt increase the price thereof, and according to the fewness of years thou shalt diminish the price of it; for according to the number of the years of the fruits doth he sell unto thee. By this rule the price of the land was regulated according to the number of crops still remaining till the next Tear of Jubilee: if the buyer would get many crop, the prince was high; if the purchaser would get but a few crops until the land had to be restored to its original owner, the price was low. V.17. Ye shall not therefore oppress one another by overreaching contrary to this commandment; but thou shalt fear thy God; for I am the Lord, your God, whose punishment was sure to strike the offender. V.18. Wherefore ye shall do My statutes and keep My judgments, both the special precepts and those based upon the natural law of love, and do them; and ye shall dwell in the land in safety, securely, free from all care and worry. V.19. And the land shall yield her fruit, and ye shall eat your fill, not merely enough to sustain life, but a surplus, and dwell therein in safety. V.20. And if ye shall say, What shall we eat the seventh year? Behold, we shall not sow, nor gather in our increase. V.21. Then I will command My blessing upon you in the sixth year, and it shall bring forth fruit for three years. The crop of the forty-eighth year would be sufficient for all their needs, not only during the forty-ninth, as a regular Sabbatical Tear, but also during the fiftieth, as the Jubilee Year, to the harvest of the fifty-first year, in fact. V.22. And ye shall sow the eighth year, at the time of the fall rains, and eat yet of old fruit until the ninth year; until her fruits come in, ye shall eat of the old store. V.23. The land shall not be sold forever, with a clear, absolute title to the purchaser; for the land is Mine; for ye are strangers and sojourners with Me, the Lord's lessees in holding any real estate. No person could hold farm land absolutely, if he purchased it between years of jubilee, any purchase in reality being only a temporary lease for a number of years. V.24. And in all the land of your possession ye shall grant a redemption for the land; the seller was always to have the right of redeeming the land which he had sold, as shown in the regulations following to the end of the chapter. Christians mill also never lose sight of the fact that they are but strangers and pilgrims here on earth, that they hold their possessions only by the bounty of the Lord, and that their true home is above.

CONSIDERATION FOR THE POOR AND FOR SLAVES. V.25. If thy brother be waxen poor, and hath sold away some of his possession, land or houses in the country, and if any of his kin come to redeem it, the man upon whom this duty devolved, v.48, then shall he redeem that which his brother sold, buy it hack for the former owner. V.26. And if the man, the original owner, have none to redeem it, and himself be able to redeem it, if he finds himself in a position that he can buy back the land which he sold, v.27. then let him count the years of the sale thereof, since the sale was made, and restore the over-plus, whatever price had been paid for the crops still remaining till the next Year of Jubilee, unto the man to whom he sold it, that he may return unto his possession. V.28. But if he be not able to restore it to him, if he cannot raise the money needed to regain possession of his land in this way, then that which is sold shall remain in the hand of him that hath bought it until the year of jubilee; and in the jubilee it shall go out, and he shall return unto his possession, for the provision was that all leases, called sales, should terminate in the Year of Jubilee. V.29. **And if a man sell a dwelling-house in a walled city, then he may redeem it,** for the purchase price, **within a whole year after it is sold; within a full year may he redeem it.** V.30. **And if it be not redeemed within the space of a full year, then the house that is in the walled city shall be established forever to him that bought it throughout his generations; it shall not go out in the Jubilee.** This was a distinct exception to the rule which applied to land in the open country and in towns. V.31. **But the houses of the villages which have no wall round about them shall be counted as the fields of the country; they may be redeemed, and they shall go out in the Jubilee.** V.32. **Notwithstanding the cities of the Levites and the houses of the cities of their possession may the Levites redeem at any time.** In their interest exceptions were always permitted. V.33. **And if a man purchase of the Levites, then the house that was sold and the city of his possession,** that is, the house on its location in the city of the Levites, **shall go out in the Year of Jubilee,** be restored to the Levite, the original owner, without cost to him; **for the houses of the cities of the Levites are their possession among the children of Israel.** V.34. **But the field of the suburbs of their cities,** the open meadow-land surrounding their cities, used for pasturing their cattle arid flocks, **may not be sold; for it is their perpetual possession,** and community property, at that. V.35. **And if thy brother be waxen poor, and**

433

fallen in decay with thee, having failed entirely in his business, **then thou shalt relieve him, - yea, though he be a stranger or a sojourner, - that he may live with thee.** Here provision is made for the second contingency, namely, that connected with a man's having sold himself into bondage on account of poverty. The paragraph is introduced with an admonition to help the poor brother who is in need of financial assistance. V.36. **Take thou no usury of him or increase,** neither interest in the case of money nor an added amount in the case of other necessaries of life; **but fear thy God; that thy brother may live with thee.** V.37. **Thou shalt not give him thy money upon usury, nor lend him thy victuals for increase.** V.38. **I am the Lord, your God, which brought you forth out of the land of Egypt to give you the land of Canaan and to be your God.** Because the Land of Promise was to the Israelites a gift of God's merciful goodness, therefore they were not to forget kindness and mercy in dealing with their poor brothers. V.39. **And if thy brother that dwelleth by thee be waxen poor and be sold unto thee, thou shalt not compel him to serve as a bond-servant,** not treat him as a slave nor have him perform the labor of a slave, v.40. **but as an hired servant and as a sojourner,** as a worker under contract, **he shall be with thee, and shall serve thee unto the year of Jubilee; v.41. and then shall he depart from thee, both he and his children with him, and shall return unto his own family, and unto the possession of his fathers shall he return.** This ordinance supplements Ex. 21, 2-6, for it would come into effect both if the servant had not yet been with a master seven years, or if lie had declared his willingness to remain with his master and had received the mark of bondage in his ear. V.42. **For they are My servants, which I brought forth out of the land of Egypt,** they were God's peculiar property; **they shall not be sold as bondmen.** V.43. **Thou shalt not rule over him with rigor,** as over a true slave, **but shalt fear thy God.** V.44. **Both thy bondmen and thy bond-**

maids which thou shalt have shall be of the heathen that are round about you; these only could be kept in true slavery; **of them shall ye buy bondmen and bondmaids. V.45. Moreover, of the children of the strangers that do sojourn among you, of them shall ye buy, and of their families that are with you which they begat in your land; and they shall be your possession,** and could be kept arid treated as slaves. V.46. **And ye shall take them as an inheritance for your children after you, to inherit them for a possession; they shall be your bondmen forever,** this applying to heathen slaves of Hebrew masters only. **But over your brethren, the children of Israel, ye shall not rule one over another with rigor.** V.47. **And if a sojourner or stranger wax rich by thee, and thy brother that dwelleth by him wax poor,** the non-Israelite growing wealthy in the same proportion as the Israelite grew poor, **and sell himself unto the stranger or sojourner by thee, or to the stock of the stranger's family,** that is, to the descendants of immigrants who were not citizen; V.48. **after that he is sold, he may be redeemed again; one of his brethren may redeem him,** in order not to have the disgrace of being in bondage to an outsider resting upon him; v.49. **either his uncle or his uncle's son may redeem him, or any that is nigh of kin unto him of his family may redeem him**; or if he be able, if he finds ways

435

'and means of raising the money, **he may redeem himself. V.50. And he shall reckon with him that bought him from the year that he was sold to him unto the Year of Jubilee; and the price of his sale shall be according unto the number of years, according to the time of an hired servant shall it be with him.** The purchase price was to be divided by the number of years which he would have to serve till the next Tear of Jubilee, and the time which he had already served was to be valued in terms of a hired servant, this amount being subtracted from the entire sum. V.51. **If there be yet many years behind, according unto them he shall give again the price of his redemption out of the money that he was bought for,** as much as his services would have been worth to his master until the Pear of Jubilee V.52. **And if there remain but few years unto the Year of Jubilee, then he shall count with him, and according unto his years shall he give him again the price of his redemption,** in this case a relatively small sum. V.53. **And as a yearly hired servant shall he be with him,** as such he should be regarded by his master; **and the other shall not rule with rigor over him in thy sight,** so that the people would become aware of it: for as soon as such treatment were known, the government was supposed to act. V.54. **And if he be not redeemed in these gears, then he shall go out in the Year of Jubilee, both he and his children with him.** V.55. **For unto Me the children of Israel are servants; they are My servants whom I brought forth out of the land of Egypt. I am the Lord, your God.** Thus the Year of Jubilee became a year of freedom and of mercy to the entire people, but especially to the poor and oppressed, and a year of rest from toil and drudgery. In this respect, it was a type of the acceptable year of the Lord, in which the Gospel is being preached to the meek, in which the brokenhearted are being bound up, liberty is being proclaimed to the captives and the opening of the prison to them that are bound, this time being in itself a foretaste of the day when the sons of God will be received into the perfect and eternal liberty provided for them, Is. 61, 1-3; Luke 4, 17-21.

68

Leviticus 26

Promises and Threats.

B LESSINGS PROMISED TO THE OBEDIENT. - V.1. **Ye shall make you no idols,** literally, nothingnesses, vain, empty deities of your own imagination, **nor graven image,** one carved or chiseled from wood and stone, **neither rear you up a standing image,** a pillar of commemoration used for idolatrous purposes; **neither shall ye set up any image of stone,** a stone shaped or hewn to represent some real or imagined creature, **in your land to bow down unto it; for I am the Lord, your God.** V.2. **Ye shall keep My Sabbaths,** as the days set a part for His special worship, **and reverence My Sanctuary,** stand in awe of the place where the holy God revealed Himself to them. **I am the Lord.** These two verses, containing substantially the entire Law of God as applied to the Jews in particular, serve admirably as a basis of the following promises and warnings. V.3. **If ye walk**

LEVITICUS 26

in My statutes and keep My commandments, both the general precepts of the natural law and the special ordinances pertaining to the children of Israel, and do them, v.4. **then I will give you rain in due season,** the showers at the two periods of the year when the land needed moisture for fruitfulness, Deut. 11, 14, **and the land shall yield her increase, and the trees of the field shall yield their fruit.** The extraordinary extent of the blessings is shown next. V.5. **And your threshing shall reach unto the vintage, and the vintage shall reach unto the sowing time.** Threshing in Palestine was done on the great open floors, beginning with the harvest, in April; the grapes were usually ripe in September; and sowing for the new crop began at the end of October or the beginning of November. **And ye shall eat your bread to the full, and dwell in your land safely,** without cares and worries about the necessaries of life. V.6. **And I will give peace in the land,** perfect security, **and ye shall lie down,** in peaceful settlement, like a herd which is safe from the attacks of beasts of prey, **and none shall make you afraid. And I will rid evil beasts out of the land, neither shall the sword go through your land,** because the enemies that might venture an attack would be driven back triumphantly from their borders. V.7. **And ye shall chase your enemies, and they shall fall before you by the sword,** since the Israelites would be rendered invincible by the Lord. V.8. **And five of you shall chase an hundred, and an hundred of you shall put ten thousand to flight,** a proverbial expression for the absolute certainty of victory for Israel's arms, Deut. 23, 30; Is. 30, 17; **and your enemies shall fall before you by the sword.** These promises were abundantly fulfilled, as the history of Israel and Judah shows,

439

e.g., in the case of Gideon. V.9. **For I will have respect unto you,** turning His face upon them in goodness and mercy, **and make you fruitful and multiply you,** giving increase upon increase, blessings which were properly appreciated in those days, **and establish My covenant with you,** which had promised such unusual blessings, Gen. 17, 4-6. V.10. **And ye shall eat old store,** grain of last year's crop, **and bring forth the old because of the new,** since the old would not even he consumed by the time the new harvest would be filling the granaries. V.11. **And I will set My Tabernacle among you,** as the visible sign of His merciful presence; **and My soul shall not abhor you.** V.12. **And I will walk among you,** in gracious communion through the worship offered to Him, **and will be your God, and ye shall be My people.** Cp. Deut. 23, 15. V.13. **I am the Lord, your God, which brought you forth out of the land of Egypt that ye should not be their bondmen,** held in shameful slavery by a heathen nation; **and I have broken the bands of your yoke, and made you go upright.** The deliverance from Egypt was a proof and pledge of the fulfillment of God's promises, and the fellowship which the children of Israel enjoyed in Him was symbolic of the perfect communion which the children of God have entered upon with Him through the redemption of Christ. If we Christians believe and trust in God with all our heart, and walk in the ways of His commandments, then He will remain with us with His Word and Sacraments. Therefore we should also love and trust in Him and gladly perform the demands of His holy will.

THE CURSE UPON THE DISOBEDIENT. - V.14. **But if ye will not hearken unto Me, and will not do all**

LEVITICUS 26

these commandments, v.15. **and if ye shall despise My statutes, or if your soul abhor My judgments, so that ye will not do all My commandments, but that ye break My covenant,** willfully set it aside, v.16. **I also will do this unto you: I will even appoint over you terror,** order it to strike them, to fill their hearts with nameless dread, **consumption, and the burning ague,** a consuming fever, **that shall consume the eyes, and cause sorrow of heart; and ye shall sow your seed in vain, for your enemies shall eat it,** they would find no difficulty about entering the country and taking the standing grain or the contents of the granaries. V.17. **And I will set My face against you, and ye shall be slain before your enemies,** with no chance of overcoming them; **they that hate you shall reign over you; and ye shall flee when none pursueth you,** which is characteristic of the godless and wicked, Prov. 28, 1; Ps. 53. 5. After this preliminary summary the Lord now announces the form which His punishment mould take in a carefully graded series which reaches its climax in the last part of the chapter. V.18. **And if ye will not yet for all this hearken unto Me, then I will punish you seven times more for your sins.** V.19. **And I will break the pride,** the majesty, the glory, the boast, of your power; **and I will make your heaven as iron and your earth as brass,** withholding both the rain above and the fruitfulness below; v.20. **and your strength shall be spent in vain,** in the fruitless endeavor to coax the land into producing; **for your land shall not yield her increase, neither shall the trees of the land yield their fruits.** That was the first degree of the increased punishment: an absolute lack of fertility in the land. V.21. **And if ye walk contrary unto**

Me and will not hearken unto Me, I will bring seven times more plagues upon you according to your sins, as the second step of the intensified curse. V.22. I will also send wild beasts among you, the larger predatory beasts and birds, which shall rob you of your children, and destroy your cattle, and make you few in number; and your highways shall be desolate on account of the reduced number of inhabitants. These were the two punishments of the second increased degree: loss caused by beasts of prey and bereavement. V.23. And if ye will not be reformed by Me by these things, if they would not learn their lesson as held before them by the Lord, but will walk contrary unto Me, v.24. then will I also walk contrary unto you, be engaged in continual acts of aggressive enmity, and will punish you yet seven times for your sins, as the third step in the increased revenge. V.25. And I will bring a sword upon you, permit the scourge of war to sweep their country, that shall avenge the quarrel of My covenant; and when ye are gathered together within your cities, where the greater density of the population made the spread of diseases easier, I will send the pestilence among you; and ye shall be delivered in to the hand of the enemy, for war and epidemics usually come together. V.26. And when I have broken the staff of your bread, which is here also represented as the staff of life, the proverbial expression denoting the infliction of extreme scarcity, ten women, of as many households, shall bake your bread in one oven, where formerly ten were needed, and they shall deliver you your bread again by weight, in careful rations; and ye shall eat, and not be satisfied. That was the third stage of God's increased punishment: war, pestilence, and famine.

V.27. **And if ye will not for all this hearken unto Me, but walk contrary unto Me,** v.28. **then I will walk contrary unto you also in fury,** in consuming anger; **and I, even I, will chastise you seven times for your sins,** in some last horrible catastrophes. V.29. **And ye shall eat the flesh of your sons, and the flesh of your daughters shall ye eat,** in a madness of cannibal hunger brought on by the severe famine. V.30. **And I will destroy your high places,** where idolatrous worship was carried on, **and cut down your images,** the pillars erected to the heathen deities, **and cast your carcasses upon the carcasses of your idols, and My soul shall abhor you,** be filled with loathing at their sight. V.31. **And I will make your cities waste, and bring your sanctuaries unto desolation,** the houses of idolatry erected in spite of the warning of Jehovah; **and I will not smell the savor of your sweet odors,** the burnt sacrifices which they brought in the insolence of their hypocrisy, as though the Lord would accept the mere outward work, without faith of the heart. V.32. **And I will bring the land in to desolation; and your enemies which dwell therein shall be astonished at it,** even they would be surprised at the distinct marks of God's punitive justice, as they were in evidence everywhere. V.33. **And I will scatter you among the heathen,** in a shameful captivity equivalent to slavery, **and will draw out a sword after you,** drive them from their homes with a drawn sword; **and your land shall be desolate and your cities waste.** That was the climax of God's revenging justice: destruction of all idols and their sanctuaries, complete overthrow of the cities, desolation of the land, and deportation of its inhabitants. These threats hold good even today. If we turn away from God, deny Him faith and obedience, and despise His commandments, He will take away His blessings, peace and prosperity, from us and even visit His anger upon us. Therefore we should fear His wrath and not act contrary to His commandments.

THE EFFECTS OF THESE VISITATIONS AND THE RESTORATION OF THE COVENANT. - V.34. **Then shall the land enjoy her Sabbaths, as long as it lieth desolate, and ye be in your enemies' land; even then shall the land rest and enjoy her Sabbaths.** It is here implied that Israel, in its revolt against Jehovah and His commandments, would omit the observance of the sabbatical years, and that the land, suffering under the oppression of this greed, would feel the relief brought about by the deportation of the owners. V.35. **As long as it lieth desolate, it shall rest, because it did not rest in your Sabbaths when ye blood upon it.** V.36. **And upon them that are left alive of you I will send a faintness into their hearts in the lands of their enemies,** filling their hearts with a cowardly fear, with the despondency of an unreasonable terror; **and the sound of a shaken leaf shall chase them; and they shall flee, as fleeing from a sword; and they shall fall when none pursueth,** victims more of their own terror than of any harm done to them by their enemies, V.37. **And they shall fall one upon another, as it were before a sword, when none pursueth; and ye shall have no power to stand before your enemies.** V.38. **And ye shall perish among the heathen, and the land of your enemies shall eat you up.** Cp. Num. 13. 32; Ezek. 36. 13. V.39. **And they that are left of you shall pine away in their iniquity in your enemies' lands,** PO long as they remain in their unrepentant attitude toward God; **and also in the iniquities of their fathers**

shall they pine away with them; for if the children follow in the footsteps of their sinful parents, the sins of the latter are visited upon them also. But now the mercy of the Lord comes into the foreground Again. V.40. **If they shall confess their iniquity and the iniquity of their fathers,** the guilt which they brought upon themselves by their misdeeds, **with their trespass which they trespassed against Me, and that also they have walked contrary unto Me,** an open confession being necessary to show the sincerity of their repentance; v.41. **and that I also have walked contrary unto them, and have brought them into the land of their enemies,** thereby freely acknowledging that they were suffering a well-deserved punishment; **if then their uncircumcised hearts be humbled, and they then accept of the punishment of their iniquity,** v.42. **then will I remember My covenant with Jacob, and also My covenant with Isaac, and also my covenant with Abraham will I remember,** with all the blessings promised therein; **and I will remember the land,** turn back to it with thoughts of love and kindness. V.43. **The land also shall be left of them, and shall enjoy her Sabbaths, while she lieth desolate without them,** being free from the oppression of a population that disregarded the will of the Lord; **and they shall accept of the punishment of their iniquity,** bowing their backs to the Lord's chastening rod; **because, even because they despised My judgments, and because their soul abhorred My statutes.** V.44. **And yet for all that, when they be in the land of their enemies,** when it seems that they are absolutely forsaken by God, **I will not cast them away, neither will I abhor them to destroy them utterly,** for that had not been the purpose of His punishment in the first place, **and to break My covenant with them; for I am the Lord, their God,** who always has mercy upon the repentant sinner. V.45. **But I will for their sakes remember the covenant of their ancestors, whom I brought forth out of the land of Egypt in the sight of the heathen. I am the Lord.** In this way the punishment of the Lord would finally result in blessing the people, in bringing them back to the fellowship of the covenant which He had never repudiated. V.46. **These are the statutes and judgments and laws which the Lord made between Him and the children of Israel in Mount Sinai by the hand of Moses.** The history of Israel, as foreshadowed in this chapter, is an example of warning to all men. Unto those that are disobedient to the truth the Lord will render tribulation and anguish, Rom. 2, 8. 9. He will in flaming fire take vengeance on them that know not God, that obey not the Gospel of our Lord Jesus Christ, 2 Thess. 1, 8. 9. But His mercy is always ready to turn to those that come to Him with a sorrowful and repentant heart.

69

Leviticus 27

Of Vows.

OF MEN AND BEASTS. - V.1. **And the Lord spake unto Moses, saying,** v.2. **Speak unto the children of Israel and say unto them, When a man shall make a singular vow,** an exceptional, unusual, special promise to the Lord, which involved the offering of his own body to the Lord for some service in His worship, **the persons shall be for the Lord by thy estimation;** the redemption from the obligations of the promise had to be made in accordance with the estimate given out, first by Moses and later by the priest in charge. The fulfillment of the vow consisted in this, that the person concerned paid the price of the estimation to the Sanctuary. V.3. **And thy estimation shall be of the male,** in the case of a man, **from twenty years old even unto sixty years old; even thy estimation shall be fifty shekels of silver, after the shekel of the Sanctuary** (about $32). V.4. **And if it be** a female, then thy estimation shall be thirty shekels (about $19.20). V.5. **And if it be from five years old even unto twenty years old, then thy estimation shall be of the male twenty shekels** (about $12.80) **and for the female ten shekels** (about $6.40). V.6. **And if it be from a month old even unto five years old, then thy estimation shall be of the male five shekels of silver** (about $3.20), **and for the female thy estimation shall be three shekels of silver** (about $1.92). V.7. **And if it be from sixty years old and above,** at the time of life when the bodily strength usually will not permit strenuous service; **if it be a male, then thy estimation shall be fifteen shekels** (about $9.60) **and for the female ten shekels** (about $6.40). V.8. **And if he be poorer than thy estimation,** if he cannot afford the price of redemption according to the priest's estimate, **then he shall present himself before the priest, and the priest shall value him,** fix the price of redemption in proportion to the person's ability to pay; **according to his ability that vowed shall the priest value him.** This special ordinance made it possible even for the very poor to dedicate themselves to the Lord by a vow; for the Lord's mercy and kindness at all times stands out with special force. V.9. **And if it be a beast whereof men bring an offering unto the Lord,** that is, if the vow concerns such an animal, **all that any man giveth of such unto the Lord shall be holy,** dedicated to Him, set aside subject to His orders. V.10. **He shall not alter it, nor change it, a good for a bad or a bad for a good;** for the vow, having once been made, could not be recalled; **and if he shall at all change beast for beast, then it and the exchange thereof shall be holy,** both of them devoted to the Lord, subject to His disposal, those without blemish being used for sacrifices, those not perfect being allotted to the priest. V.11. **And if it be any unclean beast, of which they do not offer a sacrifice unto the Lord, then he shall present the beast before the priest; v.12. and the priest shall value it, whether it be good or bad; as thou valuest it, who art the priest, so shall it be.** The priest was to fix a medium price, neither too high nor too low, for the proceeds of the sale were used in the interest of the Sanctuary. V.13. **But if he will at all redeem it,** for his own use, **then he shall add a fifth part thereof unto thy estimation,** as a sort of compensation for his act in taking the animal back for his own use.

OF HOUSES, FIELDS, AND FIRSTLINGS. - V.14. **And when a man shall sanctify his house to be holy unto the Lord,** in a vow devoting its value to the service of Jehovah, **then the priest shall estimate it, whether it be good or bad; as the priest shall estimate it, so shall it stand,** his medium valuation should be final. V.15. **And if he that sanctified it will redeem his house,** desiring to have it back for his own use, **then he shall add the fifth part of the money of thy estimation unto it, and it shall be his.** V.16. **And if a man shall sanctify unto the Lord some part of a field of his possession,** the price of its valuation being intended for the use of the Sanctuary, as a gift, **then thy estimation shall be according to the seed thereof,** according to the amount of seed used in putting the field to grain; **an homer** (a little over eight bushels) **of barley-seed shall be valued at fifty shekels of silver** (about $32.40). V.17. **If he sanctify his field from the Year of Jubilee,** immediately after its close, when the land was again cultivated, **according to thy estimation it shall**

stand. The valuation once fixed would hold good till the nest Tear of Jubilee, and the one that made the vow would be obliged to make his yearly payments accordingly. V.18. **But if he sanctify his field after the Jubilee,** after some years had elapsed, **then the priest shall reckon unto him the money according to the years that remain, even unto the year of the Jubilee, and it shall be abated from thy estimation.** In the case of a field of barley, for instance, if twenty years still remained till the nest Tear of Jubilee, then the person concerned would have twenty shekels to pay, plus the one-fifth which was added for the sake of compensation, if it was so arranged. V.19. **And if he that sanctified the field will in any wise redeem it, then he shall add the fifth part of the money of thy estimation unto it, and it shall be assured to him.** V.20. **And if he will not redeem the field,** by the regular payment of the price of valuation, **or if he have sold the field to another man, it shall not be redeemed any more;** if a person lapsed in his payments, he forfeited his ownership of the field. V.21. **But the field, when it goeth out in the Jubilee,** out of the hands of the man that bought it in the mean time, **shall be holy unto the Lord, as a field devoted,** and thus the property of the Sanctuary; **the possession thereof shall be the priest's.** V.22. **And if a man sanctify unto the Lord a field which he hath bought, which is not of the fields of his possession,** does not belong to the land which is the perpetual inheritance of his family, v.23. **then the priest shall reckon unto him the worth of thy estimation, even unto the Year of the Jubilee,** the total sum due as the price of redemption; **and he shall give thine estimation in that day,** make payment of the required sum at once, **as a holy thing unto the Lord.** This provision obviated the possibility of the land's being devoted to the Sanctuary and thus being lost to the original owner, who was to regain possession of it in the year of the Jubilee. V.24. **In the year of the jubilee the field shall return unto him of whom it was bought, even to him to whom the possession of the land did belong,** and who could not dispose of it absolutely, but only until the year of redemption. V.25. **And all thy estimations shall be according to the shekel of the Sanctuary,** the standard of weight for all money transactions; **twenty gerahs shall be the shekel.** V.26. **Only the firstling of the beasts, which should be the Lord's firstling,** Ex. 13, 2. 12, no man shall sanctify it: these animals could not be used in the event of vows; **whether it be ox or sheep; it is the Lord's.** V.27. **And if it be of an unclean beast,** one that could be used neither for sacrifices nor as food for the priests, **then he shall redeem it according to thine estimation, and shall add a fifth part of it there to; or if it be not redeemed, then it shall be sold according to thy estimation,** for the benefit of the Sanctuary. V.28. **Notwithstanding, no devoted thing that a man shall devote unto the Lord of all that he hath, both of man and beast, and of the field of his possession, shall be sold or redeemed,** while it is under the vow; **every devoted thing is most holy unto the Lord,** a gift which cannot be redeemed, surrendered to the Lord to be disposed of at His will, irrevocably cut off from all common use. V.29. **None devoted, which shall be devoted of men,** dedicated to the Lord in this special sense, **shall be redeemed, but shall surely be put to death;** the person was irredeemable, and Jehovah's sentence of destruction was sure to be carried out. V.30. **And all the tithe of the land, whether of the seed of the land or of the fruit of the tree, is the Lord's; it is holy unto the Lord,** absolutely at His disposal, and Jehovah executed the ban. V.31 **And if a man will at all redeem aught of his tithes, he shall add thereto the fifth part thereof,** as a penalty or compensation. V.32. **And concerning the tithe of the herd or of the flock, even of whatsoever passeth under the rod,** that is, under the staff of the shepherd, who keeps a careful record of the animals in his care, **the tenth shall be holy unto the Lord,** the tenth part of the annual increase was set apart for the use of the Lord and His Sanctuary. V.33. **He shall not search whether it be good or bad, neither shall he change it,** v.10; **and if he change it at all, then both it and the change thereof shall be holy; it shall not be redeemed.** V.34. **These are the commandments which the Lord commanded Moses for the children of Israel in Mount Sinai,** this last chapter on vows being an appendix to the Book of Leviticus, the types of whose sacrifices point forward to the Lord, our Righteousness; for they were prescribed to the Jews of the Old Covenant because of transgressions, until the promised Seed should come.

Made in the USA
Middletown, DE
14 January 2023

22144006R00272